Empress

To the Ancestors of India's Women

And to Our Plural Heritage

Empress

THE ASTONISHING REIGN OF
NUR JAHAN

Ruby Lal

W. W. NORTON & COMPANY

Independent Publishers Since 1923

New York | London

For information about permission to reproduce selections from this book, write to
Permissions, W. W. Norton & Company, Inc., 500 Fifth Avenue, New York, NY 10110

For information about special discounts for bulk purchases, please contact
W. W. Norton Special Sales at specialsales@wwnorton.com or 800-233-4830

Manufacturing by LSC Communications, Harrisonburg
Book design by Chris Welch
Production manager: Anna Oler

ISBN: 978-0-393-23934-8

W. W. Norton & Company, Inc., 500 Fifth Avenue, New York, N.Y. 10110
www.wwnorton.com

W. W. Norton & Company Ltd., 15 Carlisle Street, London W1D 3BS

1 2 3 4 5 6 7 8 9 0

CONTENTS

DRAMATIS PERSONAE

THE MUGHAL RULERS

Akbar: the third Great Mughal emperor, son of Humayun

Babur: the first Great Mughal emperor

Dawar Bakhsh: Mughal ruler with the shortest reign, son of Khusraw, used to forestall Shahryar's bid for the crown

Humayun: the second Great Mughal emperor, son of Babur

Jahangir (né Prince Salim): the fourth Great Mughal emperor, co-sovereign with Nur Jahan

Nur Jahan (née Mihr un-Nisa): co-sovereign with Jahangir, the first and only female ruler of the Mughal Empire

Shah Jahan (né Khurram): the fifth Great Mughal emperor, son of Jahangir, rebelled against his father

NOTABLE WOMEN

Arjumand Banu (Mumtaz Mahal): wife of Shah Jahan, in whose memory the Taj Mahal was built

Asmat Begum: Nur/Mihr's mother

Dai Dilaram: Nur/Mihr's wet nurse and mentor, prominent harem officer

Gulbadan Banu Begum: daughter of Babur, led a royal women's pilgrimage to Mecca, author of the *Ahval-i Humayun Badshah*

Hamideh Banu Begum: revered mother of Emperor Akbar

Jagat Gosain: mother of Shah Jahan, rival of Nur Jahan

Ladli Begum: only daughter of Nur Jahan and Sher Afgan, married Shahryar

Ruqayya Begum: Akbar's childless wife, key matriarchal figure for Mihr/Nur as well as Jahangir

Salimeh Sultan Begum: senior wife of Akbar and later mentor to Mihr/Nur

NOTABLE MEN

Asaf Khan (né Abul-Hasan): son of Ghiyas Beg, brother of Empress Nur, father of Arjumand Banu, loyalist of Shah Jahan

Ghiyas Beg (I'timad ud-Daula): Nur/Mir's father, wazir of the Mughal Empire under Jahangir

Jadrup: Vaishnavite ascetic and spiritual mentor of Jahangir

Khusraw: Jahangir's eldest son, rebelled against his father

Mahabat Khan (né Zamana Beg): fought to quell Prince Khusraw's rebellion, then turned against Jahangir, kidnapping him

Shahryar: son of Jahangir, married Ladli and was favored to rule by Nur, as opposed to Shah Jahan

Sher Afgan (né Ali Quli): Mihr/Nur's first husband, a functionary under Akbar

SCRIBES, ARTISTS, AND HISTORIANS

Abdal-Qadir Badauni: historian at Akbar's court

Abdur-Rahim Khan-i Khanan: poet, military general and translator of the *Baburnama*, loyalist of Jahangir

Abul-Hasan: painter and portraitist favored by Jahangir

Farid Bhakkari: financial officer in the time of Jahangir, author of *Dhakhiratul Khawanin*

Khafi Khan (Hashim Ali Khan): military figure and chronicler of the Mughal Empire, author of *Muntakhab-ul Lubab*

Niccolao Manucci: military figure, quack doctor, and author of *Storia Do Mogor*

Muhammad Hadi: contemporary of Aurangzeb, contributed late sections of *Jahangirnama*

Mulla Kami Shirazi: poet whose works celebrate the life of Nur Jahan

Mu'tamad Khan: Jahangir's paymaster of troopers and memoirist

Sir Thomas Roe: British ambassador to Mughal India who wrote a detailed account of the empire

Empress

ONE

Queen of Queens,
an Introduction

In the autumn of 1619, when the days were clear and cool, perfect for travel, the royal cavalcade of Emperor Jahangir and Empress Nur Jahan, his twentieth and favorite wife, set out from Agra, the capital of Mughal India, headed for the Himalayan foothills. The people of Mathura, a popular pilgrimage site along the emperor's route, were anxious for his arrival. For months, a tiger had been attacking villagers and visitors, then disappearing into the forest, evading local hunters. No divine intervention seemed to be forthcoming from Lord Krishna and his consort Radha, the Hindu deities worshipped in Mathura's temples. But the emperor could solve the problem. Killing tigers had long been a royal prerogative.[1]

Jahangir—his name meant Conqueror of the World in Persian, the language of the court—was the fourth of the Mughal emperors, a Muslim dynasty established by invasion early in the sixteenth century. Descendants of the Central Asian nomad kings Chingiz [Genghis] Khan and Tamerlane, the Mughals ruled much of Hindu-majority India for more than three hundred years.

According to one excited observer, the imperial procession included "fifteen hundred thousand" people—men, women, and children; courtiers, soldiers, and servants—along with ten thousand elephants and a great deal of artillery.[2] The procession halted near Mathura, and attendants began erecting hundreds of magnificent tents, with the harem quarters marked with intricately carved red screens. While the traveling court was still being set up, a group of local huntsmen appeared and begged Jahangir to do something about the tiger.

Unfortunately, the emperor was obligated to decline. Several years before, Jahangir had taken a vow to give up hunting when he turned fifty. After that, he'd promised Allah, he would injure no living being with his own hands. He was two months past that milestone birthday, and had recently renewed the vow as an offering on behalf of a favorite four-year-old grandson, traveling with him, who suffered from epilepsy. Shooting a tiger was now out of the question for Jahangir. The empress, however, was there to protect her subjects.

Beautiful and accomplished, Nur Jahan was the daughter of nobles who'd fled persecution in Persia. She was also the widow of a court official implicated in a plot against Jahangir, but that didn't stop the emperor from falling hard for her. She was thirty-four when they married, nearly middle-aged in the Mughal world. Since their wedding in 1611, the same year that Shakespeare premiered *The Tempest*, Nur Jahan (Light of the World in Persian, the name bestowed by her husband), had proved to be a devoted wife, a wise and just queen, a shrewd politician—and an expert markswoman. Her shooting skills were already legendary. A few years earlier, she'd amazed her husband and his courtiers by slaying four tigers with only six shots.

On October 23, 1619, Nur Jahan mounted an elephant and settled into the howdah, the elaborate litter on the animal's back, holding a musket. The mahout, the elephant handler, led her along the sandy track toward the forest. Nur Jahan accompanied her husband, Jahan-gir, on his own elephant, and they were followed by a long line of courtiers, some on superbly ornamented elephants and horses and others in red and gold jeweled palanquins with silken seats, decorated with garlands of flowers and carried by attendants. Portraits of Nur Jahan from the period suggest that she was wearing a regal turban, much like the ones favored by the emperor and distinguished noble-men, but highly unusual for a woman; a knee-length tunic with a sash around the waist over tight trousers; and earrings and a necklace of rubies, diamonds, or pearls. Her shoes were open at the back, expos-ing the henna designs on her feet.[3] At forty-two, she was still praised by her contemporaries for her luminous beauty.

Local hunters on foot guided the party past fields of barley, peas, and cotton, lush from the recent rains. Along the way, they spot-ted herds of cattle, goats, and blackbuck with long corkscrew horns. When they reached the forest, the emperor and empress could barely see beyond the dense wall of creepers, bushes, and trees—lofty *nim*, thorny *babul*, and many others.[4] The hunters showed the empress and her retinue the spot where the tiger was likely to appear, and they waited.

Soon Nur's elephant, in the lead, began groaning and stepping ner-vously from side to side; the mahout couldn't make it stand still, and Nur Jahan's howdah lurched precariously. From his own elephant, Jahangir looked on, silent and focused. Later, he would recall the moment in the *Jahangirnama* (The memoirs of Jahangir), a journal he began when he ascended to the throne in 1605 that would serve as the public record of his reign. "An elephant is not at ease when it smells a tiger, and is continually in movement," he wrote, "and to hit with a gun from a litter is a very difficult matter."[5]

The tiger emerged from the trees. Nur lifted her musket, aimed between the animal's eyes, and pulled the trigger. Despite the sway-ing of her elephant, one shot was enough; the tiger fell to the ground, killed instantly. Jahangir was delighted. A woman shooting publicly was rare; a woman shooting with such expertise was unheard-of.

Nur's shooting skill wasn't the only thing that made her highly unusual. She held a position in the empire never before filled by a woman: co-sovereign. For more than a decade and a half, from a few years after their wedding until Jahangir's death, Nur Jahan ruled along with her husband, effectively and prominently, successfully navigating the labyrinth of feudal courtly politics and the male-centered culture of the Mughal world. She issued her own imperial orders, and coins of the realm bore her name along with her husband's. In Islamic thought and practice, the edicts and the coins were convincing technical signs of sovereignty. Furthermore, Nur sat where no other Mughal queen had sat before or would after, in the *jharokha*, an elaborately carved balcony projecting from the palace wall, from which government business was conducted.[6] Subjects gathered below the *jharokha* to pray for her health, and getting a look at her was considered auspicious. More important, nobles sometimes presented themselves below the imperial balcony "and listen[ed] to her dictates," according to a contemporary historian. "At last her authority reached such a pass that the King was such only in name . . . Repeatedly he gave out that he bestowed the sovereignty on Nur Jahan Begam."[7]

A generation earlier, Jahangir's father, Akbar the Great, had ordered all royal women—wives, daughters, and concubines—to be sequestered behind harem walls. He called them "the veiled ones." But three decades after Akbar's dictate, Nur Jahan was on view in the most male and public of places. A new kind of power was on display.

Nur Jahan was the only woman ruler in the long dynasty of India's great Mughals. How did she do it, in that time and that place? How did the empress's extraordinary strengths, the emperor's lamentable weaknesses, the twists and turns of seventeenth-century politics, and the power of their love combine to defy a time and a culture that ought to have made the reign of Nur Jahan impossible?

I first met Nur Jahan when I was a restless nine-year-old growing up in Dehradun, India, 150 miles north of Delhi. I loved stories, and my mother had a bagful of wondrous tales for my two younger sisters and me. She would dish out selections as she played with us on hot summer afternoons, oil our hair, or put us to bed, even when she was tired after a long day of running the household.

Though some of my mother's stories were about animals—a parrot who advised its owner; a clever fox that fooled some peasants—most were about unusual women, though I didn't notice this at the time. We heard about the brave Rani of Jhansi who fought against British rule, and also the British Queen Victoria; Heer of the eternal love story Heer-Ranjha, India's *Romeo and Juliet*; the goddess Parvati, who stood up to her husband, the terrifying Shiva; and Sita, the dutiful princess at the center of the Hindu epic *Ramayana*, admirable in her own way. Mother sang songs based on the epics, and reminded us to behave more like these amazing women when we got overly mischievous. On weekends, my father, a civil engineer, often listened from the sidelines, hidden behind his newspapers.

One afternoon, my mother and I were sitting on the floor playing *gaind-gitta*. Similar to the American game of jacks, *gaind-gitta* involves bouncing a small ball with one hand and moving five dice into prescribed arrangements with the other hand while the ball is in the air—creating, for example, a cave with the left hand and placing one die at a time in it with the right as the ball danced up. A game of fine balance, *gaind-gitta* required close concentration. Still, at some point, I grew bored. "I want a story," I said to my mother. I can't remember whether we finished the game, but she did tell me a story, one I hadn't heard before, about Nur Jahan, wife of the seventeenth-century Mughal emperor Jahangir.

My mother called her *Maharani*, Queen of Queens in Hindi.

Though some of the details of that day's story are hazy, what stuck with me was that while Nur ruled the empire alongside her husband, dispensing justice and masterminding daring rescues, she also wrote poetry and designed clothing, gardens, and buildings. Still vivid are the glint in my mother's eye as she spoke, and the spark ignited in me by Nur's accomplishments and allure. She felt more real to me than other heroines my mother spoke about. I turned to my father, seemingly immersed in his reading, but eavesdropping on my mother's story. "I am Nur Jahan." I declared. "You are Jahangir!" He laughed and on many occasions repeated my words to others.

At some point, that fascination with Nur's story translated into my love for the history of the Mughal world—for Mughal women, to be precise. In time I became a feminist historian. After I'd published two books that examined duty, aspiration, and degrees of freedom among women in premodern and early modern India, both of which challenged conventional notions of what constitutes historical evidence of women's lives, I was invited to write a biography of Nur Jahan.

Hers is a household name in South Asia. Nur Jahan has been the subject of at least eight movies, several plays, an opera, and numerous historical romances in Hindi, Urdu (the national language of Pakistan), Punjabi (spoken in both India and Pakistan), English, and other languages of the subcontinent.[8] Travel to India or Pakistan today and you'll find tour guides, custodians of Mughal tombs, and local visitors to these sites who delight in recounting legends of Nur. As I began researching this book, one of my first tasks was to explore that oral tradition: what exactly the public knows (or thinks it knows) about Empress Nur.

I engaged a graduate assistant in Lahore, Pakistan—once part of the Mughal Empire—who asked thirty men and women ranging in age from twenty to thirty-five what they knew about Empress Nur. The majority responded enthusiastically with a famous legend about how Nur and Jahangir met. So did a comparable number of Indian tourists, tour guides, and history buffs I interviewed myself in Agra and Delhi. Every retelling of the tale was similar to the version published by the nineteenth-century Urdu writer and critic Maulana Muhammad Husain Azad:

> In the prime of his youth, Mughal Emperor Jahangir [then, Prince Salim] strolled into a garden. He had just been to the Meena Bazaar, the renowned market in the capital where royalty and nobility wandered among merchants displaying the curiosities of the world. Jahangir had a pair of invaluable pigeons in his hands. He saw a flower he wanted to pluck, but his hands were not free. Just then a young woman passed by. Asking her to hold on to the pigeons, he turned to pluck the flower. On turning back to the woman, he saw that she had only one pigeon in her hand. He asked about the other. She replied: "Your Highness, it has flown away." "How did that happen?" the astonished Prince asked. She stretched her hand, loosened her grip and let the second pigeon go. "Like this," she said. The prince was stunned: he lost not only his rare pigeons, but his heart as well.[9]

Only two of the young Pakistanis knew that Nur had been a politically powerful queen, and an accomplished poet—and they, too, began with the pigeon story said to have launched a royal romance. Both in Pakistan and India, the people we talked to generally invoked two dates—Nur's birth in 1577 and her marriage in 1611—and explained their importance in a few lines: *She was born on the road outside Kandahar* [in modern-day Afghanistan] *as her destitute parents made their way from Iran to India. They abandoned her; then she was restored to them. Jahangir and Nur Jahan met in the Meena Bazaar. He fell in love with her. They married.* Popular works about the empress focus on this imperial love story, and Nur's birth on the road is the favorite opening scene of films, plays, and novels. Most of them revel in her use of feminine wiles to gain influence in the harem and the court, and nearly all of them end, as did the interviewees' responses, with Nur's marriage.

Though modern South Asians embrace the legends of Nur with affection, gusto, and pride, the emphasis on her romance with Jahangir truncates her biography in a way that diminishes her. In the popular imagination, Nur's story seems to stop at the very moment when her life's best work began.

Between 1614 and 1627, the year of Jahangir's death, Nur served as her husband's co-sovereign, a decisive player in courtly and succession politics, and a commanding strategist. She defended her subjects against oppressive landlords and otherwise championed social justice. At the height of her power in the 1610s and '20s, princes and courtiers sought her advice and followed her commands; she had the faith and trust of her husband. In 1626, when Jahangir was taken prisoner by a rebellious nobleman, it was Nur who led her imperial troops to rescue him. *Amar Chitra Katha*, a popular comic-book series read by Indian children and adults, highlights that episode on the cover of an issue about Nur; the illustration shows her astride a war elephant leading the battle to save the captive emperor. But inside, the narration of her bold military and political endeavors is sketchy and tepid; more of the comic is devoted to Nur's romance with Jahangir. Secondary school textbooks mention Nur briefly, but they don't discuss her as a leader.

The Mughal family into which Nur married had a tradition of strong and prominent elder women—assertive royal wives, influential mothers and aunts whose opinions were valued. But no woman had ever openly and fully taken charge of the empire. It would be another 350 years, when Indira Gandhi became India's first female prime minister, before another woman ascended to such heights in Indian statecraft.

Many of her male contemporaries were in awe of Nur, whom they saw as a person of uncommon political and cultural acumen, and a remarkable leader. But in a conservative patriarchy, they had trouble accepting, despite empirical evidence, that she could be both womanly and a sovereign. Some commentators pronounced her cunning and conniving, precisely the way certain authoritative women are described to this day. Thomas Roe, the British ambassador to Jahangir's court, saw Nur as manipulative and mysterious: "[Jahangir's] course is directed by a woeman, and is now, as it were, shut up by her soe, that all justice or care of anything or publique affayres either sleepes or depends on her, who is more unaccessible then any goddesse or mistery of heathen impietye."[10] In the view of Peter Mundy, a merchant with the British East India Company who visited Agra in 1630, Nur was "hautie and stomakefull"—that is, stubborn.[11]

Europeans like Roe and Mundy seemed especially bewildered by the phenomenon of Nur Jahan. She hadn't inherited an empire, as had Queen Elizabeth I of England, crowned twenty years before Nur's birth, nor was she exactly a favorite, the familiar adviser-minister figure they knew, a staple of European courts but always a male. They couldn't quite wrap their minds around a woman's coming to power because of her own talents, but they could understand a wily consort winning the indulgence of a love-blind emperor.

Jahangir's marriage to Nur in 1611, the critical moment thought by many to explain her rise, launched a multitude of legends about every phase of Nur's life—her birth, her first marriage, harem life, an alleged early affair with Jahangir when he was a young prince, her meeting and marrying Jahangir, her power over her husband. The legends soon engulfed the truth, overshadowing her actual personal history. Narrations of the royal romance became more extravagant in nineteenth-century British colonial histories that were steeped in the orientalism of the day, embracing exoticized stereotypes of Asia—depraved despots, a shockingly sensual harem.[12]

Historians writing in the 1960s and '70s (and even in the early 1990s, after an extensive gap), strove to cast Nur in a fuller biographical mode, as a distinguished queen on par with great rulers such as

Elizabeth I or Indira Gandhi. Unfortunately, these studies offered
only bullet-point synopses of Nur's life: *she issued orders, coins were
struck in her name, she designed clothes and gardens.* There is no palpable
sense of the anger or playfulness we'd expect of a living woman, no
details about her support of Jahangir, her deep investment in the life
of the empire, her political maneuvers and countermaneuvers, her
raw ambition, her vulnerability as well as her strengths, or the very
human way in which she fought to build and preserve her husband's
and her own sovereign rights. Little in these biographies suggest that
royal women played any crucial role in Mughal imperial life, let alone
that one of them, Nur Jahan, was rewriting history.[13]

Even into the late twentieth century, academics disparaged the
legends about Nur as gossip, and leaned on love as the explanation
for her extraordinary rise rather than attributing it to her talents.
They dismissed Jahangir as an inebriated, ineffectual king, interested only in aesthetics, philosophy, and mind-altering substances, so
besotted—with alcohol, opium, and Nur Jahan—that he handed over
the running of his realm to her. Yes, the emperor was a drinker and
he smoked opium. Yes, he was deeply in love with this wife. But that's
not why she became a ruler to be reckoned with.

A key problem for twentieth- and twenty-first-century scholars has
been that they've had no model for producing a layered social history
of the Mughal world. They inherited a widely accepted caricature of
a mysterious and unchanging harem that was supposed to represent
the sum of Mughal private life. The following remarks on the Mughal
harem and Nur Jahan, taken from a serious and sympathetic biography of the empress that came out in 1993, demonstrate the pervasive
hold of that skewed representation:

> Finding a productive and satisfying place in a society where
> pleasure (in all its forms) was the main competitive commodity
> was a substantial task [for Mughal women] . . . the enjoyment of

palace life was enhanced . . . by the frequent use of drugs and alcohol. Intemperance was the Mughal family's main affliction, and despite public abjurations and the clear ban on the use of liquor by Islam, it remained not only a private curse but a public habit . . . Jahangir's harem was, from all accounts, a rowdy and exuberant place to live and Nur Jahan's fulsome charisma played out profitably against its many walls.[14]

The more deeply I investigated the life and times of Nur Jahan—you can learn more about my methods and sources in the note at the end of the book—the more clearly I saw that the reasons for her rise were intriguingly complex, and that neither the popular legends nor conventional scholarly works fully tell her story.

Carefully assessed, the unusual sources I used have yielded details that allow me to offer plausible answers to the two questions that come up again and again. *How did she do it?* I'm asked each time I teach or give a talk about Nur Jahan—the same query that was already familiar four centuries ago; the same sense of puzzlement at a woman's supremacy. *How did it happen back then, and in India?* Many people—students, audiences at my public lectures in the West and the East, an enthusiastic undergrad who waited on me at a restaurant, friends in private discussions—find it difficult to picture a powerful woman rising in a seventeenth-century Muslim dynasty.

But the common conception of past times as always more repressive and unenlightened than today is a misjudgment. Seventeenth-century India—the empire that called itself Hindustan, known to Persians and Arabs as Al-Hind, the land beyond the Indus River—had a surprising openness and diversity of religion and thought, despite the weight of patriarchy. During his reign, Akbar forcefully set in place an ethos of coexistence. The highly plural culture of Akbar's India was one in which you could be Shi'a or Sunni Muslim and yet marvel at the esoteric messages of Sufi mysticism or Hindu asceticism, question Jesuits about the life of Jesus, or tease a youthful monk about the pleasures of the flesh, all of which Nur Jahan did. Nur, a Shi'a Muslim woman, married a Sunni king who had a Hindu mother and both Hindu and Muslim wives and concubines.[15]

Of course, not all of Mughal life was benign; arbitrary rule was accompanied by acts of ferocity that would make subjects shudder with fear. A young Emperor Akbar, for example, dispatched a rebellious foster brother by having him tossed off a building, And in 1573, a year after Akbar had conquered and annexed the sultanate of Gujarat, he quelled a revolt there and ordered his men to make a minaret out of the heads of a thousand rebels who'd fallen in battle, as a warning against further insurrection.

But Akbar's general commitment to tolerance enabled the advent of new styles of sovereignty on which Jahangir and Nur would build. Ironically, though Akbar was the first Mughal to sequester women in a grand palace harem, his policies of openness allowed Nur to flourish.

The personalities and circumstances of the people close to Nur helped shape her unprecedented rise. She became the ruler she was because of Jahangir's strengths and weaknesses—and yes, his capacious and abiding affection and admiration for his wife. I certainly don't intend to undo the imperial romance; Nur and Jahangir earned their love story. But other factors are just as important, perhaps more so. Nur's parents were enlightened nobles who took great pains with their daughter's education, which continued in Jahangir's harem, where elder women mentored Nur. Life there was far richer and its matriarchs more politically astute than most accounts suggest. Her leadership skills deepened and broadened on the road. Jahangir admired the wandering lifestyle of the first Mughal emperor, Babur, and emulated it. He believed a sovereign should be constantly on the move throughout his realm—observing, interacting, making notes, and taking stock—and Nur traveled with him on most of his journeys between 1611 and 1627. Jahangir's penchant for the itinerant life meant more liberties for Nur and other women of the Mughal household. They came out of the walled quarters to which they'd been relegated by Akbar and into open country, where the tented harems of the royal encampments afforded them more freedom of mind and body.

Jahangir's mobility contributed to Nur's co-sovereignty. Making his wife increasingly responsible for governing released the emperor from state duties and freed him to pursue his interest in nature, geography, art, and philosophy, though he remained the de jure ruler. Thomas Roe wasn't terribly approving of the arrangement, which allowed Nur more power:

> I am yet followeing this wandering King over mountaynes and thorough woods, so strange and unused ways that his own peo-
> ple . . . blaspheame his name and hers that (it is said) conducts all his actions . . . I feare hee will not long stay any wher, whose course is directed by a woeman.[16]

Perhaps it happened because the stars were aligned. In Nur and Jahangir's world, all of human existence was bound up with the movement of the planets and other celestial objects. Royalty and common folk alike consulted seers and stars, judging auguries before embarking on journeys, scheduling weddings, naming newborns, and making peace with the end of a life. Mystics, dream interpreters, seers, and astrologers shaped Nur's universe. According to these oracles, the planetary conjunctions seem to have been on her side from the moment of her birth.

TWO

Miracle Girl

When a large comet passed startlingly close to Earth in the autumn and winter of 1577, astronomers, astrologers, philosophers, and monarchs all over Europe and Asia, including the Mughal emperor Akbar, were spellbound. The distinguished Danish astronomer Tycho Brahe made precise measurements of its path, findings later used by his student Johannes Kepler to formulate the laws of planetary motion.

Known for his curiosity and open mind, thirty-five-year-old Emperor Akbar was in the twenty-first year of his reign when a comet, Zu-Zanab—literally, "possessed of a tail"—became visible in the skies over India, bright enough to be seen in daylight. The celestial body that Europeans called the Great Comet provoked intense discussion in Fatehpur-Sikri, then the Mughal capital. Akbar invited astrologers to give their opinion on the form, appearance, and effects of Zu-Zanab's flight.

Ancient Indian astrology books described more than a hundred kinds of comets, some possessing tails, others forelocks, that could herald both good and bad fortune in the countries they crossed. Akbar's royal astrologer, Jotik Rai, informed him that Zu-Zanab had traveled over Tibet, western China, Turkestan, Farghana (a principality in Uzbekistan), and Khurasan province in northern Persia, modern-day Iran, where it was observable for eighty-five days. The comet would produce serious disturbances in those lands, Jotik Rai said. Persia especially would suffer. The astrologer's predictions were confirmed early in the new year, when trusted visitors reported to Akbar that the Persian monarch Shah Tahmasp had died and his kingdom was suffering economic woes and bloody political upheaval.[1]

What Akbar didn't know was that the season of the comet had brought another momentous event, one that would someday affect the fate of his empire. On the road outside Kandahar, in what is now Afghanistan, a girl had been born to a couple leaving repressive Persia for Akbar's empire, a land they hoped would be more welcoming to their liberal views on politics and religion. They were part of a caravan making the long and arduous journey to India along a stretch of the Silk Road, the ancient web of trade routes linking East and West. The baby arrived before the turn of the year, a Sagittarius or Capricorn entering a world where people believed that comets, eclipses, and arrangements of the zodiac shaped an individual's disposition and attitudes. They called their daughter Mihr un-Nisa, "Sun of Women."

The Great Comet was glowing overhead when Ghiyas Beg and his wife, Asmat Begum, pregnant with Mihr, left their home in Herat, the capital of Persia's Khurasan province, a vibrant commercial center at the crossroads of several major trade routes.[2] Both were educated people from noble families, liberal members of the ruling class in a Persia where liberality went in and out of fashion and often contended with fundamentalism. Ghiyas, a trim man of twenty-two with gentle brown eyes, was considered exceptionally wise and open-minded, an expert letter-writer who loved poetry and historical prose. He and his wife, Asmat, described later in Mughal records as a lively, large-spirited woman, already had two sons and a daughter.[3]

In India, the couple would become luminaries, with Ghiyas prominently discussed in the official archives of Akbar's son, the Great Mughal Jahangir. (The first six Mughal emperors, through the end of Aurangzeb's reign in 1707, are known as the Great Mughals, and the kings who followed and ruled until 1858 as "the later Mughals." Europeans sometimes used the term Grand Mughal to describe each of the Greats.) Jahangir would praise his trusted and admired finance minister Ghiyas as capable, generous, and sincere, and bestow upon him the title I'timad ud-Daula, Pillar of the State. But when Ghiyas and Asmat left Persia, the future was uncertain.

Mystery surrounds the precise troubles that forced their departure. Several sources echo the eighteenth-century account of a Mughal chronicler named Khafi Khan, who wrote, "After his father's death, as a result of unfortunate circumstances, Ghiyas started for India as a fugitive . . ."[4] What exactly were these unfortunate circumstances? We can't be sure, but the historical evidence suggests several credible reasons for his departure.

Ghiyas's father died in 1576, the same year as Shah Tahmasp, whom Ghiyas had served as a highly valued revenue collector. Histories written long afterward suggest that without the financial support of his father, the young man had gone into debt. And without royal protection from Tahmasp, the freethinking Ghiyas most likely worried about the disfavor of the intolerant new shah, Isma'il II, son of Tahmasp. Imprisoned for years by his father, Isma'il II had succeeded him through murderous machinations in a short reign with a high body count. He died not long after Ghiyas left Persia, poisoned, some suspect, by rivals for the crown.

When Isma'il II became shah, a centuries-old tradition of religious pluralism and harmonious coexistence, maintained to some degree during most of Tahmasp's fifty-two-year reign, even in periods of repression, gave way to ever more rigid official intolerance. Ghiyas's leanings were liberal and rational. He might reasonably have thought his life was in danger, debt or no debt.

An acceptance of diversity had marked the first three hundred years of Persia's Safavid dynasty, which evolved from a thirteenth-century order of Sufis, tolerant Muslim mystics. The rulers who descended from the order's founder respected a variety of faiths, and all had prospered: mystics, Sunni and Shi'a Muslims (differing then, as now, over who were the rightful heirs to the Prophet Muhammad and thus the appropriate leaders of the Muslim community), Turkish tribes that practiced animism, and Armenians and other Christians.

Gradually, however, the Safavid rulers became less accepting and more militant. Shah Isma'il I, who ruled during the first two decades of the sixteenth century, proclaimed himself to be divine, a rightful successor to Muhammad, and established Shi'ism as the only legitimate basis for the kingdom's social-political order. Sunni religious institutions weren't entirely wiped out, but they lost their endowments from the state, and many Sunni clergymen and legal experts were executed or exiled. Over time, Isma'il I became so severe about what he considered to be the principles of righteousness and lawfulness that he cut off the hands of anyone playing a musical instrument.[5]

The Safavid state under Isma'il I singled out anyone sympathetic to religious practices other than Shi'ism and punished them with public chastisement, prison, or death. Sufism, which emphasizes a direct, personal experience of God, was officially discouraged, though its practice continued in private. Since the founding of the Safavid dynasty, rigidity and freedom had always existed simultaneously, though the ratios were sometimes wildly skewed toward repression. A town would have its mosques—and its opium dens. A mullah might denounce Sufism from the pulpit, then debate one of its practitioners over coffee.

Under Isma'il's successor, Tahmasp, Persia offered more opportunities for experimentation in literature and thought, despite some official intolerance. Ghiyas and Asmat, born into cultured and edu-cated noble families, were raised in an atmosphere of intellectual pursuit and inquiry, where reflection and interpretation were valued. Men of the upper classes gathered to eat, drink, recite poetry, and talk politics. Aristocratic women, highly accomplished in the arts of reading, writing, and calligraphy, were also likely to share with one another poetry they had composed. In groups they might shop for clothing and lace in the marketplace and visit the *hammam*, the bath-house, where they could laugh together, share secrets, mull over mar-ital problems, and speak frankly about sex. Men and women would discuss literature: epics, fables, poetry, accounts of travel, stories of territorial rivalry and battles among the rulers, with their claims and counterclaims of cultural supremacy. Although social interaction was largely segregated by sex, respectable men and women might mix at family dinners, picnics, or musical gatherings at home, with wine and song.[6]

With both his father and Tahmasp gone, however, Ghiyas appears to have felt this way of life was threatened. An understandable next step would be to head for India. For more than two hundred years, Persians seeking economic opportunity or protection from perse-cution had left for wealthier, more tolerant Al-Hind. Adventurers sought their fortunes in the diamond mines of the Deccan, the pla-teau between northern and southern India. Traders sailed between ports in the Indian Ocean; Sufis practiced in peace; poets composed eulogies for Indian patrons from Bengal to Kashmir. The transplants also included craftsmen, soldiers, sages, theologians, physicians, cal-ligraphers, musicians, dramatists, and dignitaries. According to one scholarly estimate, from 1501 to 1722, 750 Persian poets relocated to India.[7] During that same period, Persian migrants with expertise in mathematics, astronomy, history, ethics, logic, metaphysics, and statecraft advised Indian monarchs.

Persians had long had a place in Mughal courts. In 1540, Emperor Humayun, Akbar's father and the second Great Mughal, was driven into exile by an Afghan ruler. Akbar was born on the road after the emperor, his family, and his retinue fled. Eventually they were given refuge in Persia by Shah Tahmasp. When Humayun successfully fought to reclaim his throne fifteen years later, he was accompanied by a number of Persians. And when Akbar succeeded his father, he welcomed Persian artists, craftsmen, poets, scholars, and philosophers to his court, and encouraged Persians to join his imperial service.

Though people moved from India to Persia, most migration was in the other direction (and there's no evidence that any Indian gained a significant position at the Safavid court). One good reason for the discrepancy was that Mughal India, Hindustan—today's north and central India, modern Pakistan and Bangladesh, and parts of Afghanistan—was one of the world's wealthiest states. Its fertile agricultural lands supported nearly 100 million people in the 1600s, a population matched only by Ming China. A range of export commodities brought a flow of foreign currency into the Indian ports.[8]

The Safavids, on the other hand, controlled a massive swath of rugged land—the territory of modern-day Iran, northwest Afghanistan, and parts of Georgia, Armenia, and Azerbaijan—that was populated by no more than 10 million people and not terribly productive. Though silk and silk thread were the region's principal and greatly valued exports, basic food items such as rice and sugar and spices, as well as cotton and indigo, came to Iran from India.

At the time Ghiyas and his family left Persia, migration to India had become even more attractive. Akbar's court had acquired the distinction of being *dar-al-aman*, the abode of peace, a place of refuge. In the second half of the sixteenth century, leaving Persia for India meant not only material comfort but the hope of freedom of thought.[9]

While the move might have offered better prospects, it must have been wrenching. To ease the anguish of farewells, a very pregnant

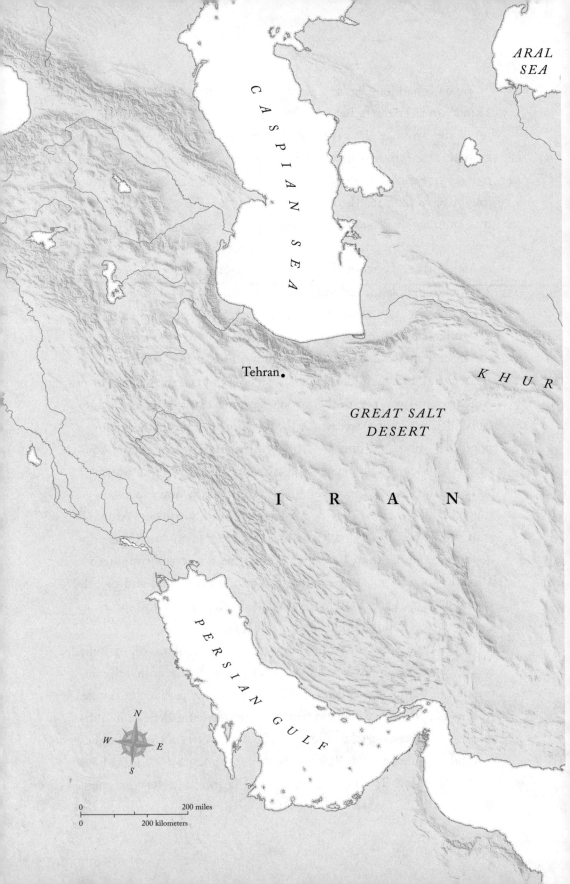

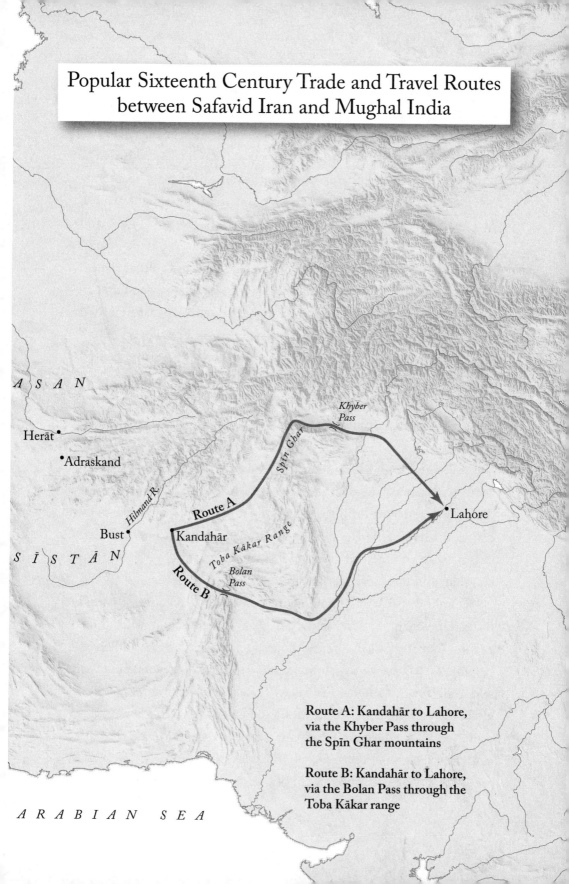

Popular Sixteenth Century Trade and Travel Routes between Safavid Iran and Mughal India

Route A: Kandahār to Lahore, via the Khyber Pass through the Spīn Ghar mountains

Route B: Kandahār to Lahore, via the Bolan Pass through the Toba Kākar range

Asmat, a concerned Ghiyas Beg, and their anxious but supportive friends and relatives would have shared a ritual series of elaborate meals, discussing the journey and expressing faith in the divine as the children played and servants scurried about. Ghiyas's cousin Shapur, who had visited India twice on business, would have been present, describing the atmosphere and promise of the Mughal world. The couple wouldn't find it such an alien place; Persian culture and customs thrived in Al-Hind. Akbar's poet laureate Abul Faiz "Faizi" claimed that Mughal mastery of Persian language and culture rivaled that of Persia itself.[10] In Al-Hind there would be relatives and associates to help Ghiyas; an uncle of Asmat's had already distinguished himself by fighting an important and successful campaign on behalf of Akbar against local rulers in western India, and he'd put in a good word for his nephew-in-law. But first, the couple had a journey of several months ahead of them.

Caravans were a common mode of travel in sixteenth-century Iran, Central Asia, and India. The cavalcades of kings stretched over several miles and included family members, courtiers, soldiers, and servants, with camels, horses, and elephants by the thousands carrying tents and provisions for huge encampments that replicated the royal court. Traders carried goods by caravan, and sometimes travelers joined those commercial caravans. That's what Ghiyas, Asmat, their children, and their servants did.

According to Khafi Khan's eighteenth-century account of Mihr's birth, a merchant named Malik Masud led the caravan in which Ghiyas and Asmat traveled. Horses, mules, and camels carried saddlebags or pulled carts packed with merchandise as well as tents, supplies, and grain for the animals. Travelers replenished their store of water along the way. Masud probably followed one of the well-known trade routes established by Arab explorers between the eighth and eleventh centuries. The most conspicuous indicator of the route that Ghiyas and Asmat took is the one detail of their journey that contemporary and later historians agree on: Nur Jahan was born outside the city of Kandahar, 350 miles southeast of Herat.

Herat was surrounded by a wall with five gates. The caravan led by Masud no doubt exited from the Kandahar Gate to the south, crossed the Hari Rud River, then moved through low hills and gently sloping valleys with springs and rivers, vineyards, cotton fields, and farms and orchards that supplied melons and apples to India.[11]

Anyone who encountered Ghiyas, Asmat, and their children on the road would know they were aristocrats. If their formal dignity, elegant clothing, and soft, nimble speech didn't make that clear, their status would be obvious from the presence of the attendants who would have traveled with them.

Moving south, the caravan would cross the Great Salt Desert, blistering during the summer and desolate all year. Its scorching winds would have given them a preview of India's summer heat. Eventually they'd come to the town of Adraskand, a well-cultivated area with plenty of sweet water—an excellent resting place. Caravan travelers determined their halting points by how far a camel could go in a day. A decade or so after Ghiyas and Asmat's journey through these parts, the next Persian monarch built a number of caravanserais, roadside inns, on the way to Kandahar. Given the importance of this trade route, some caravanserais likely existed even at the time of Asmat and Ghiyas's passage. But most often travelers camped in open country, pitching their tents near water, under the shade of trees or in a garden, depending on the season.

The caravan probably passed alongside the lakes and marshes of the fertile Sistan region, where the travelers would have seen, in the distance, houses made of clay. Masud may have led his party on through Bust, a depository for wares in transit to India, and found a camping spot close to the Helmand River, not far from Kandahar, a pleasant area but dangerously isolated. Attacks by thieves were not uncommon on these journeys. Caravans were often robbed of sup-

plies, merchandise, and animals by bandits armed with swords and
known to wound and even murder travelers. Father Bento de Goes,
a Jesuit missionary, wrote in the early sixteenth century that while
traveling on horseback through Northwest Afghanistan, he lagged
behind his caravan and was approached by four riders. When he realized they were robbers, the missionary tossed a costly turban as far
away as he could. As the thieves quarreled over this prize, Father de
Goes spurred his horse and sped away. A little farther on, his group
was attacked again, by a different set of robbers. That time, several
travelers were killed.[12]

Everyone in the caravan with Ghiyas and Asmat, the aristocratic
men, women, and children who rode and the servants and tradesmen
who walked, would be tired and their animals exhausted. As remedies
for fatigue, travelers ate garlic, onions, and dried apricots, and fed
them to their animals. Sometimes burdened horses and mules in a
caravan suffered to such an extent that they collapsed on the journey.
Spare camels and horses traveling without loads came in handy.

Just before Masud's caravan crossed the Helmand, legend has it,
they were set upon by brigands, and Ghiyas and Asmat lost everything they owned except for a couple of mules. The historical records
don't say whether Masud's caravan traveled with guards who fought
the thieves, whether anyone died in the skirmish, or whether there
was a skirmish at all. If there was an attack, a shaken Ghiyas would
have had to restock supplies along the way.

Asmat's due date was approaching, making the journey potentially
more perilous. As an Iranian saying had it, "From the day of conception on, a woman has one foot in this world and one foot in the other."
To ward off accidents during pregnancy, folk wisdom suggested,
women should sew a few seeds of wheat or millet and a gold coin into
a piece of cloth, and keep the sachet with them all the time.[13]

Somewhere just short of Kandahar, Asmat delivered her baby, a
girl. The birth was most likely attended by a small band of servants,

including a midwife, perhaps Dai Dilaram, the woman who would serve as Mihr's wet nurse and remain with her when she became Empress Nur Jahan. The servants would have erected a separate tent or enclosure to ensure privacy for Asmat. Men weren't allowed to view or help with the birth of a child; the code of modesty required that only women be present.

If she followed the custom of the day, Dai Dilaram would have asked Asmat to squat facing in the direction of Mecca with a large copper platter containing a little dirt beneath her, so that the newborn child would immediately come into contact with the earth. Asmat, already a mother three times over, would be familiar with all the necessary rituals of birth. Dai Dilaram would tie the umbilical cord with a thread and cut it, then clean and purify the baby with a ritual bath and wrap her in a white cloth, as prescribed in Islam for both male and female newborns. (In death too, the body was covered in white, marking the completion of a life cycle.) Dai Dilaram would then assure others outside the tent, Ghiyas and well-wishers, that mother and baby were fine. Hearing the news, Ghiyas would have offered prayers of thanks for the safe arrival of his new daughter, Mihr un-Nisa. A beautiful infant in all legendary accounts, she surely brought a moment of pleasure to the caravan community amid the hardships of the road.

Besides her parentage and her name, only one thing is certain about Mihr's birth: She entered the world outside Kandahar in the winter of 1577, on the road to India. During her time as empress and after, in chronicles and legends, several key embellishments were added to the tale. By the eighteenth century, three fascinatingly different versions of her birth story had been published, each revealing a great deal about the teller and his times (the writers were all men), including prevailing attitudes about politics, gender, and religion.

Niccolao Manucci was an Italian who came to India in 1653, eight years after Mihr/Nur's death, and spent nearly sixty years there as an artilleryman, foreign correspondent, linguist, and quack doctor; he claimed to have been the chief physician of the last Great Mughal, Aurangzeb, though he had no formal medical training. Fascinated by tales of Nur's birth and accomplishments, Manucci decided that the model for the narrative of Empress Nur's nativity should be nothing less than "The Flight into Egypt," the famous story of Jesus's infancy told in the Gospel of Matthew and employed as a potent motif by European painters. In Manucci's 1705 *Storia Do Mogor* (History of the Mughals), he wrote:

> I was anxious to find out about the descent of this queen, and I came to know for a certainty that she was the daughter of a Persian who arrived from Persia as a camel-driver in the service of some Armenian merchants. He brought with him his wife, who was enceinte. On the way, near the fortress of Candar [Kandahar], she was delivered of a child, and one of the merchants lent him an ass on which to convey the woman in that state of distress. The child that was born in that miserable plight came to be this famous queen (Nur Jahan).[14]

The image of Ghiyas leading a donkey bearing a pregnant Asmat brings to mind the biblical passage in which Saint Joseph, fleeing the murderous King Herod, guides the Virgin Mary and baby Jesus to safety in Egypt. Lively, shrewd, and observant, Manucci, a devout Catholic, was aware that this episode in the life of Jesus was well known in India. Not only did Jesuit visitors to the Mughal capital tell the story, but artists in the court of Jahangir copied the engravings and woodcuts of Albrecht Dürer, including *Flight into Egypt*, which depicts the scene.[15]

More than 150 years after Nur's birth, the rather eccentric, quick-witted trade agent turned Mughal chronicler, the aforementioned Khafi Khan, popularized a more melodramatic version of Nur's birth,

adding a shocking detail. In his telling, Ghiyas and Asmat made a
desperate decision when their daughter was born. Fearful that they
wouldn't be able to provide for the newborn because they'd been
robbed, they abandoned her by the roadside in the dead of night. In
the morning, the caravan leader Masud, wandering up and down to
oversee arrangements, spotted her by chance. Struck by her beauty
and moved by her helplessness, he picked her up. Then, searching for
a nurse in the caravan, he noticed Asmat, and (knowingly or unknow-
ingly) gave Nur back to her mother.[16]

Khafi's vivid tale of abandonment resonated with readers of his day.
Other writers picked it up, adding flourishes with each new telling.
One such embellishment came from Alexander Dow (1739–1779), a
Scottish sailor who was five years old when Khafi died in India. Dow
made his way to Bengal, serving on a private warship. Charmed by
the eastern world, he wrote a history of India, based upon a well-
known Persian text, to which he added a dissertation on the Brah-
manic religion, an ancient form of Hinduism, and an appendix on
the last forty years of the Mughal Empire. These works shaped early
British views of India.[17]

In the third volume of his *History of Hindostan*, published in 1772,
Dow presented the story of Nur's birth for the first time in English,
adding new details to the account of her abandonment. Dow was heir
to traditions in which great historical figures showed signs of distinction from the cradle, accompanied by miracles and marks of wonder:

> To carry the child was impossible [because of their circum-
> stances]. . . . A long contest began between humanity and neces-
> sity: the latter prevailed and they agreed to expose the child on
> the highway. The infant, covered with leaves, was placed under a
> tree; the disconsolate parents proceeded in tears. When they had
> advanced a mile from the place . . . [Asmat] gave way to grief;
> and throwing herself from the horse on the ground, exclaimed,

"My child! My child!" . . . [Ghiyas] was pierced to the heart . . .
He promised to bring her the infant. He arrived at the place. No
sooner had his eyes reached the child, than he was almost struck
dead with horror. A black snake . . . was coiled around it . . .
extending his fatal jaws to devour the infant. The father rushed
forward. The serpent, alarmed at his vociferation, retired into
the hollow tree. He took up his daughter unhurt, and returned
to the mother. He gave her child into her arms; and, as he was
informing her of the wonderful escape of the infant, some travel-
lers appeared, and soon relieved them of all their wants.[18]

The snake survived as a popular ingredient in most of the colonial
writings about Nur that followed Dow's. In movies made before and
after Indian independence from British colonial rule, Nur's abandonment, the snake, and her rescue, became enduring motifs.

An Italian quack doctor, an Indian courtier, a Scottish adventurer—
each wrote of Nur Jahan's remarkable birth. The Catholic merce-
nary Manucci was interested in an imitation of Christ. For Khafi,
the Indo-Persian tales of migration and a man's compassion for his
wife were dominant. Alexander Dow and the early colonial writers
who followed him were enchanted by a romantic image of India, that
land of wonders, surprises—and snake charmers. In our time, tour
guides from Lahore to New Delhi bring additional elements to the
saga of Nur's birth—for example, that light radiated from her baby
face, in keeping with both her birth name and the one Jahangir would
give her.

✤ THREE ✤

Al-Hind

Several months after Mihr was born outside Kandahar, the family crossed the Indus River into Al-Hind. In late 1578, Ghiyas, Asmat, baby Mihr, and her siblings reached the city of Lahore, the major entry point to the Mughal Empire for those coming from the northwest.[1] Then, as now, two major routes led from Kandahar to Lahore, one via the Khyber Pass through the Spīn Ghar Mountains; the other via the Bolan Pass through the Toba Kakur range.

Ringed by the river Ravi in the agricultural region of Punjab, Lahore, today part of modern Pakistan, was earning a reputation as a grand and prosperous Mughal city. Akbar sometimes used it as a seat of government; he'd ordered the fort rebuilt in brick and stone on the foundations of an older mud structure, and other splendid buildings, guesthouses, and pilgrimage centers were erected. Lahore's bustling bazaars and delightful gardens, the potpourri of languages and cultures, added to its appeal.[2]

Newcomers to Lahore commonly found temporary lodging with relatives or others from their country. In most Indian towns and cities

of this time, nobles and landlords opened their homes not only to
visiting relatives and friends but also to travelers, merchants, workers,
job seekers, servants, and the poor, though the patron's family usually
reserved a substantial part of the residences for private use.[3] Some
lodgers stayed for free, some paid rent, and some worked for their
room and board.

Ghiyas and Asmat were introduced by their caravan leader to a
Persian man living in Lahore who made arrangements for the family
to stay in a mansion near the fort.[4] That would be their home until
the time was right for the final leg of the journey to Emperor Akbar's
court in Fatehpur-Sikri, 350 miles to the southeast, near Agra, the
former capital.

Merchants congregated outside the fort—some who plied the
Agra-Lahore axis, a lucrative route, and some who came in caravans
from the northwest selling Iraqi horses, silk thread, and muskmelons.
An official in Akbar's court called Lahore a "resort of people of all
countries whose manufactures present an astonishing display and it
is beyond measure remarkable in populous-ness and extent."[5] Asmat
and Ghiyas would have walked along streets crowded with houses,
perhaps exploring the bazaars that pulsated with energy, packed
with buyers, sellers, and passersby exchanging greetings and news.
One section of the bazaar, a series of intricate lanes, was set aside for
women only. Women took their time gazing at the bold patterns and
colorful embroidery on the finest muslins, silks, and velvets. Many
wore flowers in their hair, and toe rings and anklets with charms or
little bells, and chewed betel leaf to redden their lips. Married women
wore *maang*, red color in the parting of their hair; or the *sekra*, seven
or more strings of pearls that hung from a band at the forehead; or the
laung, a clove-shaped stud ornamenting the nose.

From the food stalls wafted the aroma of cooked food and whiffs
of raw meat. Rice was central to Persian cuisine, but in Lahore, it
was served in piquant dishes unfamiliar to Asmat and Ghiyas, such

as biryani—rice with meat, onions, peppers, cinnamon, cumin, and other spices; or its variants, yakhni (rice and meat cooked in a gravy or broth with onions) and yulma (a sheep scalded in water until its wool came off, and then prepared like yakhni in potage). Accompanying these dishes were breads large and small, baked in the oven or made in skillets.

Everywhere Ghiyas and Asmat would hear the melodious tones of their mother tongue, which had become the favored language of the Mughal elite. A large number of Persian-speakers had settled in Lahore, among them scholars and literary figures from Safavid Iran and neighboring Central Asian regions. Booksellers in the markets of Lahore, Delhi, and Agra sold anthologies of Persian poetry. The fourteenth-century Iranian poet Hafiz had predicted that Persian was so irresistible a language that someday "all the Indian parrots [poets]" would relish "this Persian candy."[6] Quoting in Persian from admired poets was as common among the cognoscenti in India as it was among intellectuals in Iran. Persian infiltrated everyday phrases and exclamations, as well: *In the name of Allah; at the door of the grave; may you be damned in hell.*

But there were words in the vernacular of Lahore that Ghiyas and Asmat wouldn't have recognized. In India, Persian mingled with Gwaliyari, Braj, Kashmiri, Punjabi, and other rich dialects that contributed to Hindavi, the evolving language of Mughal India. Words, metaphors, and ideas from the Indian world had been integrated into the Persian language. Sufi centers in India played a vital role in this commingling. More than two centuries before Ghiyas and Asmat arrived in India, a new form of poetry was born, the genre known as *Sabk-i Hindi*—Persian poetry in the Indian style. From its beginnings, the form embodied the constant exchange between India and Iran, and the potential fruits of coexistence.[7] Pre-Mughal Sufi poets Amir Khusraw and Hasan Sijzi of Delhi, for instance, urged in their Persian poetry the transcending of religious and sectarian differences—

ideas that entered Indo-Persian culture and, later, deeply influenced
Emperor Akbar's promotion of tolerance.

The caravan was Mihr's first nursery, and Lahore her second. The
family stayed only a few months, a necessary stopover during which
Asmat could rest and the children adjust to a new environment—the
sight of grand Indian elephants, green parrots, and bright-blue peacocks; the absence of cypress trees. Ghiyas had time to think his way
forward, considering the best possible plans. That Asmat's uncle was
still favored by Emperor Akbar was a promising sign of good fortune
ahead. The uncle had already found a place in Akbar's court for a
cousin of Asmat's, a young man who'd risen in the imperial ranks.
Now it would be Ghiyas's turn.

Ghiyas Beg's first encounter with Emperor Akbar took place sometime between late 1578 and early 1579. From afar, as Mihr's family approached Fatehpur-Sikri, they would have seen the pinnacles
of the red sandstone harem, its multilevel stone pavilions crowned
with umbrella domes. The capital was a stunning example of visual
harmony. All its buildings were made from the same red sandstone,
sang-i surkh, and its many gardens were cooled by the leafy shade
of mango and neem trees and lush henna bushes. Hundreds of feet
below Akbar's harem was the caravanserai, the travelers' lodging,
from which Ghiyas and Asmat could gaze up at the majestic heights
of the women's quarters.

Ghiyas and Asmat would have known the legend of the founding
of Fatehpur-Sikri before they arrived in the city. Nearly a decade earlier, when Agra was the capital of Mughal India, Emperor Akbar was
in despair. Although several children had been born from his many
marriages, none had survived. His courtiers suggested that he seek
the blessings of the Sufi saint Salim Chishti in the village of Sikri.
When Akbar visited Salim Chishti, the saint blessed him and foretold
that he would have three sons. Prince Salim, n amed after the mystic,
was born on August 30, 1569, to the first of Akbar's Hindu wives,

Harkha. The grateful emperor announced that as a tribute to the saint he would build the city of Fatehpur-Sikri.[8] Fatehpur means City of Victory. Construction began two years after the birth of Prince Salim, who would one day take the name Jahangir, and continued into the 1580s.

Studded with domes and cupolas raised on columns, the tiled rooftops of the palace extended as far as the massive Jami Mosque. Near the palace was a great tower called the Hiran Minar, decorated with mock elephant tusks that commemorated Akbar's capture and domination of elephants. On the *maydan*, a large open space, Akbar and his court enjoyed polo, elephant fights, gladiatorial battle, acrobatics, and the flying of trained imperial pigeons. A court historian described Fatehpur-Sikri, surrounded by desert, as "Paradise on the brink of the precipice."[9]

Akbar gave two audiences every day. The first, for the general public, usually took place after he had finished his morning ablutions and prayers. He would appear at one of the balconies of the palace, showing himself, at a distance, for the *jharokha darshan*, the public viewing during which he blessed his people from on high.[10] One scribe grandiloquently described the Mughal emperor during such an appearance as "the sun of heaven of great fortune . . . who gives asylum to the world, the splendor of whose forehead illuminates the eyes of the world."

> At the rise of the sun, as is customary, the kettledrums of rejoicing and success are sounded . . . fleet-footed horses, with jeweled trappings . . . and female elephants are displayed . . . before the imperial gaze . . . On every side, a wave of tumult of God-given magnificence rises . . . Renowned princes, exalted offspring of kings . . . khans, sultans, mirs and mirzas of Iran and Turan . . . exalted lords of pen, high-ranking amirs, amirs' sons in service, a variety of swordsmen, triumphant elite servants, nimble quiver

bearers . . . Arabs, Persian, Turks, Tajiks, Kurds, Tartars . . . various groups and castes of learned men from Hindustan . . . from all the perfected imperial realms . . . are honored to kiss the threshold.[11]

It would not be surprising if Ghiyas and Asmat went to view His Majesty upon arriving in the new capital. After all, Ghiyas was preparing for an audience with Akbar, and seeing the Mughal's majesty would prime him for their meeting.

Akbar held a second, more exclusive audience each day, for local nobles and officials as well as ambassadors and trade representatives from other parts of the world.[12] Typically, this took place in the State Hall, usually toward the close of the day or at night. There the emperor announced court appointments, facilitated by contacts and associates. It was at such a gathering that Ghiyas Beg was introduced to Akbar.

According to the inventive Khafi Khan, the historian who popularized the legend of Mihr's abandonment, the caravan leader Malik Masud served as Ghiyas's intermediary as he sought the monarch's favor. Or perhaps Asmat's uncle was the key. In any case, Ghiyas's family and personal connections, and his previous service to the Persian shah were definite advantages in gaining access to Akbar.

The spacious State Hall was located at the eastern extremity of the palace, at the opposite end of the city from the harem. Tucked into one side of this meetinghouse was the pillared courtyard of the Audience Hall, the Dawlatkhana or Abode of Fortune. Here Akbar sat cross-legged on an elevated platform bearing a rug-draped red sandstone throne, clad in a knee-length gold-embroidered silk cloak tied at the waist with a delicately embroidered *kamarband*, the imperial dagger hung at his side. He wore a lamb's wool shawl, tasteful necklaces of gold and pearls, finger rings, and gold-embroidered shoes with pointed toes. The emperor chose his clothes according to the traditional color of the day's reigning planet, a practice his father had begun and that he continued.

The beating of a large drum and incantations to the divine inaugurated the assembly. Body guards, princes, grandees of the court, and men like Ghiyas Beg, who had permission to attend, stood barefoot in their designated places. Prince Salim, age ten, Akbar's longed-for eldest son, was near him, at a distance of a yard or so when standing, and a yard and a half to six yards when sitting. The second little prince, Daniyal, stood a little farther off, and the third, Murad, farther still. Railings of gold separated the king and the princes from the devoted nobles, next highest in rank, and these men were divided by a railing of silver from a group comprising the senior nobles, some lesser nobles, and other officials. A wooden railing set apart the rest of the men in the hall. Learned men and accomplished craftsmen paid their respects; imperial clerks presented petitions; and officers submitted their reports. From distant lands and fabled ports, merchants and traders came bearing expensive gems and other valuables, rarities and goods. Agile gladiators and wrestlers, singers, and entertainers waited in readiness for an imperial command.

The master of ceremonies, the courtier in charge of protocol, would have called out the name of Ghiyas Beg, who'd step forward dressed in the manner of a typical sixteenth-century Indo-Persian noble, in a white flowing cloak and elaborate turban, tasteful attire emphasizing his temperate demeanor in the presence of the almighty king. He would have worn no red, scarlet, or yellow; those colors were reserved exclusively for Akbar. Ghiyas would place the palm of his right hand upon his forehead and bend his head forward, performing *kornish*—a sign of the saluter's humility and submission to the royal presence, and his readiness for any service that may be asked of him. Akbar was known for his polite address to those present in official assemblies. He spoke to all comers with "the correctness of his intentions, the unbiasedness of his mind, the humility of his disposition,

the magnanimity of his heart, the excellence of his nature, the cheer-
fulness of his countenance, and the frankness of his manners."[13]

Silence was an important part of court decorum. Those admitted
to the emperor's presence weren't entitled to initiate a conversation.
Ghiyas Beg would have stood before the Grand Mughal in stillness. If
the emperor turned to look at a courtier or raised an eyebrow toward
him, that courtier would be pleased; if the emperor spoke, he would
feel blessed.

Khafi Khan reports a charming exchange between Akbar and the
caravan leader that may or may not have actually occurred. Akbar
remarked to Malik Masud that the caravan leader hadn't brought fine
presents this year as he had in previous years. Masud was pleased. Art-
fully, he responded that he had in fact brought a living present such
as had never come from Iran or Turan [Central Asia].[14] The emperor
took the measure of Ghiyas Beg, who, well schooled in courtly etiquette, stood humbly, head slightly bowed, hands folded, awaiting
any royal directive. Following the audience, he was given employment
by the Grand Mughal.[15]

Akbar had devised a complicated system for assigning warrior-
nobles, mature princes, and elite officers numerical rankings called
mansab—ranging from 10 to 10,000—that determined their salaries.
Nobles and officers served in a variety of capacities: as provincial governors, commanders of strategic fortresses, heads of military campaigns, revenue collectors who oversaw local tax collectors, provincial
judicial officers, and chief town officials.

Ghiyas's first job and starting rank in Mughal service are unrecorded.[16] But sources note that when he became the diwan (fiscal or
a revenue officer) of Kabul in 1595–96, he was granted a mansab of
300. By the time Akbar's son succeeded him as emperor early in the
seventeenth century, Ghiyas's rank had soared to 7,000—near the top
of the line.

As he left his first audience with Akbar, Ghiyas would have offered the emperor *taslim*, a salutation that involved placing the back of his right hand on the ground, then raising it gently until he stood erect, putting the palm of his hand upon the crown of his head. Repeating the *taslim* three times to indicate that he was ready to give himself as an offering, Ghiyas Beg would set forth on his new Indian career.

FOUR

The Cupolas of Chastity and the Perfect Man

A s Ghiyas and his family began settling into their new life in Fatehpur-Sikri, two events were still the talk of the town. One was the fire that ravaged a workshop known for producing the finest textiles in the country; piles of fine wool carpets made by Persian weavers and 10 million yards of velvet, silk, satin, and brocade had burned to ash. The other was far more momentous: A few months earlier, several older women of the imperial harem had left on an unprecedented pilgrimage to Mecca. Akbar's elderly aunt Gulbadan Banu Begum—her name translates as Princess Rosebody— had informed her nephew that she wished to go to Mecca with other women from the harem so she could fulfill her pledge to God that she would visit the holy places. Until recently, however, the route had been unsafe because of squabbles with Portuguese traders who commanded extensive trade rights in the Indian Ocean and issued passes to pilgrims. Once the Portuguese and the Mughals settled their differences, Gulbadan brought up the matter again. Akbar gave her permission to proceed, along with provisions and a large sum of money.[1]

Gulbadan, cerebral and observant, in her seventies at the time of the pilgrimage to Mecca, was the daughter of the first Mughal, Babur. She left for posterity the only historical chronicle written by a woman in the age of the classical Muslim Empires—the Ottomans of Turkey, the Safavids of Iran, and the Mughals of India—providing extraordinary insight into the lives of Mughal court women.

Accompanied by thirteen senior harem women, and their servants, reciters, and singers, Gulbadan departed from Fatehpur-Sikri in the fall of 1578, just as Asmat and Ghiyas were leaving Lahore. The women planned to cut southwest through the province of Gujarat in western India, where they would board a ship for Mecca. Akbar directed his six-year-old son Murad to lead the pilgrims on their journey to the sea. In the Mughal world of the seventeenth century, a little boy was considered man enough to escort the most senior women of the dynasty. But when Gulbadan made the point that precisely due to his tender age Murad should be left behind, the emperor acquiesced. Three older men escorted the convoy.

The women decided that Akbar's mother, Hamideh Begum, and a trusted servant woman who was her confidante should remain in the capital to counsel the emperor. Akbar often relied on his mother for support and advice. The two were mutually devoted. Hamideh had a habit of traveling to visit her son unannounced when he was away from the capital. Earlier that year, for instance, the emperor was hunting in the forests of Punjab when his attendants announced to him that his mother had arrived at the camp and was anxious to see him; Akbar was delighted to receive her. He clearly admired her mettle. Once when he went to Kabul to settle scores with a rebellious stepbrother, he left his mother in charge of the province of Delhi.

Gulbadan's pilgrimage to Mecca with other senior royal women, and their insistence on leaving Emperor Akbar's mother behind as his counselor, reveals a great deal about the workings of the Mughal harem.

A few years before Ghiyas and Asmat arrived at the capital, Akbar had declared that women of the royal household were to be segregated in a well-ordered, high-walled harem. To ensure their seclusion, he built a large enclosure and gave each woman a separate apartment. According to the first official history of the Mughals, *Akbarnama* (The history of Akbar), commissioned by Akbar and written by historian Abul-Fazl, the harem housed five thousand women—but Father Antonio Monserrate, a Jesuit priest visiting from Portugal, reported the number as three hundred. The movement of the sequestered women was restricted, and rules governed who could visit them and who could not. The harem was under constant surveillance. Women superintendents watched over each section—the most trusted in the emperor's quarters, which were guarded by eunuchs. A contingent of Rajputs, a Hindu warrior clan, patrolled the perimeter of the women's palace.

The harem played a role in Akbar's grand plan for solidifying political networks and expanding his territory. Early in his reign, Akbar was unsatisfied with the size of his empire. Though he controlled a large central area that included the fertile plain of the river Ganga, in the east, large areas of Bengal were still under the command of local rulers, and in the west, Ajmer was in the hands of Rajputs, while Gujarat and adjoining states had a tributary status. Akbar set out to change that, acquiring territory through massive and bloody military campaigns across India, battles that won him the sultanate of Gujarat and the state of Bengal, among others. He also grew his empire through shrewd alliances. He recruited advisers, governors, and officers of diverse ethnic, regional, and religious backgrounds, and married into the families of several of these men. Having both Muslim and Hindu wives allowed Akbar to create the political networks that helped him rule a Hindu majority and set the foundation for expanding Mughal authority.

Furthermore, the seclusion of women in the harem, which Fazl called *the fortunate place of sleep*, contributed to what amounted to an imperial rebranding. In the early 1570s, the emperor began casting himself as a sacred figure, an infallible spiritual authority. Fazl, the official historian, amplified the emperor's illustrious genealogy, hinting at divine roots. The inviolability of the royal harem, penetrable only by the emperor—housing glorious and untouchable women, fitting consorts of a godlike king—was meant to be further proof of his near-divinity. The terms used by Akbar's court historian to describe the harem—for example, *cupolas of chastity* and the women within it—the *chaste secluded ladies*—were meant to make clear that Akbar's was an unpolluted line. The harem also served as a symbol of the emperor's strength and virility. Fazl's assertion in the *Akbarnama* that the harem held five thousand women was vital proof of the emperor's power.[2]

Of course, the Great Mughal (or *Grao Mogor, Groote Mogul, Grand Mogol*, as the Portuguese, Dutch, and French called Akbar, respectively) wasn't inventing a completely new body of rules for women. His nomadic ancestors had maintained firm codes of modesty and separation, but their peripatetic lives made complete segregation of the sexes impossible. Akbar carried the process much further by permanently secluding his women, whom he called *the veiled ones.*

But Gulbadan's journey, and the fact that Hamideh stayed behind as a wise adviser, proved that, while Akbar wanted to render women invisible, that invisibility wasn't complete or inviolable. A group of senior royal women decided that they were not going to be simply locked away in the harem of Fatehpur-Sikri, making a bold claim to self-expression and resourcefulness by insisting on traveling to Mecca, a culturally accepted journey. This *hajj* led by the emperor's aunt—a rare event then and later—underlined the point that women had been, and would continue to be, active players in political decisions and the future of the empire, despite Akbar's move to segregate them.

Even in dealings with women from subordinate princely states, the emperor didn't always get his way. For example, Pravin Ray, poet and courtesan of the raja of Orchcha, refused Akbar's summons to come to the court and join his harem. She sent the following couplet in response: "Pay heed, wise emperor, to what Pravin Ray has to say. Only low caste people, crows, and dogs eat off the plates used by others."[3] Standing boldly in solidarity with his lover—the raja likewise had refused to surrender to Mughal authority.[4]

Growing up in her father's house, Mihr would hear about intrepid Gulbadan—though not about bold Pravin Ray—from the women around her: her mother, Asmat, and Asmat's friends, who likely invoked the story of the *hajj* and of the imperial adviser Hamideh as inspiring examples of Mughal women's imagination and leadership.

An ardent inquirer, Akbar rejected religious orthodoxy and aimed to build a new philosophy, which he called "Universal Peace." He was drawn to the ideas of the great Sufi thinker 'Ibn al-Arabi (d. 1240), especially his opinion that a king who fulfilled the obligations of divine regency was a "Perfect Man." Aspiring to perfection, Akbar, the self-styled Chosen One of God, felt called to initiate a policy of tolerance. He took part in Muslim rites and practices, sent money to Mecca, and swept the floor of the great mosque in Fatehpur-Sikri. He also admired the liberal philosophy of the Nuqtavis, a Persian Sufi sect; held the New Testament in high regard; embraced yogic practices; experimented with vegetarianism; and was so keen to understand the power that Hindus experienced in worshipping the sun that he memorized the 1,001 names of the sun in Sanskrit. Akbar's chroniclers subtly linked him with traditions of the Hindu Rajputs, the cultural heritage of many of his wives. The ancient Rajputs traced their aristocratic lineages from the sun (*suryavamshi*) or the moon (*chandravamshi*). Kunti, one of the protagonists in the ancient epic

Mahabharata, a famous version of which was illustrated in Akbar's workshop, conceived a son immaculately through the rays of the sun. Rama, the great god-king of the epic *Ramayana* (also illustrated in Akbar's atelier) belonged to the sun lineage. And some of Akbar's Rajput subjects raised him to the same status.[5]

Traditions regarding the sun and moon had entered Islam as part of various philosophical and occult systems. Akbar was aware of Persian Neo-Platonic philosophers known as Illuminists—chief among them the twelfth-century thinker Suhrawardi (d. 1192)—who believed that all life comes into existence through constant blinding illumination from God, the Light of Lights, revealed to man by a chain of dazzling angels. At their head was the angel Gabriel, identified with the spirit of Prophet Muhammad. All men possess a divine spark, said Suhrawardi, who recognized five levels of wisdom. Only those in the top three were the masters of their age. Among them were Suhrawardi himself, Plato, and, according to Akbar's official historian, Akbar. The emperor also knew that the Illuminists who interested him had been influenced by the ancient Greek philosopher and mystic Hermes Trismegistus, who regarded the sun as a manifestation of divinity.[6] Akbar's interest in light and celestial bodies would be of particular importance for his successors, Emperor Jahangir and Empress Nur.

The wise and accomplished Akbar is said to have been illiterate; his son Salim would mention this in his memoir when he became Emperor Jahangir. Was it true? Or was Akbar's claim of illiteracy a way of putting himself on par with Prophet Muhammad, who also couldn't read? In any case, records suggest that official documents, scriptures, poetry, and stories were read out loud to Akbar. One of the readers was the son of a storyteller to the Iranian monarch Tahmasp, Ghiyas Beg's former employer and sovereign.[7] Akbar loved tales from the *Hamzanama*, the chronicle of Hamzeh, the Prophet Muhammad's uncle, who traveled the world to spread the doctrines of Islam.

In Fatehpur-Sikri, there was tension between the open-minded emperor and the orthodox Sunni clergy. They were suspicious of Sufi mystics, who regularly entered a trance and had visions; they could be insulting to the Shi'a, and they sometimes disapproved of Akbar's actions and interests. Clerics weren't the only critics. The historian Abdal-Qadir Badauni, known as Badauni, served in the emperor's court and wrote a rather huffy counternarrative to the *Akbarnama*. "Hindustan is a wide place," Badauni observed, "where there is an open field for all manner of licentiousness, and no one interferes in another's business, so that everyone can do as he pleases. . . ."[8] He didn't mean this as a compliment.

Around the time that Ghiyas Beg was inducted into the Mughal court, Akbar assumed greater control of religious affairs. He issued a public edict declaring himself the supreme arbiter of religious matters in his realm, taking precedence over Muslim religious scholars and jurists. In disputed matters, according to the edict, the emperor would decide which opinion was authoritative and hence binding for all Muslims. The edict also declared that Akbar was the caliph, although modern scholars differ on whether he intended to be the supreme authority over Muslims only in his domain, or over Muslims globally, thus rejecting subordination to the Ottoman king who'd claimed the title of caliph since taking control of the holy cities of Islam in 1517.[9]

Rumors spread that the emperor had turned against Islam. Reports traveled to Iran, Central Asia, Portugal, and Spain that Akbar had committed sacrilege by claiming to be the new Prophet. His true motivation was perhaps more spectacular. According to scriptural predictions, an Islamic messiah would one day inaugurate a new epoch of peace and prosperity. Akbar dreamed of being declared the awaited Mahdi, the Renewer, the messiah who would banish evil and usher in a just world order. Whichever philosophical basis for his sovereignty appealed to Akbar most—the "Perfect Man" of al-Arabi, the scriptural notion of the Mahdi, or the concept of divine light—all converged on the point that he was an agent of God who would maintain the "rhythm and balance of the cosmos."[10]

While Persian migrants of status like Ghiyas felt welcomed in Akbar's court, the finer details of his control and the machinery of government were less immediately apparent.[11] With time Asmat and Ghiyas would decipher the written and unwritten rules, exceptions to those rules, and possible avenues of advancement open to a newcomer. The factions and fissures in Akbar's court were continuously shifting. The comfortable coexistence of Hindu rajas and the Mughals, of Hindavi and Persian, the Bible and the Quran, the orthodox and the heterodox—in sum, the diversity of beliefs and practices that made Akbar's India a charmed place—was difficult to maintain. So was Akbar's goal of completely confining the chaste secluded ladies of the harem.

FIVE

The Wak-Wak Tree

The legendary island of Wak-Wak lay at the edge of the world, in a sea where fish danced. On it stood a talking tree, with the heads of humans and demons growing from its branches amidst leaves and flowers, and the heads of beasts sprouting from its roots—lions, tigers, dragons, cows, elephants, and mythical flying creatures called simurghs.

The story of Wak-Wak, which first found popularity in *Shahnama*, the Book of Kings, an eleventh-century epic poem by the celebrated Iranian author Firdausi, would have been an important part of Mihr's childhood, along with other fables, poems, and histories from the Islamic world. These works were the earliest components of her education—literary, moral, and practical—as she was growing up in her father's *haveli*, his mansion, restricted to the women's quarters, where no men could enter except Ghiyas, his sons, and the male servants of the house. There Asmat and Ghiyas would tell stories to Mihr and her siblings—her older brothers Asaf and Muhammad, her older sister Manija, and their younger siblings Khadija and Ibrahim, born in India.[1] Along with the story of Wak-Wak, Ghiyas and Asmat may have shared the delights of the *Tuti-Nama*, a fourteenth-century Persian collection of tales told by a wise parrot to distract his mistress from having an affair while her merchant husband was away on business. Mihr might have thought that the clever bird was a bit like the sagacious storyteller Scheherazade in the *Thousand and One Nights*, with which her parents were also likely to have entertained and educated their children.

As in any noble Muslim household, Asmat and her daughters were forbidden to enter the men's area, the *mardana*. Female servants were also barred. The main entrance to the house was a large gate on the street that opened into a courtyard leading to the *mardana*. Behind this front row of rooms a verandah led to another courtyard, around which the rest of the household would be arranged, perhaps on two floors. The women's sections would most likely have several private rooms on the upper floor and communal rooms, kitchens, and toilet facilities below. Off the courtyard, on the outskirts of the women's area, were storerooms, stables, and servants' quarters, with back doors opening onto the street.

When men came to the house to discuss official matters or to socialize with Ghiyas, a male servant led them to a waiting room, and then to the curtained and carpeted reception hall of the *mardana*, where niches in the walls held vases of flowers. There Ghiyas Beg would greet his guests with *Salaam 'Alaikum*, "peace be unto you," and invite them to sit on mattresses cushioned with pillows. The guests responded *Valaikum Salaam*, "and upon you, peace." Ghiyas and his social equals hailed one another in affectionate terms such as *bhai* (brother) or *baba* (father). He'd offer them betel leaf and a *huqqa*, a water pipe, and if a meeting extended into mealtime, an attendant would spread an embroidered *safra* on the floor and bring out food from the inner quarters. When Ghiyas met with men of lower status, probably in the waiting room or outside the *haveli*, they addressed him as the *benefactor of the poor*, or with the phrase *"I eat your bread and salt."* A servant might say to Ghiyas, with deference, *"I live by you."*[2]

Women visitors to the *haveli* were ushered from a waiting room in the women's area to one of the communal rooms by a female servant. In the women's quarters, visits from friends were part of daily life shaped by a flurry of household activities. Under the watchful eye of Asmat, a female housekeeper would distribute foodstuffs to the cooks. Another servant inspected storerooms and checked the *haveli* accounts. Dai Dilaram, the wet nurse who perhaps helped deliver Mihr and still served the family, had her own ceaseless rounds as Asmat's right hand—caring for the children, helping in the kitchen, reminding servants to dust the carpets, light torches in the evening, and water the pots of reeds set in windows to cool the inner quarters during blistering summers. She would feed the pet parrot, clean the silver fruit trays, and keep rose water ready so that guests could cool their hands and faces with a refreshing splash. When a servant arrived from the men's area with a request for a snack or a meal, Dai Dilaram would hurry to instruct the cooks to prepare, at a moment's notice, dressed rice, spiced and roast meats, a variety of lentils and bread. She might have taught the children chess and Persian backgammon.

A reliable intermediary between the world indoors and the one outside, Dai Dilaram was responsible for buying food from local tradespeople.[3] Women selling vegetables, fruit, fish, meat, spices, and cloth also came to the back doors of the *haveli* near the servants' quarters. A servant might bring them something to eat as they waited inside the gate, where Dai Dilaram or another member of the staff would inspect their wares and make purchases. The tradeswomen would chat with the servants, relating news of the town, and picking up gossip about the lives of "big" people. They would sing songs and recite verses in Braj, the dialect of Hindavi spoken by locals in the region, impromptu performances that Mihr and her siblings would have understood and enjoyed.

Ghiyas's days were devoted to administrative matters—obligatory appearances at court, meetings with men petitioning for help or seeking guidance on issues of finance, and writing reports for senior Mughal officers. During his tenure as diwan, minister, in the revenue department, he brought into order accounts that had long been in arrears.

Asmat spent most of her time in the women's quarters with the children, overseeing household affairs, reading, or socializing with visitors. Sometimes she and the children might visit bazaars or riverside gardens with male family members or servants as chaperones. But rather than traveling public streets, elite girls and women often used rooftops as protected avenues of passage from one home to another. On these connecting terraces, they took a break from the confinement of the lower floors. Mihr, her mother, and her sisters likely gathered on the roof with friends to chat, dry or oil their hair, view the busy streets from above, or recite poetry while helpers hung up wet laundry and looked after grains and pickles drying in the sun.

The *haveli* of Ghiyas may have been among the mansions on the half-mile-long main street of Fatehpur-Sikri, which was interrupted in the middle by the *charsuq*, the central market, with lanes going in four directions, each lined with shops and stalls. Five times a day, the exalting sound of the *azan*, the call to prayer, from the Jami mosque would drown out the tinkle of workmen's tools; the grunts of cattle, sheep, and goats; and the conversations of passersby, shoppers, and merchants selling fireworks, fish, wood, soap, building materials, and more in the Mughal bazaar. These were the sounds Mihr would have heard from the roof of her home.

It was here in the Fatehpur-Sikri *haveli*, bound by the distinct rhythms of the men's and women's quarters, that Mihr took her first steps; wrote the first letter of Persian script, *alif*, (literally, "commencement"); and learned Hindavi: the name of a vegetable or a constellation, the word for summer dust storms, *jhakkhar*, or *Ram Ram*, a common greeting invoking Ram, the popular Hindu deity.

When Mihr was about eight years old, Akbar left Fatehpur-Sikri because of its inadequate water supply, shifting the Mughal capital to Lahore. Around then, Ghiyas moved the family to nearby Agra, another center of royal government that would later become the capital. For Mihr and her family, life in their new mansion and town would have been very similar to life in Fatehpur-Sikri. Mihr would remain in her father's Agra *haveli* until her marriage.

As Mihr and her sisters were growing up, festivals, ceremonies, and ritual observances would give them opportunities to interact, indirectly, with the world beyond their father's house. After the month-long fast during the days of Ramazan, and the appearance of the moon of 'Id, Muslims celebrated 'Id ul-Fitr, the breaking of the fast. Emperor Akbar gave a feast, where "magical minstrels administered the medicine of wisdom" to courtiers who also watched archers on horseback and games of polo. Akbar distributed alms and gifts; as the official account of his reign puts it, "crowds of men obtained their wishes."[4] Mihr's father and brothers would regale the girls with descriptions of the events.

On the morning of 'Id ul-Qurban, the Feast of Sacrifice, commemorating the Quranic story of Ibrahim's readiness to sacrifice his son Isma'il at the command of God, Muslim men gathered at the place of prayer, the *'Id-gah* (literally "the place of rejoicing"), usually an open space outside a town or a village.[5] Afterward, families held a big feast at home. Noble households gave new clothes and sheep or goats to the needy, ensuring that the poorest were able to offer sacrifice and rejoice. For Mihr and her siblings, the main message of this feast day would be the importance of faith—Ibrahim's faith was tested at the command of God—and generosity, which would allow them to earn spiritual merit.

In the month of Muharram, Shi'a Muslims observed a period of mourning to mark the martyrdom of Husain, son of Ali, the fourth caliph. Men carried imitation mausoleums in public processions. At the first sight of the moon of Muharram, people exchanged greetings as a new year began according to the Islamic lunar calendar. Other major events included Shab-i Barat, the Night of Salvation, when people considered past sins and resolved to sin no more; the Prophet's birth anniversary; and Nauruz, the Iranian spring festival. Though aristocratic women rarely attended most of these commemorations, they observed rituals in private. They gave alms to the poor, sent presents to family and friends, remembered deceased ancestors, and feasted. If Mihr didn't participate publicly, these observances would connect her, even from indoors, with the greater world.

As the children grew older, the boys were offered opportunities not given to the girls. For one thing, boys in Mughal India had tutors; girls didn't. Family members, mainly the women of a household, took the initiative in pushing girls to learn, though sometimes fathers or grandfathers taught them arithmetic, and the art of writing. Ghiyas, a master calligrapher, might have demonstrated the beauty of good penmanship to both his sons and his daughters.

There were no educational requirements or schools for aristocratic Muslim girls or those of other Indian communities. For Muslim girls, the emphasis was on memorizing verses from the Quran to be recited at ritual festivities and gatherings. The equivalent was true in elite Hindu families. A knowledge of certain scriptures was part of a girl's education, along with singing devotional songs. But although the Hindu goddess Saraswati was the patron of learning, women were not to learn the Vedas or any other branch of the Shastras, ancient Hindu law books. No Hindu girls went to the pundits, the scholars, to study: if any of them did learn Sanskrit it was within the family. Mihr would know Hindu girls in her neighborhood who were raised, like her, to learn scriptures by heart and read moral tales that stressed responsibility and discipline, but suggested limited possibilities for women.

Still, later in life, Nur would write poetry of a sophistication that showed she was not only highly literate but well read in the Persian literary tradition. As empress, she would often seek counsel from her father on urgent matters of governance, which suggests a long-standing close relationship between them. Perhaps it was Ghiyas who introduced her to Iranian masters such as the wise poet Hafiz, or the Anatolian mystic Rumi, whose rhyming couplets, composed between 1258 and 1273, were collected in the *Masnawi*, and told her the legend of the miraculous Baka flower, brought to Rumi's wife by flying saints from India. Mentioned in the earliest Indian medical treatises and holding a prominent place in the Ayurvedic pharmacopoeia, the flower was used to heal diseases of the eye.[6]

In various seasons, Hindus recited tales from the glorious epics, *Ramayana* and *Mahabharata*, marking the triumph of good over evil. Mihr may have read Persian translations, or learned about the characters in Hindu epics and fables from the non-Muslim employees of the household. They would tell the children the stories of women such as Shakuntala (the wife of a king who overcomes the curse separating them) and Draupadi, a major character in the *Mahabharata*—and gently reprimand the children when they misbehaved by reminding them of the morals of these stories: be brave, be obedient, learn from elders.

As she matured, Mihr would note the subtlety of the tales she heard and read, picking up insinuations of the earthy and the divine in poetry and fables. She would learn that the story of the Wak-Wak tree appears in a Quranic verse that calls it the Tree of Zakkum and says that its fruit was the head of a demon. (The tale may have even deeper roots; a sixth-century Chinese writer mentioned a similar legend.) A great intellectual in the ninth-century court of the Abbasid dynasty in Baghdad described the tree as a cross between plant and animal. In tenth-century Arabic literature, it was noted that the tree grew in India, though over the centuries various writers conjectured that it could be found in the Indian Ocean, on Madagascar or islands off the coast of East Africa, on the Pacific Rim near Japan. Asmat or Ghiyas might have told her that Alexander the Great was said to have visited the talking tree of Wak-Wak; male and female heads on the tree prophesied his death.[7] The many rich variations of this story may have sparked her love of literature and poetry.

Ghiyas and Asmat would have seen early signs of Mihr's agile mind, her ingenuity and literary imagination. She would continue a tradition, a way of thinking and being, that Ghiyas and other Persian migrants like him longed to nurture. In Nasir al-Din Tusi's *Akhlaq-i Nasiri* (Nasirean ethics), one of the detailed and dogmatic child-rearing manuals popular with Muslim parents, the author declared that well-bred girls and boys should keep away from "frivolous poetry, with its talk of odes and love and wine-bibbing . . . for poetry can only be the corruption of youth."[8] Ghiyas disagreed; lyrical sensibilities ran deep in his family. His father, Muhammad Sharif was an accomplished poet, as was his brother, who took the pen name Wasli, the One Who Seeks Union with the Divine. His cousin Shapur, who had visited India before Ghiyas, produced a collection of poems. To these men, the boundary between the human and divine was porous; longing across differences was the great unifier. Poetry and mysticism shared this desire to dissolve dualisms.

In Safavid Iran, speaking of direct union with God, extolling the majesty of love and youth, even displaying a questioning or introspective attitude had come to be viewed as heretical. Poets, mystics, and thinkers were persecuted or killed for what was considered blasphemy.

In India, Ghiyas was able to nurture his expressive inheritance. His *haveli* became a haven for poets such as Hakim Arif, who was so moved by Ghiyas's love for the genre that he wrote a panegyric poem in his honor. Ghiyas also welcomed Talib Amuli, whom he would one day introduce to Jahangir. Amuli so impressed the monarch that he awarded him the title Malik us-Shu'ara, the King of Poets.[9] Perhaps when she was a little girl, Mihr sneaked up close to the men's quarters and hid in a corner to hear the visiting poets recite.

While Mihr would acquire a taste for narrative and poetry informally, from listening to stories and poems and from her own unfettered explorations of literature, and from memorizing the Quranic verses—becoming familiar with the torments and travails of Quranic characters—her reading would have also had to follow certain parental and societal prescriptions. She and her sisters would be expected to read aloud the elegant, lyrical prose of *Gulistan* (The rose garden), written in 1258 by Saadi, the Shakespeare of Persian literature. The spirit of the book would suit Asmat and Ghiyas's mild temperaments. Within Saadi's parables lay instruction for handling the challenges of adulthood and guidelines for wise leadership, as in the first chapter, "The Conduct of Kings," where Saadi calls for prudence and justice in a ruler.[10] Mihr and her parents never dreamed that she would someday put this advice to practical use in ruling their adopted homeland along with her emperor husband. Such a position—or anything close to the exercise of political power by a woman—was simply not part of their world.

What mattered most to noble Muslim families of Mughal India was strengthening character—teaching children what a growing boy should learn in order to be a gentleman; how a girl should behave in order to be an ideal woman. Such instruction covered every aspect of their lives: where they slept; how they dressed; what they learned; what and how they ate; whether they drank wine or composed poetry; whether and where they played with kites or pigeons; how and where they mixed socially, and with whom.

Among Tusi's prescription for girls in *Akhlaq-i Nasiri*, first published in 1235 and one of the five books that Emperor Akbar regularly had read to him:

In the case of daughters, one must employ . . . whatever is
appropriate and fitting to them. They should be brought up to
keep close to the house and live in seclusion (*hijab*), cultivat-
ing gravity, continence (*'iffat*), modesty and other qualities we
have enumerated in the chapter on Wives. They should be prevented from learning to read or write, but allowed to acquire
such accomplishments as are commendable in women.[11]

Two centuries earlier, another guide to conduct, *Qabus-Nama*, also
a favorite among kings and aristocracy, spoke of a girl's lot in more
starkly negative terms:

If you have a daughter, entrust her to kindly nurses and give her
good nature. When she grows up, entrust her to a preceptor . . .
[to] learn the sacred law and the essential religious duties. But
do not teach her to read and write; that is a great calamity. Once
she is grown up, do your utmost to give her in marriage; it were
best for the girl not to come into existence, but, being born, she
had better be married or be buried . . . daughters are captives of
their parents . . . helpless and incapable of finding employment.
Make provision for her . . . fasten her about someone's neck so
as to escape from anxiety for her.[12]

Although the idea of universal education for women didn't exist,
there was a tradition in Persia and Al-Hind of men acknowledging
the intellectual achievements of women. Poets and compilers of biographical compendiums wrote of women who were literary stars, and
of those learned in religion. According to these books, thirty-two
female scholars lived in Baghdad in the eleventh century; two hundred "noteworthy" women lived in Damascus in the twelfth century.
A fifteenth-century Egyptian, Al Sakhwai, wrote *Kitab al-Nisa*, an
extensive collective biography of several women in his time who were

transmitters of the traditions of the *hadith*, the records of the Prophet's words and deeds.[13] Mihr would learn about awe-inspiring, well-remembered queens and princesses in the Islamic world, such as Pari Khan Khanum, a daring Safavid princess and fine poet from Asmat and Ghiyas's native Iran, and, from their adopted land, Gulbadan, Akbar's bold and independent memoirist aunt.

As for boys, in almost all manuals of comportment that parents or tutors would use, the discipline of the senses was primary. "Let [the boy] also from time to time adopt the custom of eating dry bread," Tusi counseled. "Such manners, albeit good in poor men, are even better in rich. . . . He should be accustomed not to drink water while eating and he should on no account be given wine and intoxicating drinks before he reaches early manhood." Boys shouldn't be allowed to sleep too much, or during the day, Tusi said, because that produced "deadness of mind." Walking, riding, and exercise were to be "customary pursuits." To be humble and gracious with peers, they were not to boast about wealth or possessions or what they ate or wore. Boys must be taught to refrain from arrogance and obstinacy. The tutor who imparted this guidance, Tusi counseled, should be intelligent and religious, well versed in the training of dispositions, "with a reputation for fair speech and gravity, an awe-inspiring manner, manliness and purity; he must also be aware of the characters of kings, the manners involved in associating with them and addressing them . . ."[14]

The evidence of Mihr's later accomplishments suggests that the gentle Asmat and Ghiyas didn't follow Tusi's harsher dictates. But even without the stern advice of strict authorities like Tusi or the author of the *Qabus-Nama*, they would insist that all their children embody such virtues as patience, discernment, and the dutiful practice of their faith. Asmat and Ghiyas would teach their sons and daughters the value of courtesy and proper demeanor. Gravity and courage would mark a man; gravity and modesty, a woman. Indelicate language was not allowed under any circumstances. *Short* and *refreshing* were the "watchwords of conversation."[15]

Mihr's parents would make sure that their daughters would be known for intelligence, piety, self-control, good judgment, tenderness, and temperate speech. In their sons, they cultivated the strength, dexterity, daring, resolution, and loyalty that led to the advancement of noble men in the Mughal court. Being skilled in the martial arts, archery, swordsmanship, riding and managing elephants and horses, along with the craft of calligraphy and polished discourse, would also come in handy.

As Mihr and her siblings grew older, the social, political, and cultural universe of her brothers became ever more separate from that of their sisters. Muhammad, Asaf, and Ibrahim would accompany Ghiyas Beg to festivities and ceremonies at court, where they witnessed Akbar's embrace of Hindu social rituals. On special occasions, the emperor applied a vermillion mark to the foreheads of select political subordinates in the court. Twice a year, he had himself weighed against a variety of goods and materials that were then distributed as alms. He worshipped the sun publicly, facing the east and prostrating himself before a sacrificial fire as Hindu clerics recited the names of the sun in Sanskrit—even as he bowed to Mecca in the west for the five times' daily Muslim prayer.

Akbar took great care in rearing his beloved son Salim to be the next heir. Ghiyas, in grooming his own sons to be worthy aristocrats, could use the Mughal princes as prime models. Just as a well-selected tutor was vital to the training of noble boys, so was a guardian, or *ataliq*, crucial in the training of princes. The *ataliq* supervised a prince's studies of the Quran; various Islamic sciences, including rhetoric, epistolary style, proper speech, and prosody; and military skills—strategy, tactics, and the correct use of weaponry. After their circumcision and the start of formal education, *bismillah khani* (pronouncing the name of God), usually at the age of four or five, Mughal princes received a daily stipend and began their integration into the life of the empire.

As an energetic and willful teenager, Salim took part in imperial processions and accompanied Akbar on royal hunts. Ghiyas and his sons would see Salim on many occasions, and in many roles. (Whether Mihr ever saw him is a matter of dispute.) Emperor Akbar ordered that, every month, a day should be set aside for an imperial bazaar where merchants displayed goods from around the world. This was also a day when ordinary men could present their grievances to the emperor.[16]

Akbar, his harem women, and women of other noble households were invited to attend the bazaar. Languages crisscrossed: Persian with Braj, Pashto with Bhasha. Travelers and traders told tales of places far and near—the wonders of the world, made even more delicious in romantic renderings. It is not hard to picture Mihr in the bazaar, along with Asmat and Dilaram. And it's possible that, as legends say but no official records prove, Mihr visited the Mughal palace on numerous occasions and could have been spotted by Prince Salim long before he became emperor and married her.

As adults, Muhammad, Asaf, and Ibrahim left the *haveli* for the world outside. Muhammad, embroiled in an act of treason against the Mughals, was executed in 1605. Asaf married the daughter of an eminent Persian man, who served in various military and financial capacities under Akbar—she remains nameless in Mughal records that speak of him—had children, and lived a long life as a distinguished Mughal noble. In due time, references to Ibrahim would appear in court histories, along with Asaf.

Mihr, Manija, and Khadija would leave the *haveli* too—but not for the court, the hunting lodge, or the imperial harem, nor the domain of imperial offices. When they left the *haveli* of Asmat and Ghiyas, it would be for marriage; their new lives would be bound by familiar routines of domestic life and cultural propriety handed down to generations of women.

Asmat and Ghiyas chose young, rising Mughal officers, men of good inheritance, as their sons-in-law. Manija was married to Qasim Khan, an excellent poet who earned distinction as a treasurer under the governor of Bengal. He became famous as Qasim Khan Manija, the name of his wife, by which the court wits addressed him.[17] (What does it tell us about Asmat and Ghiyas's home that Manija too grew up to be such a strong person that her husband came to be called by her name?) Khadija was married to a nobleman, Hakim Khan, an official in the court of Emperor Jahangir. Except for stray references to their husbands, there is nothing else in the records about Manija or Khadija.

The matrimonial career of their sister, Mihr, however, would eventually generate volumes of praise, blame, conjecture, and legend. It began with her first wedding to an ordinary provincial Mughal officer.

SIX

The Mirror of Happiness

Carved in graceful floral patterns, a wooden screen separated the men's section of the wedding ceremony from the women's. Asmat, her daughters and daughters-in-law and their children, Dai Dilaram, and a host of other women surrounded the bride, seventeen-year-old Mihr. Dark-eyed and slender, she would have worn a knee-length shirt and shalwar, long breeches, of muslin or fine silk. Both were white, the color of blessedness, with heavy brocade, gold for luck, decorating the sleeves and hem of the shirt. Seamstresses would make sure that Mihr's wedding shirt wasn't sewn with any knots; they were inauspicious and would fetter fortune. A taboo on buttons had been relaxed by this time, as with other Indian and Iranian practices that had undergone changes in the Mughal world. Jackets with prized jeweled buttons made of ruby and cornelian were in vogue among kings, queens, and nobles, and Mihr may have worn such a garment over her wedding clothes.[1]

She wore jeweled earrings—rubies, perhaps, or pearls—and a shimmering veil of transparent silk, embroidered with gold filaments, would be draped loosely over her head, showing her exquisite face.[2] Kohl lined her almond-shaped eyes, a feature that stands out in her later portraits.

On the other side of the screen sat the groom, Ali Quli Beg, a Mughal government official and former military officer, dressed in a flowing silk top and trousers embroidered in gold. He was accompanied by Mihr's brothers; Asmat's uncle, the first member of the family to arrive at the Mughal court; cousin Jafar Beg, who reached India a little before Asmat and Ghiyas; court associates; and family friends. Quli's first benefactor in India, one of Akbar's generals, would likely have been present. As was the custom, Ghiyas would have withdrawn from the room when the groom signed the marriage contract in order to leave the new husband in "complete liberty."[3]

The records don't say precisely where the 1594 wedding of Mihr and Ali Quli took place, but the most likely venue was Ghiyas and Asmat's Agra *haveli*.[4] A wedding at a nobleman's house was a big event for the community. The mansion would have been festooned inside and out with lace, tinsel, strings of bells, and colorful embroidered fringes; the trees in the courtyard would be hung with garlands of marigolds and jasmine. Before and during the ceremony, support staff would hurry in and out of the mansion—servants, singers, seamstresses, while palanquin-bearers waited inside the front gate. Women guests from neighboring houses—newlywed and the long-married, young girls and old women—would join Mihr's mother, her sisters, and her brothers' wives in the women's quarters. Some wore bracelets of small seedpods and new buds, signs of favor and love.

Marriage arrangements in aristocratic Indian households of the late sixteenth century were made according to set protocols. Mihr and Quli's union was brokered in the usual way, with one likely exception. Traditionally, the groom's mother, sisters, or another female relative would launch negotiations with the bride's family. Often this would happen after the groom's family engaged a female peddler or a wet nurse—someone with access to the women's quarters of the prospective bride's home—to surreptitiously gather information about the family's background and circumstances. Among the elite Muslims of the time, eunuchs and singers of *qawwali*, Sufi devotional music, usually carried the marriage offer from the bridegroom's family to the bride's. *Hastgari*, asking for a young woman's hand in marriage, entailed an offer of two sums of money to the bride's parents. The first, the marriage settlement, was the insurance money for the daughter in case of divorce or the death of her husband.[5] The second, an Iranian practice that Mihr's family would likely have retained, was the *chirbeha* or the "price of milk," given to the bride's mother in symbolic repayment for the milk with which she nourished her daughter. After the customary bargaining and agreement on appropriate sums, the parents of the bride would accept or reject the proposal. If the answer was yes, the groom's female relatives would then bring a shawl and a ring to the girl's house to mark the betrothal. Several festivities and rituals involving the two families followed, but the bridegroom and the bride met only on the day of their wedding.

No contemporary writer mentions who brought the marriage proposal to Mihr's family, or what kind of negotiations followed. That's probably because Quli had no relatives in India to make the arrangements. A former table attendant of Shah Isma'il II, he'd fled Iran immediately after the king was murdered in 1578. No sources reveal how he supported himself during the several years he wandered through the Persian territories. But in 1592, when he reached Multan, a city in what is now the Punjab region of Pakistan, he joined the Mughal Army. The imperial troops, led by Abdur-Rahim, were about to go into battle against the ruler of Sind, a kingdom south of Multan bordering the Safavid Empire.

Rahim, whose father once served as Akbar's vice regent, was a poet, translator, courtier, and commander. After the death of his father, Rahim's stepmother, Salimeh Begum, married her cousin, Emperor

Akbar. A woman of distinguished lineage—she was the granddaughter of the first Mughal—Salimeh was sensible and savvy. Rahim and
Salimeh Begum would become important figures in the lives of Mihr
and Quli.

The Mughal Army prevailed, but the defeated ruler of Sind delayed
his formal capitulation. Then the rains came, and the Mughal Army
ran short of provisions. In battle and afterward, a modern historian
writes, Quli distinguished himself by his "valor, courage and intrepid-
ity."[6] The Mughal forces finally consolidated their victory and headed
for Lahore, by then the new Mughal capital.[7] Rahim recommended
the heroic Quli for a government position.[8]

Around this time, mentions of Quli's political career began to show
up in public records.[9] Ghiyas probably took note of the young man's
rising prospects. He would have heard about Quli's bravery in Sind,
and may have felt sympathetic toward a Persian adventurer who had
escaped the dangers of persecution in Iran and sought a better life in
India, as Ghiyas and his family had done fifteen years earlier.

The daring Quli seemed a suitable match for a bright and accomplished young woman like Mihr. Ghiyas would have first broached
the subject with Asmat and then proposed it to Mihr. When Mihr
accepted her parents' wishes, Ghiyas, or an intermediary, spoke to
Quli.

On the night before the wedding, women of the family and neighborhood would color Mihr's hands and feet with henna designs.
They would then lay a white cloth on the floor, east to west, facing
Mecca. On it would be placed a mirror sent by Quli—"the mirror of
happiness."[10]

With no relatives nearby, Quli would come to Ghiyas's house the
next day accompanied by friends, advisers, and associates, most of
them likely fellow members of the migrant Iranian community. Ghiyas would receive the prospective husband, embrace him, and lead
him to a large room lined with divans and gold-embroidered cushions

where other male guests had assembled. Men and women sat in separate areas of the room, with the carved screen between them. On the women's side, a platter sent by Quli to Mihr would display wild rue, incense, sugar, a small sack of henna, a cake of soap, and a loaf of *sengek* bread—leavened dough made on a bed of stones, inscribed in gold or red with a wish for happiness. Asmat would have added a handful of nuts.

The Quran, a prayer rug, the platter, and the mirror of happiness set the stage for the marriage contract. Two mullahs, one representing Quli and the other Mihr, would come in and sit in the men's section of the room. Addressing Mihr through the screen, one of the mullahs would ask if she consented to the marriage. Asmat and her sisters, sitting close by, would provide moral and, if necessary, physical support. After a prescribed modest pause and polite prompting, Mihr would say "yes," or simply nod. The women sitting next to Mihr would serve as witnesses, confirming her assent. Then the mullah would ask Mihr whether she had received the agreed-upon marriage settlement. When Mihr uttered the word "yes," the mullah would have asked her whether she authorized him to marry her to Quli. Once she said yes again, the two mullahs would face each other and pronounce blessings; all the guests, women and men, would express joy and bless the newlyweds, sitting across from each other with the screen still between them. Women would immediately offer sugared almonds to Mihr, which she would crunch and swallow with her eyes closed. When she opened her eyes, she'd make sure to look upon a little boy among the guests, a ritual meant to ensure that her first-born would be a boy.[11]

The screen would be taken away, and Mihr's mother and sisters would formally introduce her to Quli. He would sit next to her, gazing at her reflection in "the mirror of happiness" rather than looking at her directly. With wild rue burning in a brazier in a corner of the room to ward off evil, the family and guests would shower the couple with handfuls of sugared almonds and coins; women would rush forward to retrieve the coins. Quli would honor his first direct look at his wife by presenting her with a jewel.

Legends and later histories suggest an interesting twist in the story of Mihr's marriage, involving an alleged attraction between the young Mihr and the future emperor Jahangir, then Prince Salim.

A seventeenth-century *khyat*, a genre that blurred the court chronicle with the *katha* or popular tale, written in the land of the raja of Jodhpur in western India, had this to say: "The emperor Jahangir, when still a prince, had an amour with Nur Mahal [Mihr un-Nisa], a daughter of Itmad Dola and sister of Asap Khan."[12] (The writer used a local version of the title that Ghiyas was later known by, and Mihr's brother's name, Asaf.)

In the early eighteenth century, when Khafi Khan was at the forefront of retailing magical versions of Mihr's birth, he wrote that she had often visited the Mughal palace with her mother. Prince Salim, Khan said, pursued Mihr relentlessly during these visits. Once he found her alone in a secluded corner and caught hold of her hands to express his love. Taken aback, she freed herself and complained to royal ladies of rank. Learning of the episode, Emperor Akbar instructed Ghiyas to marry off his daughter immediately, and suggested the bridegroom—Ali Quli. As soon as the wedding took place, Akbar granted Quli land rights in Bengal and dispatched him to that distant province.[13]

The nineteenth-century British sailor turned Mughal historian Alexander Dow told yet another variation in his *History of Hindostan*. One day, wrote Dow, Salim visited Ghiyas's home. Honored guests were invited to dine. "Wine was brought on the table, the ladies, according to custom, were introduced in their veils." As soon as Mihr appeared, Salim was taken by "her stature, her shape, her gait . . ." Mihr sang, and Salim was enraptured. "When his eyes seemed to devour her, she, as by accident, dropt her veil; and shone upon him, at once, with all her charms. . . . her timid eyes . . . fell upon the Prince, and kindled all his soul into love." He was silent for the remaining part of the evening, "distracted with his passion." He didn't know what to do. Mihr had already been betrothed to Quli, a "nobleman of great renown." Salim pleaded with Akbar, who refused to undo Mihr's engagement, even in favor of the heir to his throne. The prince "retired abashed," concludes Dow, and Mihr became the wife of Ali Quli.[14]

As these legends have it, Salim's passion for Mihr, established in his youth, remained unquenchable. Mountstuart Elphinstone, an administrator in the government of British India, repeated this assertion in his 1858 *History of India*, including the story still told in India today, about Prince Salim giving Nur two pigeons to hold, which she frees, thus capturing his heart.[15] Another volume published in the late nineteenth century, Syed Muhammad Latif's *History of the Panjab*, presented the most elaborate retelling of the legend—full-blown episodes that included animated discussions between Mihr and her parents at the time of her wedding to Quli.

Asmat, Latif wrote, was in favor with Prince Salim's mother and often visited the palace accompanied by her young daughter. Mihr, "happy in mind, and endowed with all the charms of beauty and unstudied grace of movement, used to amuse the kind-hearted queen with the dances of her native land and the songs . . . [she had] a thousand charms, a thousand attractions." One day, as she was dancing, Prince Salim entered the royal apartments. "The eyes of the two met. Salem [sic] was fascinated by the graces of her person, no less than by her sprightly wit. The attachment was mutual."

Although Mihr was already betrothed to Quli, Salim met her at her mother's house on several occasions and found opportunities to court her, according to Latif. His behavior disturbed Asmat, who spoke to the prince's mother. Through her the matter reached the emperor. Salim longed to marry Mihr and petitioned his father for permission. But Akbar was "too honorable a man to commit such an injustice" to his valued minister Ghiyas, who had already arranged his daughter's marriage to Quli. The emperor recommended to Asmat that the wedding take place as soon as possible. Mihr "had no voice in her own destiny," Latif wrote. She warned her parents and one of her brothers that, by refusing her marriage to the prince, they would "incur the wrath" of Salim, who was cruel in his revenge. "In vain did she plead that his whole happiness depended on this marriage, as did hers. In vain did she point out that she had no fear of Jodha Bai, Prince Salem's principle [sic] wife, and that she would mold Salem like wax in her fingers." Nothing worked. Mihr was married to Quli and "the young but dangerous beauty was removed to a distance from her royal lover, the bridegroom taking her away to his manor in Bardwan."[16]

The legends differ in their details: Mihr and Salim had or hadn't met in their early youth. She was betrothed to Quli before she met Salim or after Salim fell in love with her. Akbar the Great was a ferocious disciplinarian, a just king, or both. But the legends agree: Salim was bewitched by Mihr.

In 1594, Mihr married Ali Quli, and they departed for the town of Burdwan in the distant eastern province of Bengal. As Mihr left her father's *haveli* with her new husband, she stepped over the threshold into the world of the householder. Like her mother, she would now be in charge of her own home. In keeping with the tradition of loyal wet nurses, Dai Dilaram, now middle-aged, would accompany Mihr, supporting her as she began a new life in a land rich with rivers, far more verdant, lush, and wild than her childhood home.

They set off east toward Bengal from Agra, along the ancient Grand Trunk Road, a well-traveled route that followed the sinuous Yamuna River. Covered coaches drawn by oxen would protect them from bad weather, driving them past villages set among groves of neem and mango trees that gave pleasant shade to travelers. Mihr, Quli, and their attendants traversed the doab, the richly cultivated land between the two great rivers, Ganga and Yamuna. On limestone columns placed at regular intervals along the road were warnings posted against pillaging. Traveling in the 1640s, the Portuguese priest Sebastien Manrique reported seeing piles of heads on the roadside and bodies hanging from the trees, punishments for robbery. The terrain was likely just as dangerous when Mihr and Quli made their journey, though as a military officer, Quli would have been armed.

After a fifteen-to-twenty-day journey of three hundred miles, Mihr and Quli would reach Allahabad, at the confluence of the Yamuna and the Ganga. There, or perhaps at the holy Hindu city of Banaras 75 miles beyond, or still farther east at the city of Patna in Bihar, the province where Buddha achieved enlightenment, the party would switch from coaches to boats. In a comfortable vessel with a canopy, powered by oarsmen, they would make their way on the nourishing waters of the wide, slow Ganga. It was still another 200 miles or so from Patna to the border of Bengal. Even though they had carefully planned the journey and carried imperial documents sanctioning passage along the river, there would have been delays. Along the way, exhaustion would give rise to anxious questions and revive memories. Mihr may have worried about what her new life would be like, far from Agra; perhaps Dilaram recalled the onerous journey that Mihr's parents took from Iran to India, prompting Quli to discuss his own adventures when he left Iran and joined Rahim in Sind.

More than a month after leaving Agra, the couple would arrive in Rajmahal, the capital of Bengal. From their boat, they would see crowds of people in ferries, traders in vessels, and, as a European visitor to Rajmahal wrote, "floating mansions, anchored in due order . . . in regular streets as it were, thus making an attractive and beautiful City."[17]

Under Mughal administrative control since 1586, Bengal had

become a province of the empire only in 1594, the year of Mihr and Quli's arrival. Quli would know Raja Man Singh, the first Mughal Bengal governor, a leading minister in Akbar's court. It was important that Quli stop at Man Singh's headquarters in Rajmahal before the couple set off for Burdwan, about 150 miles farther south. Establishing a good relationship with the governor was vital to the success of provincial officers like Quli. Although the emperor made all appointments, it was the duty of the governor, far from the center of the Mughal court in Lahore and Agra, to ensure that officers worked faithfully and in accordance with imperial directives.

Then it was on to Burdwan. Located on the northern bank of the river Damodar, seventy miles northwest of today's Calcutta/Kolkata, Burdwan was an important military outpost on the frontier of Mughal territory.[18] It was from Burdwan that the Mughals had marched to seize Bengal, formerly ruled by the Afghans. The Damodar essentially marked the Mughal administrative boundary. To the south of the river was the territory of the raja of Bishnupur, who enjoyed virtual independence even though he was formally a subordinate ally of the Mughals. Other parts of Bengal—the tribal areas west of Burdwan, the cities of Dhaka and Chittagong to the east, the beautiful mangrove forests of the Sundarbans, home of the Bengal tiger, farther southeast—had various and fluid arrangements with the Mughal government.

When Quli and Mihr arrived in Burdwan, the town had a fort, a mosque, a bazaar, and the tomb of a Sufi saint, Bahram Sakka, a humble water-carrier who had gained Akbar's admiration. The emperor gave Sakka the village of Faqirpur, near Burdwan. He died some thirty years before the newlyweds' arrival. Mihr must have been moved by the villagers' tales of Sakka's benevolence, and by the message inscribed on his tomb: "The rich should, according to the injunction of the Koran, with pleasure, help orphans, beggars, the afflicted and the homeless."[19] Mihr returned periodically to Sakka's tomb after leaving Burdwan, and later in her life would take it upon herself to help hundreds of orphan girls successfully arrange marriages.

The Damodar River was fordable only in the dry season. For much of the year, people crossed in small boats. Come the rains, the embankments would break and floodwaters creep into the mosques and temples, the bazaar, and the earthen residences of Burdwan's inhabitants. Swampy, stagnant pools formed along the river, breeding mosquitos.

Mihr and Quli's home would be like other *havelis* in the region, known as *bangala* or *chauchala* in Bengali. Some thirty miles east of Burdwan were large settlements of Muslims, the most prominent in the Padua and Hugli areas. Revenue collectors, learned men, merchants, and ex-soldiers lived there, and it's likely that Quli and Mihr did too. The houses of the elite, both Muslim and Hindu, were built from a combination of bamboo, the wood of the betel-nut tree, and, rarely, sun-dried bricks, some reaching as high as three stories. Spacious and beautiful, with multiple halls, the houses were flat-roofed; they had gardens with covered walks and walls to protect the residents from foxes and tigers. Mihr's new mansion would be commodious, with clean reservoirs of water for bathing. A few *bangalas* had *hammams*, hot baths—"a rare luxury in Bengal."[20]

As part of their compensation for administrative duties and revenue collection, Mughal officers like Quli were given *jagir* lands, areas under their personal supervision. On their own lands, *jagirdars* were free to conduct matters as they liked—"free to rule, and free to oppress" tenants and farmers, as one historian put it—raising their taxes, even seizing their sons and daughters.[21]

Bengali landowners squeezed the peasantry, especially at the time of annual revenue collection. In addition, the imperial government levied taxes of all kinds: on exports and imports, on the shops of workmen and retail merchants in towns, on temporary stalls in pilgrim bazaars. An inland toll collected at roadside and riverbank stations, an additional financial burden, became a big nuisance. The profusion of taxes and the multitude of officers (some without specific office) meant constant confusion for travelers and local people.

Even in remote provinces like Bengal, the Mughal emperor, not the governor, was the ultimate authority, and relations between Akbar and provincial officers were almost always direct. From time to time, he sent his personal agent to bestow money, horses, imperial robes, and other honors as a token of his recognition of a man's work. And if there were cases of disobedience or neglect among his officers, the emperor meted out punishment. The governor sent progress reports to the sovereign, but officers were also eager to inform the emperor of their own exploits—suppressing a local rebellion, perhaps, or successfully collecting taxes—sometimes sending substantial gifts along with their updates.

So employees of the Mughal court stationed in Bengal looked to two epicenters: Rajmahal and the Mughal capital. Officers visited these cities in person periodically, in pursuit of approval or advancement—and longing for a transfer to a less isolated area. Quli made trips to the provincial and imperial capitals; he was deeply caught up in news and rumors from both centers. The entanglement would grow more intense with the rebellion of one of the emperor's sons, an insurrection that was to shape the end of Quli and Mihr's years in Bengal.

Relations between the Mughals and the province of Bengal were far from stable. The imperial officers serving there were exclusively non-Bengali, both Indian and non-Indian. Except for a few of the local landed elite who were incorporated into Mughal service and could be required to participate in military campaigns, no Bengali was assigned a number in the emperor's numerical ranking system. So imperial officials were, to quote a Bengal historian, "nothing more than a body of foreigners who came to this province only as sojourn-

ers and went back at the end of their terms of service."[22] Often, there
were clashes between imperial officers and the local Bengali officers.

The region was warm through most of the year. No more freez-
ing winters, as in Lahore or Agra; no more crisp evenings near the
time of Diwali, the Hindu festival of lights celebrated in autumn.
In Bengal, sultry temperatures and high humidity during the rains
meant changes in the way Mihr and Quli dressed. The local people
wore mostly cool cotton. Quli would have been most comfortable
in trousers and a *kabaya*, a knee-length robe that folded around the
neck and closed with knots down the front. Mihr dressed in flowing
cotton drawers, trousers, and blouses, with a light cotton head cover.
Dilaram's attire would be similar. The couple's diet would change too.
Bengalis ate more rice—cultivated extensively in the province—fish,
herbs, lemons, and vegetables than Mihr's family had in Agra; green
chilies soaked in vinegar were a regional specialty.

The newlyweds were rather different from each other. Quli was a
man of the sword, strong, daring, and dogged. Prince Salim would
one day give him the title Sher Afgan, or Slayer of Tigers. Mihr was
cerebral, an aesthete, a woman of many interests, from poetry to
design to hunting. They shared the Persian language and the heritage
of the Iran he knew so well and about which she had heard so much.
He would appreciate her curiosity and innate intelligence. Rather isolated in the eastern provinces, he would be likely to lean on her and
discuss matters of trade, taxes, public grievances, the particulars of
his visits to Rajmahal, and news from the Mughal court. Mihr's later
grasp of governance suggests that Quli talked about these things
with her—or that she was very observant and perspicacious.

When her husband was away, Mihr might have pondered the new
religious and philosophical ideas she was encountering. Burdwan was
the hinterland of a hinterland, a border town aggravated by bureau-
cratic and feudal oppression. Even so, the people recognized and celebrated the beauty of the landscape and riverscape. Bengalis regarded

water as a living thing, a relationship reflected in their many water songs. An abode of shrines and temples, Bengal was rich in many modes of direct veneration of the divine—especially of the child-god Krishna, but also Ganesha, Shiva, Saraswati, Lakshmi, Vishnu, the snake-goddess Manasa, and the goddess Durga, protector from evil. Ordinary Bengali men and women were also enthralled by charismatic Sufis and Hindu holy men who moved from region to region.

In Burdwan, men and women of all walks of life incorporated many forms of natural cures, spirit worship, and trances into their everyday practices and belief systems. Among the stories going around was one about a worshipper of the goddess Kali, who, with the aid of supernatural powers, managed to dig a tunnel to rescue a captive from a Mughal prison.[23] Many Hindus had also turned to new forms of direct worship of a personal god. Devotion, not reason or knowledge, was the way of salvation in this approach to Hinduism, centered on the god Krishna. The incantation of Krishna's name was the ultimate form of worship.[24] Recitation as a way of forging harmony with the divine was familiar to Mihr. She, like other Muslim women of her time, had grown up reciting the Quran. Mihr and Quli's daughter would do the same.

Mihr gave birth to their daughter in Burdwan, in 1600 or 1601, and they named the child Ladli, the Loved One, an affectionate term for a little girl.[25] The steadfast Dai Dilaram, an experienced and cherished confidante, would have been by Mihr's side as she brought her baby daughter into the world. New traditions from Bengal would accompany Ladli's birth. Women in the mansion and from the neighborhood would light a fire with straws taken from thatching and make an offering to Shashthi, the goddess of children. They might place the skull of a cow at the door of the labor room to ward off the evil eye and avert "unnatural happenings," such as the entrance of a crow or a wild fowl into the house. Local medicine men, masters of medicine and astrological science, and Muslim hakims, wise men, could be consulted in a medical emergency.[26] Bengali and non-Bengali dancers and musicians, *luliyanis* and *kalawants*, popular among the Mughal bureaucrats, would perform at Ladli's birth. When a woman had a baby, her mother and other close relatives would visit. Asmat or one of Mihr's sisters may have gone to Burdwan.

As a toddler, Ladli would play with stone toys and tortoiseshell and seashell bracelets, Bengal specialties, and with domestic animals: goats, rams, cocks, and birds such as mynahs and parrots. She might have learned archery or dart throwing, or blown toy trumpets. Perhaps Mihr and Quli took her to see snake charmers and acrobats, even those who wound red-hot chains around their bodies.[27]

She would feed on the fresh and fragrant Bengal fish and rice, dried fruit from Persia and Kashmir, and the sweet rice-and-nut dish khirsa; she would listen to servants, neighbors, or fishermen singing magnificent water songs in Bengali, her twin first language along with Persian-Hindavi. Her parents would teach her to speak in both tongues with gentility and restraint.

The little girl would almost certainly have heard recitals on the *vina*, the stringed instrument associated with Saraswati, the goddess of learning, which was popular in Bengal at this time. She would play in the mansion garden on her own or with the children of the household staff, visit the mosque and the bazaar, or ride with Mihr to Bahram Sakka's grave in a palanquin covered with camlet, cloth made from camel or goat hair. Perhaps there'd be picnics on the river with Quli, Mihr, and attendants, and dice games, polo, elephant fights, or hunting to observe. Very likely, Ladli listened to Bengali *pathaks*, professional readers who told stories from ancient Indian books—about the mischievous Krishna, for example, dancing in his yellow robes. Eventually, like her mother, Ladli would have elementary lessons in rhetoric, logic, and the poetry of Persian masters, and she'd memorize passages from the Quran.

In Bengal in those days, seven was the ideal marriage age for a girl;

consummation came at puberty. An unmarried girl crossing twelve would bring social opprobrium upon the family. But Mihr and Quli were not likely to have followed that custom, and in any case, Mihr left Bengal to return to Agra in 1608, when Ladli was seven or eight, long before she became an old maid of twelve.

Mihr and Quli had no more children after Ladli. Perhaps their daughter's birth was so difficult that it prevented Mihr from having more children. What did the couple, or Mihr's relatives, make of this circumstance? They lived in an age and culture in which boys were prized. Kings, nobles, officers—and indeed, matriarchs, elite or non-elite—longed for sons. Mothers coaxed younger women to keep birthing until a son was born. If it took another marriage, they would urge their sons to marry again. Whatever a sonless home meant for Quli and Mihr, there is no indication that Quli ever took another wife in quest of a male heir.

Quli's official duties kept him away from home a good deal of the time, like other Mughal men who sallied forth for politics, trade, warfare, and adventure while women **and** girl-children stayed at home. And after 1599, when he was drawn into unsettling events involving Prince Salim, eldest of the emperor's three sons, Quli became an absentee husband and father.

SEVEN

Grave Matters

The year that Mihr and Quli married, Emperor Akbar suffered a serious illness, unnamed in the chronicles but so dire that his sons began vying for the throne they thought would soon be vacant. The Princes Salim, Daniyal, and Murad—aged twenty-five, twenty-four, and twenty-two—each mobilized supporters, anticipating a war of succession.

Akbar recovered and resumed full kingship, but he was keenly aware of his mortality, and the question of who would succeed him became a great preoccupation. During his reign he had dramatically expanded the Mughal Empire, from Bengal in the east to Afghanistan in the west, including Kabul and Kandahar. In the north and northeast, he held several mighty Himalayan regions. The areas adjoining the river Godavari in the south were his, even though the Deccan was not yet in Mughal control. He was deeply concerned about leaving an enlarged and thriving Hindustan in the right hands.

In theory, he had plenty of choices. Mughal monarchs didn't follow the law of primogeniture, automatically passing the throne on to the eldest son. Technically, an emperor could choose any male member of the royal family as his successor. Akbar had declared that he would choose his successor from among his own immediate family; there would be no accession of some distant cousin. But that still left plenty of room for uncertainty and anxiety among his sons, based on historical precedent. Babur, the first Mughal emperor, had for more than a decade favored his oldest son, Humayun, as his heir. Near the end of his life, however, he declared that his youngest son would follow him as emperor. After much factional squabbling among his court advisers, Babur, on his deathbed, finally did name Humayun, Akbar's father, as successor.

Akbar had groomed his three sons carefully, especially Salim, his favorite. The boy's first *ataliq*, the all-important royal tutor/guardian, was a son of the Sufi saint who had prophesied Salim's birth. The prince was taught next by a high-ranking noble of Central Asian background, and then by Abdur-Rahim, the poet-general who brought Quli to the Mughal court. Akbar saw to it that Salim attained all-around excellence. Part of the cultivation and training of the prince was learning to forge his own networks of authority, a degree of independence vital for learning the leadership skills that a future emperor would need.

But after Akbar's brush with death, he became troubled about Salim, by then a fully established adult prince with a high numerical courtly rank, provincial and military assignments, and a separate princely establishment with the attendant perquisites, including his own harem. Akbar worried that Salim's independence could evolve into rebellion.

In 1594, when he was well again, Akbar made a move that caused a huge rift between him and Salim. He gave to Salim's eldest son, seven-year-old Khusraw, a high imperial rank and a share of the revenue from the newly conquered eastern province of Orissa, adjoining Bengal. The governor of Bengal, Man Singh, under whom Quli served, was Khusraw's maternal uncle. Akbar appointed him the boy's protector. Furthermore, the emperor stated openly in court that he "loved [his] grandchildren more than [his] sons"—a sharp challenge to Salim's growing imperial ambitions.[1] Salim, who had already begun wooing nobles even before Akbar bestowed high rank on Khusraw, intensified his efforts to gain supporters.

Akbar directed Salim to lead Mughal forces against the Rajput state of Mewar, to the west. The emperor generally had fostered good relations with the Rajputs, but occasionally had to deal with a recalcitrant leader. Salim hesitated, and his supporters argued that it was vital for him to stay close to the capital, given the emperor's advancing years. But Akbar insisted that Salim go. Quli was part of the military contingent that Salim led to Mewar, and the prince was greatly impressed by the provincial officer's valor. "I gave him the title of Shir-afgan [tiger slayer]," he would later record in his memoir.[2]

Not long after he returned from Mewar, Salim, determined and ambitious, openly rebelled against his father. While Akbar was away from the capital on a military campaign, the prince had his own name read during the *khutba*, the sermon at Friday prayers, and ordered imperial coins struck in his own name—two acts that were the prerogative of the king. Salim even tried to seize control of the Agra fort, but he was turned back by imperial troops. By late 1599, he'd set up an alternate court in Allahabad, halfway between Agra and Bengal. The choice of location was strategic: Akbar had built a fort there from which Salim could keep an eye on both Agra to the west and Bengal to the east, where his son Khusraw, boosted by Akbar, was popular. Furthermore, Allahabad provided a stable agrarian base—landowners with substantial fighting forces to abet the defiant prince's plans. This would be his princely seat until 1604.

A growing number of provincial officers of both high and low rank joined Salim's court in Allahabad, including Quli. Records suggest that he may have been involved in building alliances and mobilizing fighting forces, reaching out on Salim's behalf to dignitaries and religious authorities across the North Indian plains.

Salim had wide support. He'd built connections with nobles from Kashmir, a group alienated by, among other things, Akbar's increased tax demands. He extended a friendly hand to local Hindustani Muslims, and to the Afghans, a dominant political group in northern and eastern India who deeply resented the Mughal conquest of their lands.

He also cultivated religious leaders, scholars, poets, and artists, whom he patronized handsomely. A marvelous group of twenty-one artists brought to life the eclectic tastes of the spirited prince and his Allahabad court in paintings that represented a new approach to Mughal art. Instead of depicting wars and the heroes of ancient epics, these works featured men and women in more intimate settings, such as feasts and other celebrations. Salim also commissioned a series of unusual paintings based on *Mirror of Holiness: A Life of Christ*, a text written for Akbar by Jesuit father Jerome Xavier. These new subjects and styles of painting reflected Salim's experimental bent of mind, which would come to influence not only his patronage of the arts but also his style of statecraft.

Salim relied considerably on his dedicated lieutenants, which meant that five years into his marriage to Mihr, Quli would have been absent from their home outside Burdwan for even longer periods than usual. He may even have relocated to Allahabad semipermanently. Mihr was left on her own in a remote area plagued by tigers and robbers. She had the reliable Dai Dilaram and others to help look after Ladli and household affairs. Mihr may have taken up the musket at this time so she'd be able to defend her family.

As Mihr went about her life in Burdwan, interacting with the populace in various ways—whether joining hunting parties, visiting shrines, or gathering with neighbors—she came to understand the structure and politics of governance in Bengal. She learned how imperial policies affected poor peasants, rich landlords, women, and children. She heard about the intricacies of Mughal factions, and about political and military affairs all over the empire. And she was exposed to various viewpoints on what was going on between Akbar and Salim—from conversations with her husband, a supporter of Salim; letters from her father, Akbar's loyal courtier; and the accounts of visitors.

Moving to thwart Salim's plans and win back the loyalty of those whom the prince had wooed away, Emperor Akbar arranged for two of his daughters to marry eminent men from Central Asia, a region where Salim was building alliances. He went after Salim's other networks and partisans, removing many from imperial posts and publicly disgracing them. In 1602, at the height of the prince's rebellion, Akbar called in his trusted friend and adviser Abul-Fazl, the compiler of the *Akbarnama*, to deal with Salim. The prince, in turn, commissioned the raja of Orchcha to deal with Abul-Fazl. The raja attacked and beheaded Fazl, and presented his head to Salim.[3]

That same year, around the time that Salim's relationship with Akbar began to change, Quli left Salim and his court in Allahabad. Three women in Akbar's harem—his mother, Hamideh; his wife Salimeh; and his elderly aunt Gulbadan—were attempting to bring about reconciliation between father and son. "When I came from Allahabad to wait on my revered father . . ." Salim later wrote in his memoir, "most of my attendants and people were scattered abroad, and he [Quli] also at that time chose to leave my service."[4]

Perhaps Quli was fed up with Salim's unpredictability. By many accounts, Salim strove for righteousness; some called him the "just prince" of Allahabad.[5] Yet he put a man to death and jailed two others because they'd accidentally frightened away his quarry while he was hunting. It was hard to tell when Salim would turn to violence. The *Akbarnama* notes that he had a "hot disposition."[6] Perhaps Quli broke with Salim because he felt the tug of loyalty to Akbar; or because he was repulsed by the assassination of Abul-Fazl; or because he saw that rapprochement between Salim and Akbar was imminent and worried about retribution from the emperor.

A reconciliation did, indeed, take place. Despite Salim's insurgency and the gruesome murder of Fazl, Akbar in the end forgave his son. "Loss of prudence" and "the intoxication of youth and of success" were cited in the *Akbarnama* (continued by another noble after Fazl's death)—as the pardonable causes of his recklessness.[7] Salimeh, a crucial negotiator between Akbar and her stepson, delivered the news of forgiveness to Salim and brought him back permanently to the imperial court, paving the way for his succession. Both of his younger brothers had recently died from alcohol poisoning; no foul play was suspected. Although Akbar still wanted his grandson Khusraw to be the successor, the powerful nobles of his court pointed out that the laws did not permit, as one modern scholar put it, "a son to trump the imperial claims of a still-living father."[8] The emperor acquiesced.

The 1605 monsoon season was nearly over when Emperor Akbar died in Agra. The news of his death spread faster than the news that he had chosen Salim as his successor. In the outer reaches of the realm, people felt "orphaned and insecure," remembered the poet and trader Banarasi. "Terror raged everywhere: the hearts of men trembled with dire apprehension; their faces became drained of colour." When Banarasi learned that Akbar had died, he was in Jaunpur, 450 miles east of Agra, sitting on a flight of stairs in his house. He shook with "uncontrollable agitation," lost his balance, fell down the stairs, and fainted.[9]

In fact, the whole town of Jaunpur was in a panic, according to Banarasi, who described the events thirty-five years later, writing in his native Hindavi rather than court Persian. Unaware that the matter of succession had been settled before Akbar's death, the people of Jaunpur were gripped by fear. Many hid in their houses, he writes;

Mughal Empire, 1530–1707

Samarqand

Amu Darya R.

Balkh

Kabul
Peshawar

Indus R.

Srinagar

Kandahār

Lahore · Amritsar

Multan · Sirhind
Sutlej R.

Panipat

Delhi

Jumna R.

Bikaner

Fatehpur
Jaisalmer   Jaipur   Sikri · Agra
Jodhpur · Ajmere

Gwalior

Thatta

Indus R.

Brahmaputra R.

Jaunpur · Patna
Allahabad · Benares   *Ganges R.*   Gaur

Dacca

Hooghly
Serampore
Calcutta

Ahmadabad

Narmada R.

Mahanadi R.

Chittagong

Diu   Daman
Tapti R.
Burhanpur

Bassein
Bombay · Poona

Aurangabad

Godavari R.

Pipili

BAY OF

BENGAL

Krishna R.

Masulipatam

ARABIAN

SEA

Goa   Vijayanagar

Bhatkal

Mangalore   Mysore

Cannanore

Pulicat
Madras
Pondicherry

Tranquebar
Negapatam

	Mughal Empire, 1530
	Mughal Empire, 1605
	Mughal Empire, 1707

Cochin   Madurai
Jaffna

Quilon

Trincomali

N
W · *E*
S

Negombo
Colombo

Galle

0   200 miles
0   200 kilometers

INDIAN   OCEAN

some began stockpiling weapons. Shopkeepers shut their doors, and the rich buried their jewels. Those with ready capital loaded it into carriages and rushed to safer places. To disguise their status, the rich walked the streets in the rough clothing of the poor; women shunned jewelry and dressed in "lustreless clothes."[10] Such was the power of the Mughal emperor. In life, he gave a sense of stability and security to his people; his death occasioned anxiety and bewilderment, even chaos.

When the news finally reached Jaunpur that Prince Salim had ascended the imperial throne in Agra and assumed the title Nur ad-Din Jahangir—Light of Faith, Conqueror of the World—people were greatly relieved and hailed the new *padshah*, the emperor.

Jahangir, thirty-six, became the fourth Mughal emperor of India on October 24, 1605. Compared to his father, Akbar, and great-grandfather, Babur, both of whom started their sovereign careers as boy-kings, Jahangir was a mature monarch, the father of three sons. He'd already married several times, had a flock of concubines, and was adored by senior harem women. He was long-limbed, with a stocky but supple body, although folds of flesh were beginning to appear. His skin was neither dark nor fair but somewhere in between; he had dark eyes, curved brows, and an impish smile. He was distinctly more Indian-looking than his predecessors—darker and more compact, without the Central Asian aquiline nose or high cheekbones of Babur or Humayun.

Elizabeth of England had died two years earlier; the Spanish had conquered Mexico and Peru. European sailing ships explored the world, returning from the East with wondrous tales, half-invented, of the alluring Mughals. Some voyagers declared that the Mughal dominion extended a thousand miles south from the capital, to the tip of the subcontinent. This wasn't accurate; Jahangir controlled the vast northern Gangetic belt and several regions of eastern and western India. But he certainly fancied expanding southward.

Once he ascended the Mughal throne, Jahangir, secure in his new majesty, set out to attain the excellence that a cultivated emperor must embody. He had his great-grandfather Babur's curiosity, his grandfather Humayun's love of animals and sense of justice (though perhaps erratically dispensed), and his father's energy. Akbar left his son a well-established government and a royal treasury worth approximately 150 million rupees in cash, or about 150 percent of the empire's total annual income.[11] Jahangir also inherited his predecessors' codes of law; a fine military; the excellent administrative, tax, and revenue systems that his father had arranged; and a rich and distinctive artistic tradition of court histories, miniature paintings, and architecture. He would go further and expand the philosophical and aesthetic accomplishments of his kingdom.

Six months after Jahangir took the throne, Ali Quli once again appeared in the imperial chronicles, under the protection of the new emperor. Jahangir forgave what he saw as Quli's desertion and noted, "After my accession, out of generosity I overlooked his offences." Jahangir ordered a revenue grant for Quli in Bengal.[12] But his detailed description in the memoir of Quli's behavior three years earlier—his "natural wickedness and habit of making mischief," suggests that the emperor still mistrusted him.[13] And according to one colorful nineteenth-century account, Syed M. Latif's 1889 *History of the Panjab*, no sooner did Akbar die and Jahangir become sovereign than his passion for Mihr revived.

Flamboyant visual markers of his power were of great importance to the new emperor. He traveled in resplendent royal cavalcades that stretched for miles; he ordered supersized coins struck bearing his image (Jahangir designed the largest ever Mughal gold coin, used mainly in his elaborate ceremonies), and he increased by 20 percent the size of silver coins minted for general circulation, an act that disrupted the economy. Six years later he realized that he had over-stretched, and returned to his father's standards.[14]

Along with ceremonial matters, Jahangir took on more routine political affairs. He bestowed or enhanced revenue grants for many officials of the Mughal state. Perhaps feeling guilty about the murder of his father's favorite courtier, he employed Abul-Fazl's son as the governor of Bihar. He awarded scores of nobles with court and pro-vincial positions, confirmed the ranks of several, and promoted many others. The emperor also honored Mihr's father, Ghiyas Beg, with the title I'timad ud-Daula, the Pillar of the State.

Jahangir considered himself blessed when a fourth son, Shah-ryar, was born the year he ascended the throne, his mother a con-cubine unnamed in the records. The imperial rejoicing, however, couldn't conceal troubles that had been brewing in Agra. Jahangir's son Khusraw, once his rival for the throne, was now eighteen, and relations between them were tense. Though Akbar's desire for his grandson to succeed him wasn't fulfilled, Khusraw had nonetheless quietly continued to build independent support, just as Jahangir had once done. By late 1605, the handsome and temperamental prince was playing out an oft-repeated imperial saga. Jahangir had rebelled against Akbar; now Khusraw was about to take up arms against his father.

Before his accession, Jahangir had agreed to give Khusraw the governorship of Bengal. A few months into his reign, however, the emperor changed his mind. Khusraw had supporters in Bengal, wealthy men with militias of their own, who might help the prince challenge his father.

To discourage support for Khusraw, Jahangir removed the prince's maternal uncle, Man Singh, from the governorship of Bengal. His replacement was one of Jahangir's foster brothers. In Mughal culture, the wet nurses of a prince were known as foster mothers and their sons were the prince's foster brothers, or *kokas*. Highly respected, the foster mothers were carefully chosen and had to be "even-tempered and spiritually minded" women married to men from noble families.[15] A prince and his *kokas* spent their childhoods together, and when a prince went on to become emperor, his *kokas* usually enjoyed career advantages.

Jahangir appointed other loyalists to posts in Bengal and bordering areas, and as a final step against rebellion by his son, placed Khusraw and his wife under house arrest in a palace tower in Agra. One historian notes that after he was confined, Khusraw increasingly expressed his fury and disrespect to his father's closest advisers. A European representative of the Dutch East India Company wrote that the final straw for the prince was receiving word from one of his partisans that Jahangir was considering blinding him.[16] Khusraw, fearing for his life, made plans to escape—and once again, Mihr's husband Quli was drawn into the fierce contest between an emperor and his son.

On April 6, 1606, Khusraw managed to flee Agra Fort at night on the pretext of paying a visit to the tomb of his grandfather. The number of men who accompanied him is disputed. Jahangir wrote that Khusraw left with 350 horsemen; another source puts the number at 150, and still another speaks of a small band of men.[17] According to Jahangir's memoir, Khusraw and his men looted sections of the city for money, horses, and supplies, then headed for Lahore, a more accessible staging ground for rebellion than distant Bengal.

Along the way, Khusraw and his band robbed travelers, attacked traders, burnt caravanserais and pillaged the town of Mathura. Landowners provided him with funds and soldiers, either willingly or under duress. According to one estimate, he collected 12,000 men and paid them cash that he'd seized from an imperial treasury caravan.[18]

Jahangir was enraged by his son's revolt, repeatedly noting in his journal that his fatherly affection had kept the prince in comfort and ease, and that there was no reason why Khusraw should have become his enemy. Jahangir evidently forgot, or chose to ignore, the example of his own rebellion, and the fact that Akbar had nurtured hopes of succession in Khusraw when he was a boy. The insurgency occurred, Jahangir declared, because of Khusraw's "lack of experience," which allowed him to be misled by "worthless companions" who failed to understand that "throne and diadem are not things of purchase."[19]

Whatever the causes of the rebellion, Jahangir took steps to stop it. He made sure that custodians of Sufi shrines were on his side, split his son's supporters by offering them money, and tapped men familiar with the geography of the Punjab to lead the pursuit of the prince.[20] By late April, however, Jahangir saw clearly that he would personally have to march against Khusraw in Lahore.

Khusraw's mother, the Rajput princess Man Bai, Jahangir's first wife and sister of ousted Bengal governor Man Singh, feared the fate awaiting her son. As far as Jahangir was concerned, Khusraw had repeatedly done wrong and deserved "a thousand kinds of punishment." Man Bai knew her husband, and knew that emperors could be merciless when someone challenged their authority. Anguished at her son's rebellion, distraught over what might happen to him, she killed herself with an overdose of opium. Jahangir deeply lamented the death of his wife:

> Her devotion to me was such that she would have sacrificed a thousand sons and brothers for one hair of mine. . . . What shall I write of her excellences and goodness? She constantly wrote

to Khusrau and urged him to be sincere and affectionate to me. When she saw that it was of no use and it was unknown how far he would be led away, she from the indignation and high spirit which are inherent in the Rajput character determined upon death . . . such feelings were hereditary, and her ancestors and her brothers had occasionally showed signs of madness . . .[21]

When Jahangir left for Lahore with his troops to quell Khusraw's rebellion, he appointed men he trusted to secure the Fort of Agra, which encompassed the imperial treasury and the harem. He put Ghiyas Beg in charge of the city, and asked loyal nobles to keep an eye on his cousins and other male relatives. "When such proceedings manifest themselves in the sons of one's loins what may one expect from nephews and cousins?" he reasoned.[22] From Agra to Delhi, and on to Panipat and Karnal, Jahangir and his men marched toward Lahore. He stopped at the tombs of his ancestors and those of Sufi saints, gathering blessings. All along the way, provincial officers promised to support the emperor. He promoted many and raised the ranks of others, bringing them securely into his fold.

Men loyal to the emperor were already on their guard in Lahore. Although Khusraw had hoped to take the fort by surprise, imperial orders against him had reached Lahore before he did. Accordingly, the guards had strengthened the towers and the walls, repaired broken sections, placed cannons and swivel guns on the citadel, and prepared for battle.

When Khusraw's forces reached Lahore, they burned one of the gates to the fort without breaching the walls, and looted Lahore for seven days. During the disorder, Khusraw got regular updates from his spies on the approach of the royal army. Racked by increasing doubt, he nonetheless decided to fight his father's soldiers. Armed with a spear and a sword, Jahangir followed rather than led his troops into battle, as was customary for an emperor. The imperial soldiers prevailed, and Khusraw's men scattered. Several escaped toward Kabul. A box of jewels and other precious things that the prince always carried with him fell into the hands of the imperial forces.

Men stationed at ferry crossings and on major roads in Punjab were on high alert, watching for Khusraw or his fleeing soldiers. The streets of Lahore were lined with the impaled heads of hundreds of the prince's followers.

Eventually, a party of the emperor's men found the prince. Hands tied, chains fastened from his left hand to his left foot—in keeping with the law of Mughal forbear Chingiz Khan—Khusraw was brought before Jahangir along with his key allies. The prince began to weep, trembling in fear. Royal servants wrapped and tied two of his men in fresh animal skins, one in the skin of an ox and the other in the skin of an ass, put them on asses with their faces to the tail, and led them around the city. Since the ox-hide dried more quickly, the man in it died from suffocation. The man in the ass's skin survived. Jahangir spared Khusraw's life, but entries in the emperor's memoir suggest that at some point Khusraw's eyes were damaged in retribution for his rebellion.[23]

In writing about Khusraw's actions, Jahangir reflected on his own behavior as an ambitious prince, here presenting a different view of his rebellion against Akbar. Looking back, he blamed some "short-sighted men" who urged him to defy Akbar, and noted that an empire couldn't successfully rest upon a foundation of hostility to a father. He even wrote of Akbar as his "visible God."[24] Now that he'd assumed the throne, he could see his father's point of view.

The saga of Khusraw's revolt didn't end with his capture. In August 1607, Khusraw's supporters in the imperial court, possibly without the prince's knowledge, plotted to assassinate Jahangir. Mihr's oldest brother, Muhammad Sharif, was part of this conspiracy. Ghiyas Beg—elevated as Pillar of the State—was put on probation immedi-

ately after the conspiracy was discovered, undoubtedly because he
was under suspicion as Muhammad's father.

Jahangir went after as many conspirators as possible. Mihr's
brother Muhammad and several other prominent conspirators were
executed; her father was demoted, fined, and temporarily imprisoned.
Hundreds of lower-ranking supporters of the prince were speared or
hanged; others were given jail terms, or exiled to Mecca for penance.
Some suspected of participation in the plot were put under house
arrest in Agra and Lahore.

The emperor set out to win over Khusraw's remaining supporters, making conciliatory gestures toward some who had indirectly
sided with the prince and demanding expressions of loyalty within
the court. He distributed images of himself to his supporters—most
likely in the form of pendants that could be pinned onto turbans, as
well as coins or lockets—and addressed them as his disciples, emphasizing that in serving him, they served the empire.

Court records suggest that Quli was suspected of complicity in the
1607 plot against Jahangir, and that his lands in Burdwan were con-
fiscated. Loyal courtiers advised the emperor that "it was not right
to leave such mischievous persons there [in Bengal]." So Jahangir
instructed the new governor to bring Quli to the Agra court, and if
he "showed any futile, seditious ideas, to punish him."[25]

The governor traveled to Burdwan by elephant with a detachment
of soldiers on horseback. Hearing the news of their arrival, Quli rode
on his horse to greet the dignitary, as would be expected of a provincial officer, even one whose lands had been taken away. He was
accompanied by two men. According to eyewitness Haidar Malik
Chadurah, an imperial soldier and administrator, as soon as Quli
entered the governor's camp, soldiers surrounded him. Quli's hand
went to his scabbard. He and Haidar fought with swords, and Haidar

was badly injured. Then Quli attacked the governor's elephant, but he lost control of his horse and had to dismount.[26] The governor's soldiers finished him off.

Jahangir's memoir offers a slightly different version of the encounter, presumably based on reports from provincial administrators. In this account, Quli mortally wounded the governor, whose men then cut Quli to pieces and "sent him to hell."[27] Whatever the details, Mihr became a widow.

A description of the event in an eighteenth-century compilation of Mughal biographies had Quli returning home despite terrible wounds, bent on killing his wife to save her from violence or disgrace. His weeping mother (a character who appears in no other history or legend) saved Mihr by claiming that she had already thrown herself into a well. Quli then expired. For some time, according to this telling, Mihr was in disgrace, because the governor her husband had killed was the emperor's foster brother.

In the early twentieth century, three hundred years after Quli's death, an Indian historian of antiquities, Maulawi Abdul-Wali, writing in the *Proceedings of the Asiatic Society of Bengal*, repeated this version and noted in addition that Mihr, "the real cause of the tragedy, took shelter, out of fear, in the house of Ashqa Jolaha [a weaver], in Burdwan." From there, she made her way, or was escorted, by stages to Jahangir's court.[28]

Syed Muhammad Latif, in *History of the Panjab*, had elaborated the notion that Mihr was "the real cause" of her husband's death, with as much brio as in his invented conversations between Mihr and her parents at the time of her betrothal to Quli. After Akbar's death, determined to get rid of Quli, Jahangir ordered him to fight a tiger barehanded. Quli prevailed. After that, Jahangir commanded forty assassins to attack Quli in his bedroom, but he vanquished them. Then the emperor appointed his foster brother, the governor of Bengal, "to induce Sher Afgan [Quli] to divorce his wife, and, in case of his refusal, put his hated rival to death." Quli rejected the proposal "with disdain," and was killed by the governor. "The lovely widow was sent under custody to Agra, as an accomplice, but was not prosecuted."[29]

Perhaps the most trustworthy account of Quli's death and its consequences for Mihr comes from Haidar, the military officer wounded by Quli, who wrote in detail about what happened to Mihr immediately after her husband was hacked to pieces.[30] Soldiers went to Quli's residence to check for any supporters he may have been harboring. The household staff had already been instructed by imperial representatives to bring Mihr and Ladli to the home of Haidar, who was charged with watching over them until they were summoned to Agra. "I did not spare any moment in honouring and serving her," Haidar wrote. For forty days, the prescribed period of ritual mourning, "that 'Bilqis [Sheba] of the Age' stayed in my house." Then an imperial order arrived, summoning Mihr and Ladli to Agra. That was common procedure: when a Mughal officer was killed, the emperor took charge of the surviving wife and children, and the man's property was forfeited to the treasury of the emperor.

Haidar and his brother accompanied Mihr and Ladli as far as Rajmahal, the capital of Bengal, and men sent by the emperor guided them the rest of the way.[31] Although Dai Dilaram isn't mentioned in the chronicles covering the events of this time, she would have accompanied Mihr and her daughter as they sailed westward on their way to the center of Mughal affairs in Agra. Twelve years had passed since Mihr had arrived in Bengal as a newlywed, with her relatives in positions of power in the Mughal court. Now she was a widow; one of her brothers had been executed as a traitor, and her father had been placed under house arrest. Her own fate was uncertain.

In Agra, the mourning Mihr was sent to the imperial harem rather than to the home of her father or one of her brothers. Ghiyas was released and reinstated in his position after paying a fine of 200,000 rupees, an astronomical sum for the times—a sign of imperial benevolence, or perhaps a way for Jahangir to earn Mihr's gratitude.

After defiant regional rulers or landlords surrendered to the Mughals, often they pledged their daughters in marriage to the emperor as a sign of peace and submission. Many of the royal wives in the harem had married Jahangir as part of political negotiations. Ghiyas and Jahangir may have made such a marriage arrangement—the fulfillment, if legend and later accounts have any grain of truth, of a desire long held by the emperor.

EIGHT

A Key for Closed Doors

When Mihr returned to Agra in 1608 after more than a decade in the wild and open spaces of distant Bengal, the capital was even grander and more crowded than when she left. Along the banks of the Yamuna River stood many more mansions than before, surrounded by luxuriant gardens and groves. "Everyone has tried to be closer to the riverbank," a visiting Dutch trader wrote, "and consequently the waterfront is occupied by the costly palaces of all the famous lords, which make it appear very gay and magnificent."[1] The sleepy village of Sikandara, just outside of Agra, was now bustling with workers completing the tomb of Akbar. It had been renamed Paradise Town in honor of its new status as the Great Mughal's burial place.

The Agra Fort, on the western bank of the Yamuna, was as imposing as ever. A drawbridge over a moat led to the fort's front entrance, Akbari Darwaza, or Akbar's Door, a colossal spiked gate richly decorated with golden loops and rings. That would be the first halting point for an entering regiment, where imperial orders would be presented to the guard. The equally magnificent Elephant Gate (Hathi Pol) to the west served as the public entrance; from there, an open bazaar led to the courtyard of public audiences with the emperor.

After passing through Akbar's Door, Mihr and her young daughter were taken to the harem, called the Jahangiri Mahal, though it was built by Akbar. A grand garden marked the entrance of this multistory palace for royal women, dominated by high domed turrets and separated from the rest of the fort complex by thick walls. The harem, viewed from the public courtyard, or from outside the walls of the fort, was visible only as a succession of rooftops and cupolas.

Mihr was thirty-one years old, attractive, dignified, and well trained in the behavior and duties required of noblewomen connected with palace society. She had visited the harem as a girl, and knew she would soon be part of a restrictive existence very different from her relative independence in Burdwan. But she had no idea what her precise role there would be.

The guardian of Jahangir's harem, a well-educated and reliable elderly woman named Aqa Aqayan, would have led Mihr and Ladli to its labyrinthine inner precincts.[2] Lavish relief carvings in floral patterns decorated the walls; vases were carved into niches and etched with leaves and flowers. Blue and red chandeliers hung from the cupola ceilings.

Numerous entrances and passages connected a series of open, paved quadrangular courtyards lined with trees and pots of plants and flowers, surrounded by verandahs behind which apartments were set. The roofs of verandahs and passageways were supported by slender, finely carved columns of red sandstone. Some split-level apartments had narrow winding staircases and densely carved balconies overlooking the courtyard.

Every apartment was spectacularly embellished with motifs from Hindustan, Central Asia, and Iran: stucco domes, lotus domes of sandstone, arches so intricately carved they looked like netting. Verses from the Quran may have decorated some walls. Although each passage, courtyard, and set of rooms had a distinct style—some with arches, some with carved pillars in arabesque designs, some with extended balconies—they formed a harmonious whole.

Mihr was no longer the head of her own household, but submerged in a sea of women, many of them remarkable, and all but the elders without full autonomy. Mihr was now living with the former emperor Akbar's elderly wives, among them Jahangir's mother and stepmothers, and the current emperor's wives and concubines from aristocratic families all over the empire and neighboring regions: Central Asia, Iran, Afghanistan. A grid of matrimonial alliances was crucial to any emperor's ambitions and authority. When the daughters and sisters of regional and international rulers entered the harem, an extensive network of loyalty was set in place. The emperor's wives included the daughters of noble Indian Muslims, of a Rajput chieftain from northwestern India whose family had maintained a strong alliance with Mughals, and of the rulers of Kashmir, Khandesh, Kabul, Bikaner, and Ghakkar.[3] One of Jahangir's wives was the daughter of a Tibetan raja. Many of the harem women had backgrounds as illustrious as Mihr's and all of them served the needs of the emperor and empire in some way, by producing sons, by giving counsel to the king and his court, by helping govern when menfolk were away, or by being good company.

Younger sons and daughters, such as then three-year-old Prince Shahryar, the son of Jahangir and an unnamed concubine, lived with their mothers. Teenage boys had their own apartments within the harem. Some moved out when they reached maturity—marked by either marriage or the assignment of administrative rank—and established their own households. Some, like Prince Khurram, the son of a Rajput princess married to Jahangir, stayed on; he was sixteen and had adult status when Mihr arrived, but he lived in the harem for five more years. Older wet nurses of the emperor, the foster mothers, and their families also dwelled in the harem.[4]

Within the Agra harem lived an immense staff that attended to the needs of royalty: midwives, scribes, lamplighters, pages, stewards, doorkeepers, oil keepers, cooks, tasters, tailors, palanquin bearers, tanners, water carriers, bookbinders, astrologers, perfumers, weavers, and masons. Also, throngs of *saheliyans*, companions, looked after the intimate needs of royal women and their younger offspring—nursing, bathing, and dressing children and keeping them from bodily harm, preparing the ladies' baths or filling their hookahs. The women of the harem often formed close bonds of friendship with their companions. And aristocratic women like Mihr's mother, Asmat, could visit the harem, according to rules put in place by Akbar.

In some ways, the harem offered women surprising opportunities— wide horizons behind high walls. Senior women were called upon by the emperor and court officials for counsel on matters of diplomacy. These matriarchs also instructed younger royal women, and intervened to protect young princes, as they did with Salim. Political ambition, intrigue, and aspirations cultivated in the harem were tightly entwined with courtly matters. Here, rebellious foster brothers could hide, as happened in Akbar's time; here, plots were hatched and sometimes botched, as when young Khusraw unsuccessfully rose up against his father, Jahangir.

Potential ways to thrive were available to all of the women. Treasured manuscripts celebrating the empire were housed within the harem's guarded confines; royal women read them and enjoyed the sublime illustrations. Some even inscribed their names on manuscripts as signs of ownership. Women wrote poetry and prose; they discussed matters personal and political. The harem was a diverse and dynamic place engaged in the affairs of the world in a deeply personal way, and its women lively and conflicted human beings with strong interests and desires. Although the emperor was meant to be at the center of harem life, he was not the only point of initiative, control, or imagination. The harem was not a space meant to enhance the individual ambitions of women, certainly not those of innovative younger women. But it was a place where women could take pleasure in everyday exchanges, in watching the stars, in gazing at the flow of the Jamuna below, in smoking a hookah as they dipped their feet in water in a cooling fountain.

Three elderly Mughal women, the mother and stepmothers of Jahangir, became Mihr's guardians and protectors.[5] One of them was Salimeh Begum, already part of Mihr's story. She was the stepmother of Rahim, the first employer of Mihr's husband Quli. The grand-daughter of the first Mughal emperor and Akbar's cousin, she married Akbar after the death of her first husband, his regent.[6] A wise, sensitive, and charming peacemaker, she helped guide Mihr.

Ruqayya Begum, Akbar's first wife, was another harem elder who protected and counseled Mihr. Ruqayya had no children of her own. Later, she would help raise Khurram, Jahangir's favorite son.

A late section of Jahangir's memoir notes that Mihr was entrusted to the care of Jahangir's mother, Harkha, a sage and reserved Rajput queen. She emerges now and then in her son's memoir, especially on formal occasions such as the celebration of his birthday or accession ceremonies, and sometimes when the women of the harem traveled.

The senior Mughal women's protection elevated Mihr; it signified imperial acknowledgment of her standing as the daughter of Ghi-yas. She was no "lady-in-waiting," as some European authors have described her over the centuries.

What mattered greatly to men and women of the court was the preservation of the spectacular Mughal Empire. Even during the nomadic reigns of the first two Mughal rulers, before a formal, physical harem existed and women sometimes accompanied the emperor on his journeys, they were meant to be separate and subordinate. Any anomalous behavior was remarkable. In 1519, when Babur, the first Mughal, was camped with his cavalcade near Kabul, a woman named Hulhul Anika, a member of the royal entourage, visited his tent and had a drink with Babur and his men. The emperor noted in his journal that he was doubly astonished—at her appearance among men, and at her actions; he had never seen a woman drink wine. He may have been an open-spirited poet-wanderer, but he still expected women to keep their place—cloistered in the company of other women.

Once Akbar ordered that royal women be secluded in a harem, only the occasional matriarch's name would appear in official documents. The sanctity and invisibility Akbar attached to royal women extended to keeping them anonymous in imperial records. In the *Akbarnama*, the chronicle of Akbar's reign, the passage that notes the birth of his longed-for son Salim doesn't mention the name of Harkha, the wife who produced him. Instead, it makes metaphorical references only to her womb; she is the nameless vessel that bore the long-awaited heir. Erasure was common for a woman of Harkha's time, a tradition in the Rajput region she hailed from as well as the Mughal dynasty into which she married.

Jahangir was attached to a number of women, and wrote about them in some detail and by name: among them, Harkha, Ruqayya, Gulbadan, and Salimeh, whom Jahangir portrays in his memoir as proactive and engaged in Mughal life. All had intervened on his behalf when he was estranged from Akbar. Among his wives, he was fond of his first, Man Bai, and wrote about his melancholy when she died, and his second, Jagat Gosain, mentioned in legends as an intimate.

The exact number of Jahangir's wives was a subject that preoccupied many writers. Thomas Roe, the English ambassador to India during Jahangir's reign, thought the emperor kept a thousand wives.[7] Roe's chaplain, Edward Terry, put the number at "four wives, and . . . concubines and women beside . . . enough to make up their number a full thousand."[8] William Hawkins, a sailor who accompanied Roe, recorded that the emperor had "three hundred wives, whereof foure be chiefe as queens."[9] A twentieth-century historian wrote that Jahangir, "a sensuous person . . . had nearly 300 young and beautiful women attached to his bed, an incomprehensible figure in the modern age."[10]

Jahangir himself made a list of his wives and children, emphasizing the political importance of his marriages.[11] By his count, the number of his wives was nineteen. The first was his cousin Man Bai of Amber, the Rajput princess he married in February 1585 when he was sixteen and still Prince Salim.[12] They had a daughter and a son. Three years before Mihr's arrival in Agra, Man Bai committed suicide during the last month of her son Khusraw's rebellion.

Jagat Gosain, also a Rajput princess, wed Jahangir a year after his first marriage and gave birth to Jahangir's favorite son, whose "advent made the world [so] joyous" that they named him Khurram, which means "joyous."[13] That very year, Jahangir also married the daughter of the ruler of Tibet.[14] Another wife, Sahib Jamal, whom Jahangir called Mistress of Beauty, was the mother of his son Parvez. A Rajput wife gave birth to two daughters. Though several of the children from Jahangir's many relationships died in infancy, two sons born of unnamed concubines survived. One of these was Shahryar, born in the year of Jahangir's accession.[15]

In 1608, either shortly before or soon after Mihr came to Agra, Jahangir married two more women: the granddaughter of Man Singh, whom he'd removed from the governorship of Bengal; and the daughter of the head of the Bundela clan, who ruled several small Rajput states and requested the alliance after he capitulated to the Mughal government following a revolt.[16]

The one-line entries in Jahangir's memoir covering many of the women he married confirm the extreme restrictions of their lives. They had no control over which of them the emperor visited and when, with whom he had children, to what extent he supported one or another woman—or whom he loved. Though Gulbadan wrote eloquently about the strains and jealousies of harem life, and the search for love, influence, and peace of mind, what women in the harem felt is something we will never fully know.

Whether Mihr felt stimulated by the social, intellectual, and cultural life of the harem, after her relative isolation in Bengal, or, after the relative freedom of her life in the hinterland, imprisoned—or perhaps a bit of both—is impossible to say. Nor is it possible to know how harem life affected her daughter, Ladli, who lived sometimes with her mother and sometimes in her grandparents' *haveli*.[17] And exactly how Mihr rose from being one among many to become the favored wife of the emperor too remains a mystery.[18]

What is known is that on May 11, 1611, in Jahangir's sixth year of rule, the emperor married Mihr, upon whom he bestowed the honorific Nur Mahal, Light of the Palace, the first of her two royal names. Many published accounts of their courtship and marriage exist—but none comes from Jahangir. He makes no mention in his journal of those events, though at the time the emperor was obsessively detailing most of his activities in the *Jahangirnama*. He noted, for example, that supplicants had brought him offerings of a peach "as big as an owl's head" and "a ruby the color of an onion." He spent a lot of ink describing a "very hot hunt" for red deer.[19] He wrote about increasing his son Khurram's rank, and about inspecting gems. But not a word of his wedding to Mihr.

He did, however, mention several interactions with Mihr's family. Khusraw's rebellion had posed a major challenge to Jahangir's reign, but it was clear that Jahangir held nothing against Ghiyas or his family for his son Muhammad Sharif's betrayal. In fact, as early as 1607, Prince Khurram was betrothed to be married to Mihr's niece, Asaf's daughter. Mihr's presence in the harem was a further sign of reconciliation. Another was a visit that Jahangir made in late 1608, accompanied by some royal women, to the home of Asaf Khan, now considered a relative on account of the betrothal, where he spent the night. Asaf presented him with offerings worth several hundreds of thousands of rupees—"jewels and jewelled things, robes, elephants and horses. Some single rubies and jacinths [a gemstone] and some pearls, also silk clothes and some pieces of porcelain from China. . . ."[20] Jahangir increased Mihr's father's rank twice in 1611 and gave him 5,000 rupees as a gift "on account of the sincerity of his friendship and his old services." The emperor later recorded Ghiyas Beg's promotion to *wazir*—minister—of the empire, in charge of imperial finance, land assignments, and revenue collection, the post Ghiyas would hold until his death.[21]

Shaken by Khusraw's revolt, Jahangir had set about building or repairing strategic alliances and consolidating his power. Maintaining good relationships with eminent families such as Ghiyas's was critical. He limited the prerogatives of his officers, issuing an imperial decree prohibiting provincial governors from engaging in practices reserved for the monarch—no blinding as punishment, for example.[22] Jahangir mended his relationship with Khusraw, but he still kept his son under surveillance.

In his memoir, the emperor recorded the particulars of urgent imperial matters, described his social engagements, listed the political advantages of his previous marriages, poured out his grief about Man Bai's death, and made lengthy observations of the natural world. Yet he seemed unwilling to record his most intimate thoughts about his final and favorite wife. No mention was made of Mihr, by then Nur Jahan, Light of the World, until 1614, when his journal took a new turn, launching into a remarkable record of Nur's actions, one of the finest surviving testimonies of her career and achievements. He paints an admiring portrait of Nur Jahan as a sensitive companion, superb caregiver, accomplished adviser, hunter, diplomat, and aesthete. Everything that he wrote about Nur Jahan from 1614 onward confirms a very special and unusual relationship. No other Mughal record gives such a rich and full depiction of a royal woman.

In a British Library manuscript copy of the *Jahangirnama*, there is an added note in the margins of a folio, stating simply that Jahangir married Nur Jahan at the end of May 1611, though there is no telling if it was the emperor himself who made the note.[23] Whatever the case, more detailed descriptions of Mihr and Jahangir's union do exist, like this vivid account by eighteenth-century court historian Muhammad Hadi:

> . . . the days of misfortune drew to a close, and the stars of her good fortune commenced to shine, and to wake as from a deep sleep. The bride's chamber was prepared, the bride was decorated, and desire began to arise. Hope was happy. A key was found for closed doors, a restorative was found for broken hearts; and on a certain New Year's festival, she attracted the love and the affection of the king. She was soon made the favourite wife of his majesty.[24]

NINE

Ascent

The *lashkar*, the royal encampment, stretched for nearly three miles in open country outside the town of Ajmer, in north-western India. Embroidered awnings, some worked in gold thread, shaded the entrances to magnificent trellis tents—hundreds and hundreds of them, round, arched, and rectangular—erected on supple wooden frames covered with waxed cloth, then hung with brocade or velvet. Screens of carved wood and felt pieced in floral patterns separated one section of the camp from another, and high red screens clearly marked the harem tents.

This was the Camp of Good Fortune, the Mu'askar-i Iqbal, which would be the home of Jahangir, Nur Mahal, and many members of their court for most of the next six years as it moved from place to place in western India, beginning in early 1613. The Camp of Good Fortune was an elaborate portable city suited to the tastes and inclinations of a monarch with a wandering spirit.

As in the permanent palaces of Agra and Lahore, the main entrance was the *naqqar-khana*, the Drum Room, where the arrivals and departures of important people were announced by the beating of drums. To the left of the entrance stood the imperial stables, with open-air enclosures for the horses and elephants, and tents for the supervisors and staff, and for saddles and other tack. To the right of the Drum Room was the imperial office, the *daftar*, where officers managed accounts and detailed revenue matters, daily expenses, and pay. Next to the *daftar* were tents for palanquins and carts for heavy artillery and hunting leopards.

Visitors passed through the Drum Room into the Great Camp Light—a corridor filled with lamps—and from there to the Hall of Public Audience, where Jahangir handled routine matters of government: granting promotions, for example, and awarding ceremonial robes and gifts. Behind it was the Hall of Special Audience, where the emperor dealt with confidential affairs of state, drafted edicts by his own hand, and met with the great nobles. Both audience halls were canopied spaces furnished with red and gold tapestries and rich rugs. Jahangir's traveling Hall of Private Audience was similar to that of his father, described in the *Akbarnama*, which contained 72 rooms decorated with 1,000 carpets, and had proper doors with locks. The structure was held up by ropes that stretched 350 yards and were fastened to poles set 3 yards apart.

Behind the audience halls was the harem, with a tent for each of the royal women traveling with the encampment. (Jahangir wrote collectively of "royal women," but only mentioned by name Nur; his mother, Harkha; his daughter-in-law Arjumand; and Asmat.) The imperial guard protected the harem, as well as the emperor's tent, to the right, and the princes' tents, to the left. Tents of eminent nobles such as Nur's father and brother Asaf were pitched in the vicinity of royal quarters, but at a distance; officers' tents were farther still, and no tent could be taller than the emperor's.

Beyond the quarters of the elite were the areas of the camp allotted to the rest of the imperial establishment. These sections included more stables and arsenals, treasuries, storerooms, workshops, kitchens, and quarters for artisans, laborers, servants, cavalrymen, foot soldiers, artillerymen. On the periphery of the rectangular camp were tents that served as guardhouses.[1] The Camp of Good Fortune probably held 300,000 people—royalty, courtiers, soldiers, and servants.

In February of 1614, twenty-one-year-old Prince Khurram arrived at the Camp of Good Fortune in Ajmer, accompanied by the elephant of victory, Fath Gaj.[2] In the Hall of Special Audience, Khurram greeted his father by touching his feet, a sign of respect. Jahangir, surrounded by nobles, welcomed his son and praised him for having led imperial forces and princely troops to conquer the long-recalcitrant kingdom of Mewar. Several earlier attempts to subdue Mewar had been unsuccessful, including one led by Jahangir himself, when he was still Prince Salim. But this time, after a few months of brutal fighting, Mewar capitulated.

The prince, the emperor, and key courtiers moved on to the harem, where Nur applauded her stepson and presented him with a "rich dress of honour, a jewelled sword, a horse and saddle, and an elephant."[3] Nur understood that Mughals cared deeply about precision in the preparation of gifts and the manner of presenting them. Royal gift exchanges served as public declarations of who was backing whom in this world of ever-shifting political alliances. She'd picked up the subtleties of the performance from her experienced father, from her mother, and from the elder Mughal women who were her mentors in the harem.

Two things were especially notable about the harem ceremony. The first is that it was Nur and not Khurram's mother, Jagat Gosain, who greeted and honored the prince; in fact, it seems that Jagat Gosain wasn't even part of the royal entourage traveling with the Camp of Good Fortune. After three years of marriage to the emperor, Nur had risen to preeminence in the harem. Khurram paid formal respects to both his father and his stepmother, almost as if he were reporting to a pair of sovereigns.

Nur had devoted the early years of her second marriage to building politically astute alliances and observing affairs of state with close attention. But when her influence first began to grow in the harem, it was built upon acts of kindness. Nur's generosity was "boundless and unlimited," according to Farid Bhakkari, who served the Mughal court during Jahangir's reign (and after) in various financial and military capacities.[4] Bhakkari was the author of a noted biographical dictionary of nobles, scholars, and other influential Mughals. In the chapter he devotes to the empress, he notes that she bestowed gifts of clothing, jewels, horses, elephants, and cash on the royal men and women around her, and gave plenty of money to the poor. Whenever Nur learned through one of her attendants that a destitute orphan girl wished to wed, Bhakkari noted, she helped organize the marriage and provided a portion of the dowry. In this way she supported the weddings of five hundred orphan girls, and even designed an inexpensive style of wedding dress, still used today by brides of poorer families and called a *Nur Mahali*.

The empress also initiated the marriages of her women companions, *saheliyan*, under the age of forty to Jahangir's troopers and attendants. She gave the *saheliyan* between the ages of forty and seventy the choice of either leaving the palace to look for a husband, or remaining with her.

All were outstanding interventions. By offering choices to the underprivileged and to the most vulnerable inhabitants of the harem, she had what we might call a "feminist" moment into which she folded the message of Bahram Sakka, the holy man she followed in Burdwan, who urged the rich to help orphans, beggars, and the homeless. Nur accomplished all of this charity work, Bhakkari wrote, with humility and courtly conduct, which were her forte.

Nur's acts of generosity earned her goodwill and admiration from many, but most important, from Jahangir. As Jahangir's favorite wife, Nur became a force within the harem. He was so infatuated with the "strength of her personality," said Bhakkari, that the fabled Islamic lovers Majnun and Khusraw paled next to him.[5] By the time Jahangir first mentions Nur in his memoir, in July of 1614, his affection and trust in her are clear, and seem to be fully reciprocated. She first appears in a passage describing a bout of illness three years into their marriage, before they began traveling with the Camp of Good Fortune, a time when the emperor was "seized with fever and headache," but told no one. "For fear that some injury might occur to the country and the servants of God," Jahangir wrote, "I kept this secret from most of those familiar with and near to me, and did not inform the physicians and hakims." A few days passed in this state. "I only imparted this [the news of his illness] to Nur-Jahan Begam than whom I did not think anyone was fonder of me." Later, as part of his regular royal routine, he entered the *jharokha*, the viewing balcony, before proceeding to the *ghusl-khana*, the parlor where he held top-secret meetings. His weakness was evident and the royal hakims were called. "As the fever did not change, and for three nights I took my usual wine, it brought on greater weakness." After lighter meals and treatment with powders and syrups concocted according to his physicians' secret formulae, the emperor improved, though from then on, he suffered periodic bouts of ill health.[6]

Nur's influence—in the harem, with her husband, and, ultimately, in governance—also grew through her family connections. The year 1611 "when Nur Jahan married Jahangir, and I'timaddudaula [Ghiyas] was appointed *diwan-i kul* [chief imperial fiscal minister] appears to make a real change in the fortunes of their family," notes an eminent Mughal historian.[7] In 1612, when Ghiyas's granddaughter Arjumand became Prince Khurram's second and favorite wife, Jahangir appointed the bride's father, Nur's brother Asaf Khan, imperial steward, in charge of the royal household, treasuries, mints, and construction projects. The emperor also granted Ghiyas Beg another raise in numerical rank. A few years later, the governorship of Lahore would be added to Ghiyas's portfolio, and Asaf Khan would be named Wakil-i Hazarat, the highest minister at the imperial court without a designated department and one of the three principal positions at the court. (His father held the top post of wazir, and the third vital position was dispenser and overseer of *mansab*, numerical rankings.) Nur's younger brother, Ibrahim, would become provincial governor of Bihar.

The constellation of power was unlike any the Mughal world had seen. Jahangir was putting the most important court offices in finance, intelligence, and military appointments into the hands of Nur's father and brothers. In the 1620s, members of Nur's extended family would also govern in Lahore, Kashmir, Bengal, Orissa, and Awadh.[8]

Nur became more and more involved in an important royal observance, the ritual weighing of the emperor, a ceremony of charity that took place twice a year in the harem, on the birthday of the emperor as reckoned by both the solar and the lunar calendar. (For all other official purposes, the Mughals used the solar calendar, based on the revolution of the earth around the sun, rather than the Islamic lunar calendar, keyed to the cycles of the moon. Year One on the Islamic calendar was 622 CE, when Muhammad emigrated from Mecca to Medina.) In 1613, the ceremony took place in the Agra harem apartments of Jahangir's mother, Harkha, before the royal retinue began their travels. Jahangir was weighed against articles piled on a huge balance scale—gold, quicksilver, silk, perfumes, copper, drugs, ghee (clarified butter), iron, rice-milk, seven kinds of grain, salt, fruits, mustard oil, vegetables; the goods were then distributed to the needy, to holy men, and to courtiers. In addition, sheep, goats, and fowl in a number equal to the emperor's age were given to some lucky farmers.[9] Sometimes harem women were shown special favor with presents bestowed after the imperial weighing. Jahangir showered Nur with such gifts. Eventually she took charge of the biannual event. In 1621, Jahangir would write in his memoir, "Nurjahan Begam has made suitable arrangements for every solar and lunar weighing ceremony since she entered into marriage with me—and she has considered it a pleasure to do so."[10]

As Nur closely watched the flow of everyday life and of grand happenings, the women of the harem were closely watching her. She was a new kind of royal wife, embodying the experiences of a full and unusual past. Nur arrived in the harem widowed and already a mother, having looked after an extensive estate in Bengal, likely picking up a gun many a time during her stay there. In that turbulent land, she'd witnessed the troubles that arose when the capital and the province knocked against each other, when an emperor and his son collided, when ambition, ego, and factionalism tangled. She seemed more canny than other royal women her age about the workings of the empire, exhibiting the knowledge expected of esteemed elder women like her harem mentors.

The winter after Khurram's wedding to Arjumand, Nur lost the guidance of one of those revered matriarchs. Jahangir, Nur, and other royal women had set up a hunting camp in the Dahra Garden, on the outskirts of Agra, when a messenger arrived with the news that Jahangir's ailing stepmother Salimeh Begum had passed away at the age of seventy-four. Ghiyas Beg looked after the transfer of the body to the burial ground.[11] The death of Salimeh would have been painful for Nur, but it seems to have coincided with the reemergence—at least in written records—of Nur's mother, Asmat, as a force in her daughter's life.

Asmat made her first appearance in the *Jahangirnama* the same year as Nur. One day when Asmat was making rosewater, Jahangir noted in early December 1614, "a scum formed on the surface of the dishes into which the hot rosewater was poured from the jugs." Asmat skimmed this oily froth and realized that it emitted a lovely concentrated scent. This was the perfume or *'itr* that she presented to her son-in-law, who was much taken by it. "It is of such strength in perfume," Jahangir wrote, "that if one drop be rubbed on the palm of the hand it scents a whole assembly, and it appears as if many red rosebuds had bloomed at once." He recalled that it was Salimeh, present when Asmat offered the attar to Jahangir, who "gave this oil the name of *'itr-i-Jahangiri*, Jahangir's perfume."[12]

Jahangir's memory of the perfume's discovery was prompted by another poignant recollection. Merchants had brought him delicious pomegranates and melons from Persia, which he shared with nobles and servants of the court. Growing nostalgic, Jahangir wrote of his father's great fondness for melons, and grieved that such fruits had not come from Persia in Akbar's time. "I have the same regret," he wrote, "for the *Jahangiri 'itr* (so called otto of roses), that his nostrils were not gratified with such essences. This *'itr* is a discovery which was made during my reign through the efforts of the mother of Nur-Jahan Begum."[13] To reward Asmat for her creation, Jahangir had presented her with a string of pearls. In little ways like this, the connection between Nur's family and the emperor was further strengthened.

The perfume was more than just an experience for the senses. Its invention, presentation, name, and magical aroma deepened the intimacy among Jahangir and the women who watched him take the first delighted sniff—Asmat, Nur, Salimeh, and other harem ladies—all breathing in the intense scent. Among the poems that Nur wrote using the pseudonym Makhfi, the Hidden One, the following verse may well have been inspired by her mother's distillation of roses:

If the rosebud is opened by the breeze in the garden
The key to our heart's lock is the beloved's smile
The heart of one held captive by beauty and coquetry
Knows neither roses, nor color, nor aroma, nor face, nor tresses.[14]

Like most of the poetry of Sufi Islam written in Persian (and later Urdu), Nur's poem expresses love's splendors on both worldly and otherworldly planes.

Nur's preeminence in the harem, her husband's admiration, and her family's domination of the highest levels of government allowed her to begin shaping matters of state through alliance-building. Bhakkari wrote that Nur's graciousness and generosity "elevated and honoured" the entire house of Ghiyas Beg. She became part of an inner circle of increasingly influential imperial advisers; it included Ghiyas Beg and his son Asaf Khan; the harem elders Harkha, Ruqayya, and Salimeh, until her death; and perhaps Nur's mother, Asmat, and her lifelong supporter Dai Dilaram.

Prince Khurram and Arjumand, his wife, would soon join this group. Nur certainly helped Khurram's rise by publicly celebrating his military successes, beginning with the victory in Mewar. But her influence probably began even earlier: Jahangir had likely discussed with Nur whether to send Khurram to Mewar as commander in the first place. The emperor certainly would have consulted Nur's father and older brother, his chief advisers, about the matter, and it's not a stretch to imagine Nur, the trusted and admired wife, as part of the conversation.

Jahangir had the highest expectations for *Baba Khurram, Dear Khurram*, the third prince. Khusraw, the rebellious eldest, had essentially been removed from the political scene. Second son Parvez continued to receive military and administrative assignments, but he hadn't impressed Jahangir, and he drank excessively. Shahryar, the fourth son, was still young, nine years old in 1614. Khurram was emerging as a strong and artful prince whose rapidly increasing rank allowed him to expand his financial base, increase his household troops, and build a strong core of loyalists.

Khusraw's rebellions had shaken the emperor, leaving him emotionally fragile and worried about the future of the Mughal dynasty.

By supporting Khurram, Nur perhaps hoped to reassure her husband that the dynastic transition after his death would be smooth. She was probably also being shrewd about her own future. As the most astute and competent of the princes and the favorite of his father, Khurram was the presumptive successor. Someday, Nur might continue her influence on government as his wise adviser. Nur feted the prince repeatedly, and he, understanding that Nur was likely to be a key player in Mughal succession, extended respect to her in unprecedented ways. For example, after Khurram married Arjumand in 1612, royal women sometimes spent the night in the prince's mansion, among them his mother, Jagat Gosain, and his stepmother Nur. When they did, the prince gave presents to them all. Nur was soon among the most highly favored. And by the time of his triumphant return from Mewar to the Camp of Good Fortune in 1614, it was Nur and not his mother who received him—a rather spectacular demonstration of the ways in which the emperor's favorite son and his favorite wife would honor each other. Nur seems to have hoped that her close association with Khurram, the handsome, motivated, and ambitious prince, would be the axis of a new order. With Ghiyas, Asaf Khan, and Nur, the emperor's "first family," by Khurram's side, the prince's future, and thus the future of the Mughal dynasty, would be secure.

During the three previous Mughal reigns, many royal women had wielded authority obliquely—by providing wise counsel to the emperor and his officials, and intervening to reconcile rebellious princes with their fathers. Nur was moving toward a more direct and visible kind of power. Attuned to whatever Jahangir required of her at any particular moment, Nur eased his concerns about his health, the safety of the empire, and his sons; she anticipated his needs. Though it may be that other wives were as conscientious, caring, and intuitive as Nur, only her attentions are recorded in his memoir and only she is hailed as the one most fond of him.

As the mother of the presumptive heir to the throne, Jagat Gosain might well have felt that her own position had been usurped
by Nur. Jahangir's great-aunt Gulbadan made clear in her keenly
observed memoir that sharing a husband wasn't always easy for
royal wives. Two generations before Nur's, Emperor Humayun's
wife Bigeh Begum complained that he had been neglecting her and
other royal women. "For several days now, you have been paying
visits in this garden," Bigeh Begum said, "and not one day have you
been to our house. Thorns have not been planted on the way to it.
How long will you think it right to show these disfavors to us helpless ones . . . ?" Later that day, the emperor sent for his wife and the
other women.

> He said not a word, so everyone knew he was angry. Then after
> a little while he began, "Bibi, what ill-treatment at my hands
> did you complain of this morning? . . . That was not the place
> to make a complaint . . . You . . . know that I have been to the
> quarters of the elder relations . . . It is a necessity laid on me to
> make them happy . . . If there should be delay on my comings
> and going, do not be angry with me. Rather, write me a letter
> and say; "Whether it please you to come or whether it please you
> not to come, we are content and are thankful to you."[15]

No official records suggest resentment on Jagat Gosain's part, and
it may be that her absence from the passages in Jahangir's memoir
celebrating their son Khurram are simply the result of his general dis-
interest in writing about any wives except Nur. But this lack of documentary evidence didn't stop later historians of Mughal life from
embracing popular legends of a rivalry between Nur and Jagat Gosain. Khafi Khan, writing in the eighteenth century, presented Jagat,
not Nur, as the favored wife. He tells the tale of a hunting trip that
Jahangir took accompanied by Nur; her mother, Asmat; Jagat Gosain;

and servants. While the hunters were in the process of guiding a lion within range of imperial guns, the emperor fell asleep with the women by his side. Suddenly the lion emerged, roaring. Nur was paralyzed with fear, Khafi Khan writes. Jagat Gosain picked up the emperor's gun, fired, and killed the lion. This roused Jahangir from sleep. Seeing the dead lion and Gosain with a gun, he applauded her bravery. But he was displeased, Khafi tells us, with the terror-stricken Nur. Asmat quickly intervened, stressing that the use of arms was the function of men who had to display their bravery on the battlefield. Women were meant for soft words.[16]

Are we to believe that Nur, the best shot in the empire, was stunned at the appearance of a lion? Or that Asmat defended her powerful daughter by invoking women's softness? Khafi admired Nur, but he was drawing upon anti-Nur stories that had begun to circulate when Prince Khurram became Emperor Shah Jahan, long after the alliance between Nur and her stepson went sour.

According to an even later story, on one occasion Nur noted the sweet smell of Jahangir's mouth. He was delighted and mentioned the comment to Jagat, who said: "Your Majesty, the woman who has smelt the mouth of only one man in life cannot appreciate it. It can only be differentiated from bad odour by a woman who has seen more than one man. So only Noor Jahan can judge it."[17] In such legends, rivalry among harem women is imagined as inevitable, and the Hindu and Muslim wives of the emperor expected to be deeply antagonistic to one another.

Perhaps the biggest problem Nur faced had nothing to do with her co-wives. A twenty-first-century translator of Jahangir's memoir wonders "whether he ever drew a completely sober breath."[18] The emperor himself provided a comprehensive history of his lifelong drinking habit. When he was eighteen, still Prince Salim, he accompanied his father, Akbar, to the Punjab region, where the emperor was fighting Afghans of the Yusufzai clan. One day while hunting near the Indus

River, Salim felt weary. A gunner suggested that a cup of wine would perk him up. The *ab-dar*, water carrier, brought a half cup of sweet yellow wine.

After that, Salim gradually increased his intake until wine ceased to intoxicate him. He then turned to spirits—probably arrack, a popular liquor made from fermented rice and date-palm juice. Slowly he moved up to "twenty cups of doubly distilled spirits, fourteen during the daytime and the remainder at night." All he ate was fowl, bread, and radishes. No one was able to control his drinking, and "matters went to such a length that in the crapulous state from the excessive trembling of my hand I could not drink from my own cup . . ." The seasoned royal physician Hakim Humam eventually spoke up. In 1600, five years before he ascended to the throne, Salim cut down on alcohol, ordering that his drinks should be two parts wine and one part spirits, and brought his intake down to six cups a day. "It is now fifteen years," he wrote in 1615, "that I have drunk at this rate, neither more nor less."[19] In order to re-create the intoxication he no longer experienced from alcohol, he began taking a substance called *filuniya*, which he described as a sedative derived from a Greek drug. He soon became addicted. At some point he began to take opium instead of *filuniya*, mixing it with spirits or wine.

Alcohol and drugs were common in the Mughal world. Wine and poetry were central to gatherings of men; drinking together was a sign and seal of loyalty and royal favor. Babur, the first Mughal emperor, wrote extensively about his drinking parties. In fact, he chided his son Humayun for being aloof and reluctant to drink (though he was a self-proclaimed "opium eater") and suggested that he socialize more with his followers.[20] Jahangir's two brothers died of alcoholism.

During the first New Year celebrations after his accession, despite Islamic prohibitions, Jahangir encouraged the revelers to indulge in drinks and drugs. To justify his embrace of intoxication as a Muslim, he quoted the famous Sufi poet Hafiz:

Cupbearer, brighten my cup with the light of wine;
Sing, minstrel, for the world has ordered itself as I desire.[21]

Jahangir's continuous drinking exacerbated his chronic respiratory troubles, which may have been asthma. Only Nur was concerned and commanding enough to intervene. In 1621, the emperor wrote that "Nur Jahan Begam, whose skill and experience are greater than those of the physicians," refused to approve the prescription of his attending physician and "by degrees, lessened my wine, and kept me from things that did not suit me, and food that disagreed with me."[22]

Though Jahangir himself never portrayed Nur as angry about his addiction and wrote only about how she helped, apocryphal reports popularized by European commentators insist that Nur was enraged by Jahangir's drinking. A famous fight scene, first recounted by Niccolao Manucci in his *Storia Do Mogor*, sixty years after Nur's death, was encoded in public memory, and is still recounted today.

Nur had succeeded in making Jahangir agree to drink no more than nine cups in the evening, and only served by her. One evening, while listening to his musicians, he came to the end of his ninth cup and wanted more. Nur refused. "When he saw that the queen wouldn't give ear to his words, he fell into a passion, laid hold of the queen and scratched her, she doing the same on her side, grappling with the king, biting and scratching him, and no one dared to separate them," Manucci wrote. "The musicians, hearing the noise going on in the [other] room, began to call out and weep, tearing their garments, and beating with their hands and feet, as if someone were doing them an injury." Nur and Jahangir, "who had been struggling together," came out to find out the reason for all the cries. "Seeing that it was a pretendeed [*sic*] plot of the musicians, they fell a-laughing, and the fight ended."

But Nur's ire lingered, Manucci continued. She informed her husband that the only way she would forgive his excessive drinking was if he threw himself at her feet. "The king," Manucci wrote, "who could not live without Nur Jahan, was willing to carry out her wishes, but feared to be blamed for such an act, which would give rise to a great deal of talk among his people." He consulted a wise old woman, who advised that when the queen was walking in the garden on a sunny day, "he should place himself before her in such a way that the shadow of his body should reach the queen's feet; then he could beseech his loved one as if he were at her feet." Jahangir did just that, approaching Nur until his shadow lay before her. "Then he said to her, 'Behold, my soul is at your feet!' and thus peace was made."[23]

Manucci gathered this information, he wrote, from "a Portuguese woman called Thomazia Martins. . . . She had charge of the royal table and was much liked by Roshan Ara Begam [Shah Jahan's daughter, who was twenty-eight when Nur Jahan died] . . . through the affection she had for me . . . she informed me of what passed inside the palace."[24] Of course, the servant who gave Manucci this information was retelling a story from years earlier—a story that, even then, was likely to have been more palace gossip and invention than hard fact. As time went by, such imperial tales were passed along with embellishments, persisting because they were sensational and excited public imagination, because they brought historical characters to life, and because they suited the politics of the moment.

Despite Nur's interventions, drinking and drug-taking sometimes impaired Jahangir's ability to conduct imperial business. This was noted in accounts written by the British ambassador to the Mughal court, Thomas Roe, by Roe's chaplain, and by two representatives of the Dutch East India Company who had dealings with the Mughal Empire in the 1620s. All of these men felt that Jahangir's addictions allowed Nur to assume more and more power. One of the Dutchmen, Pieter van den Broecke, who established a textile factory in western India, went so far as to say that Jahangir "gave himself up to pleasures, allowed himself to be misguided by women, and became addicted to drink, caring very little about his kingdom . . . when he had drank [*sic*] his last cup [and] all men had departed, the queen came out in all her splendour, undressed him and put him to sleep in a hanging bed, which was constantly rocked otherwise he got no sleep. His wife knew well how to use her opportunities for he always said 'yes' and scarcely 'no' to whatever she asked or desired . . ."[25]

Mughal chroniclers who were members of the court, like Bhakkari, the biographer of Mughal nobles, would have regarded Jahangir's drinking and other excesses, even when they were occasionally disabling, simply as expected kingly behavior. Unlike van den Broecke and other Europeans, Mughal observers didn't connect Nur's ascent to her husband's use of alcohol or opium. Instead, they ascribed her rise to her own ambition, manipulation, and "mischief-making," as Bhakkari would describe it. They would find Jahangir's later delegation of some sovereign tasks to his wife problematic not because it signaled that he'd succumbed to indulgence, but because they felt that a woman shouldn't have such power.

The court chroniclers recording events in seventeenth-century India acknowledged that Jahangir, like many other monarchs, was mercurial—sometimes sensitive and civilized, sometimes tempestuous and ill tempered. They accepted that his style of kingship was different from that of his father, Akbar. Though Jahangir embraced and enhanced the Mughal ideal of cosmopolitanism and ecumenism promulgated by his father, he was more interested in the ceremonial, aesthetic, and philosophical aspects of Mughal kingship than in being a conqueror. He'd inherited a well-organized empire, one that had expanded enormously during Akbar's reign. Though Jahangir would succeed in getting Mewar to submit and keep continuous pressure on the Deccan, his imperial project was hardly the "conquest state option favored by his father."[26] Only once did he go to war himself, to protect his throne from Khusraw's rebellion. He had commanders to battle on his behalf.

Jahangir was more interested in the grand ritual acts of ideal Mughal kingship: holding weighing ceremonies, bestowing charity, encouraging courtly etiquette, offering his subjects glimpses of his semi-divine person from the imperial balcony. He exercised his majesty not as a warrior but as an enthusiastic and knowledgeable patron of the arts; an avid traveler through every region of his realm, and a naturalist absorbed in studying the land, its people, its flora and fauna. Jahangir loved books, illustrated or calligraphic, and gems, especially rubies. Obsessed with gathering statistics, he ordered the measurement not only of the Mughal territories but of a great range of things animal, vegetable, and mineral. The series of discussions Jahangir convened with clerics, astrologers, and poets right after he became emperor set the tone for his reign. He eagerly consulted with learned men and ascetics, and would always be something of a mystic and a seeker. Jahangir had numerous conversations with a brilliant young Jain monk named Siddhichandra, who grew up in the Mughal court. Jainism is an ancient Indian religion that emphasizes non-violence, non-attachment, and asceticism. In the Agra palace, before they set out for their travels in the west, Jahangir, Nur, and Siddhichandra were chatting and Nur teased the monk by asking whether the pleasures of flesh are important. A congenial but heated debate followed. The emperor used the Jain metaphysical doctrine of *syadvada*, or relativism, as his argument. "There is nothing in itself either good or bad, meritorious or sinful, but our thinking makes it so," he said to Siddhichandra. "*Syadvada* . . . is applicable everywhere for those who believe in it. Absolutism . . . would amount to heresy."[27]

Though her husband's drinking and his many intellectual and spiritual preoccupations may have given Nur unusual opportunities to exercise her gifts of leadership, Jahangir never considered his approval of her growing power as abdication. Any observer who concluded that his indulgences and interests, or the growing involvement of Nur in governance, signaled Jahangir's lack of interest in ruling would have been greatly mistaken. His habits and enthusiasms never interfered with his commitment to kingship. Jahangir directed and closely monitored his generals and administrators. He put in a full imperial workday even when he was drinking or using drugs in the evening. He'd forcefully quelled Khusraw's rebellion against him, and made sure there were no others. His sovereignty was never in doubt to him, to his family, or to his courtiers and officers. The words he inscribed in the copy of the *Jahangirnama* that he presented to his son Khurram in 1618 is a candid assertion of his sovereign rule. He calls himself "a just and equitable monarch . . . upon whose worthy form He (The Distributor of Justice) draped his *khilat* [robe of honor] . . . Imperial rule had been given to this supplicant at the divine court."[28]

A striking mark of Jahangir's reign was the mobility of his court, and that, too, worked in Nur's favor. The emperor and his retinue traveled almost constantly, even when he was based in one region for a long spell and made a series of shorter trips. Babur, the first Mughal, inherited the tradition of a traveling royal camp from his nomadic Central Asian ancestors, and his successors kept up the practice of kingship on the move even as they settled into grand headquarters in Agra, Lahore, and Fatehpur-Sikri. Akbar had traveled only for hunting, pilgrimages, and war, but, from the time he was a rebellious prince, Jahangir was the most mobile of the Mughals. He had the wandering spirit of his great-grandfather Babur, who often took his whole court on the road to live in tents. Jahangir traveled for many reasons: to follow military campaigns like the one in Mewar, to hunt, to observe and catalog the characteristics of his country, to experience the pleasure of novelty. Perhaps most important, however, the moving imperial camp served as a formidable sign of royal power.

[It was] a permanent reminder of Mughal sovereignty . . . a constant threat to any obstreperous zamindar [landowner] considering disobedience or revolt. Since the camp showed the imperial grandeur on permanent display all over the empire, actual fighting could often be avoided . . . [furthermore, a] camp in open fields was the ideal setting for stately ritual . . . welcoming ceremonies (*istiqbal*), paying homage (*kornish*), grand receptions and banquets of reconciliation . . .[29]

Jahangir married Nur during an unusual period of repose in Agra. For nearly two years after the wedding, the couple undertook a range of short, festive outings in the area. One day, the emperor, Nur, and other royal women went by boat to visit a melon garden downriver, planted and tended by Khwaja Jahan Kabuli, a distinguished man renowned for having guarded Agra from attack during Khusraw's rebellion. The boat reached the garden at dusk, and while servants set up the tents where the royal party would spend the night, the emperor and company spent the evening walking among the melon beds. Suddenly, sharp winds sprang up; the tents and the screens surrounding them were blown down. Jahangir, Nur, and the other women slept on the boat. They spent part of the next day again strolling in the melon garden before returning to the city.[30]

By late 1613, Jahangir, motivated partly by a wish to be closer to the Mewar campaign but mostly by his wanderlust, was eager to tour his territories in western India, accompanied by his favorite wife, Nur. In the early days of the dynasty, the Mughals' peripatetic culture allowed women greater freedom than they might have had otherwise, and than they would during the reigns of later emperors. This freedom lingered as independence of mind even after Akbar sequestered women in the grand harems of the imperial palaces. Now travel with her husband brought Nur out of confinement; by the end of her life, she would travel the breadth of the empire. It was from a tent that she would, in the not-too-distant future, issue her first imperial order.

After having moved several times, the Camp of Good Fortune

was back in Ajmer on March 20, 1616, when Jahangir honored his wife in a novel way. The emperor, Nur, and a group of royal women paid a visit to her father's tent, "in order to add to his dignity," Jahangir wrote. Ghiyas presented "exceedingly rare" offerings to the emperor—pearls and rubies worth a fortune, and elaborate clothing. "A pleasant assembly was held," wrote Jahangir; nobles and servants drank cups of wine. After the festive gathering, Jahangir begged Ghiyas to excuse him. He went back to his imperial tent and issued an edict: "I ordered Nur-mahall Begam to be called Nur-Jahan Begam," changing his wife's name from Light of the Palace to Light of the World. [31]

Names had a very special significance among royalty of the Islamic world. Monarchs regularly conferred exalted and poetic titles and names upon members of the family or court as indications of status and privilege. Akbar and his court historians, for example, favored senior women of the harem with epithets that spoke of purity and sanctity, such as the Abode of Mary, the Great Lady of the Age, Liberality of Good Things, Bounty of the House, and Wisdom of the Court. [32] Though Jahangir called some royal matrons the Fortunate Lady, the Exalted Queen, and the Powerful Lady, most of the names he gave to his wives, concubines, and entertainers suggest his taste for beauty and opulence, like his wife Sahib Jamal, Mistress of Beauty, the concubines he called Bold-Eyed and Pretty Body; or dancers and singers he dubbed Pearl, Ruby, Diamond, Rose, and Saffron.

When Jahangir renamed his wife Nur Jahan, Light of the World, he moved onto a loftier plane, linking her name to his by references to illumination and strength. The emperor's full name was Nur ad-Din Muhammad Jahangir. Nur ad-Din, Light of Faith; Jahangir, Seizer or Conqueror of the World. [33] Jahangir's father, Akbar, subscribed to the Persian Neo-Platonist notion that all life came into existence by the constant blinding illumination of God, the Light of Lights. In Persian, *nur* means "light," and in Pashtu, a language of Afghanistan familiar to the Mughals, it means "rock." The name the emperor gave to his newest wife embodied both meanings: brilliance and solidity. The Light of the Palace was elevated to Light of the World, and the honorific Begum clinched her status as a highly exalted woman.

Celebrations followed Nur's renaming. A week afterward, Shahanshah Jahangir and Nur Jahan Begum—effectively the emperor and the empress—visited Asaf Khan's tent-mansion, roughly two and a half miles from the imperial lodgings. For half that distance, Asaf covered the road with velvet and brocades to honor his elevated sister and her emperor husband. He presented them with gifts: jewels, gold vessels, fine textiles, four horses, and a camel. Immediately after this event, Jahangir raised Ghiyas's rank yet again, and granted him a *tuman tugh*, a horsetail banner, a custom begun by the Mughals' Central Asian ancestors and a prerogative reserved for royalty—an extraordinary sign of imperial favor.[34]

Jahangir turned to Ghiyas for advice on a matter with which he was obsessed: trouble in the Deccan Plateau, the vast expanse of territory to the south of the Mughal Empire that today constitutes large parts of the states of Maharashtra, Karnataka, and Andhra Pradesh. Throughout Mughal history, the sultanates of the Deccan had successfully resisted takeover by their northern neighbor. Even Akbar had been able to win only a tiny corner of the Deccan, the fort of Ahmadnagar. And now the chief minister of the independent Ahmadnagar state, a former slave from Ethiopia named Malik Ambar, skilled as a soldier and politically adroit, was rallying other Deccan states to win back the fort and resist Mughal incursion into the south.

Ambar had been bought as a slave years before and pressed into service as a soldier by the chief minister of Ahmadnagar. Freed by the minister's widow, Ambar married and became a lancer. In 1595, when Akbar's forces attacked the fort and city of Ahmadnagar, aiming to annex the whole state, Ambar and the small contingent of troops he headed broke through the Mughal lines but were ultimately overpowered. Ambar and his men withdrew deep into the countryside to regroup.

The Mughal Army fought the soldiers of the sultan of Ahmadnagar intermittently for the next five years, but the best they could do was capturing the Ahmadnagar fort and taking the sultan prisoner in 1600. They failed to conquer the rest of the state. When the fort fell, Ambar, who now headed a 7,000-man army in the independent part of Ahmadnagar, successfully pushed for a twenty-year-old member of the royal family to become a replacement for the imprisoned sultan. The young man married Ambar's daughter, and Ambar became his son-in-law's regent and the chief minister of Ahmadnagar.

Since becoming emperor in 1605, Jahangir had dispatched general after general to do away with Ambar and the puppet sultan, without success. Jahangir believed that because Prince Khurram had been victorious in Mewar, he was the commander best suited to lead a campaign to the Deccan and finally defeat Ambar. Ghiyas, Nur, and the rest of the imperial inner circle of advisers agreed. Khurram said he would go on one condition: that his eldest half-brother, Prince Khusraw, still a darling of the harem women, be placed in the charge of Asaf Khan, a form of house arrest. Khusraw had been making overtures to the emperor, hoping for a complete reconciliation, and Khurram feared that while he was away, Khusraw could work his way back into their father's good graces and become a rival for succession.

On the day that Khusraw was handed over to Asaf Khan, surrounded by soldiers, according to Thomas Roe, "divers weomen in the seraglio mourne, refuse their meate, crye out of the king's dotage and crueltye . . . The king gives fayre words, protesteth no intent of ill toward the Prince . . . and sends Narmahall [Nur] to appease these enraged ladyes; but they cursse, threaten, and refuse to see her. The common people all murmer."[35] Harkha, Jahangir's mother and Khusraw's grandmother, strongly opposed handing the prince over to Asaf Khan, arguing that physical harm might befall him. Nur managed to calm Harkha's fears. Other high-ranking supporters petitioned the emperor to grant more freedom for Khusraw, but Jahangir remained, as one historian put it, "steadfast in his commitment to punish his son . . . [which] Nur Jahan and Khurram undoubtedly encouraged.[36]

After Khurram departed for the Deccan states in October 1616, the traveling court returned to activities more congenial than preparing for war and arguing over Khusraw's ongoing house arrest. Jahangir ordered repairs on two large, deteriorating reservoirs and a broken dam. He and Nur made nine visits to the tomb of a revered Sufi saint in Ajmer, and traveled to Pushkar Lake, a Hindu sacred site, fifteen times. The imperial encampment moved, stayed in one place for a short while, and moved again.

A month after Khurram's departure, the emperor and empress left the encampment for Ramsar, with a small party of royal women, courtiers, officers, and servants. Ramsar, a *jagir* twenty miles southeast of Ajmer, was the first of two large estates, encompassing whole villages, that the emperor would bestow upon Nur Jahan. Estates were usually given to nobles with rank; a *jagir* came with lucrative fiscal rights—to tax revenues, a share of profits from goods sold, and taxes on goods coming in. Not only was Nur given her own estates, but her holdings were mentioned in lists of landowners counted as imperial officeholders.

The party spent eight nights in Ramsar; Jahangir fished and hunted—gazelle, antelope, and waterfowl—and Nur looked after estate business, conferring with her treasurer. On the last night of their stay, she ordered a feast. "On all sides and in the middle of the lake, which is very broad, lamps were displayed," Jahangir wrote. Gems, jeweled vessels, fine gold-beaded textiles, and a variety of other offerings were displayed before the emperor. The next day the royal entourage moved on.[37]

Jahangir and Nur spent the rest of 1616 in this itinerant mode. Among their many stops was the village of Lasa, in the conquered kingdom of Mewar, which would also become Nur's property. There, Jahangir hunted and he and Nur arranged to send twenty-one winter robes of honor for amirs—top commanders—assigned to the Deccan. On the road, they celebrated Khizri, the feast-day honoring Khwaja Khizr, a saint considered to be immortal and revered by both Muslims and Hindus. The figure of Khizr was an amalgam of the prophet Elijah, who appears in the Old and New Testaments and in the Quran; the Mesopotamian demigod Gilgamesh; and Alexander the Great's legendary love, his cook Andreas, who accidentally fell into the fountain of youth and gained eternal life. Associated with water, fish, and rejuvenation, Khizr roamed the world invisible, at times appearing to mortals to impart wisdom. For Sufi mystics, he was the repository of the mysteries of the universe. The festival of Khizri would have a special meaning for Jahangir, for he too was one who wandered, and loved probing the mysteries of nature. After Khizri festivities in the tents of Nur's father, Jahangir issued an order that the harem women were not to veil their faces from Ghiyas. There was nothing to hide from this elder, he said, who, like a wise Sufi, was a model of the art of living and being.

Through much of the spring of 1617, the Mughal camp traveled in Malwa, a temperate region five hundred miles southwest of Agra dotted with lakes, green valleys, stately palaces, and 360 notable Hindu shrines and temples, as noted in the gazetteer of Akbar's reign. Willows and hyacinths lined the banks of calm rivers; wheat, poppy, sugarcane, mangoes, melons, and grapes grew in abundance. By late 1617, the Mughal camp was set up outside of the fortress town of Mandu in Malwa. A celebrated and solitary ascetic named Jadrup was staying nearby. After many years of religious retreat in a far corner of the desert, the venerable hermit had returned to a spot near the ancient city of Ujjain. Jahangir decided to visit him.

Jadrup lived in a tiny cave dug into the middle of a hill. The passage leading to the small pit where he sat, Jahangir reported, was six feet long, three feet high, and just under two feet wide. The emperor seems to have braved the passage in order to talk with Jadrup in his cave. There was no mat, no straw. Jahangir wrote:

> In the cold days of winter, though he is quite naked, with the exception of a piece of rag that he has in front and behind, he never lights a fire . . . He bathes twice a day in a piece of water near his abode . . . He takes by way of alms five mouthfuls of food . . . which he swallows without chewing, in order that he may not enjoy their flavor . . . he has thoroughly mastered the science of Vedanta, which is the science of Sufism. He spoke well, so much so as to make a great impression on me. My society also suited him.[38]

Through Jadrup, a noted Vaishnavite—a Hindu who worships Vishnu as the supreme god—Jahangir came to believe that the Vedantic philosophy of Hindus and the beliefs of Muslim Sufis were "more or less identical." Based on the Vedas, the sacred scriptures of India, Vedanta affirms the divinity of the human soul and the harmony of all religious traditions, and is one of the ancient philosophical foundations of Hinduism.

Jahangir would seek out Jadrup many times.[39] For the emperor, part of the joy of wandering was nourishing his soul and mind in the company of ascetics, poets, scholars, and artists—masters of penance, scriptures, art, thought, and the turmoil of human existence.

After the first entry about Nur in Jahangir's memoir, his admiring references to her began to proliferate. Many of the most appreciative passages deal in detail with her hunting prowess—a subject deeply meaningful to Mughal rulers. When Jahangir praises Nur's skill as a hunter, he is not so obliquely endorsing her ability to rule.

Hunting was much more than a leisure activity. For Mughals, hunting symbolized imperial dominance, as it had for their Mongol and Turk ancestors. Stalking and shooting allowed a ruler to display his ability to tame the wild and to publicly assert his bravery in the open theater of the hunting grounds.[40] In addition, hunting served some of the same vital purposes as royal travel in general. The emperor and his officers could gather local intelligence and amass data about land revenue, trade, and production. A ruler had the opportunity to meet his people—peasants or traders, who might appear to pay respects or make complaints—and form close ties with local chiefs. Sometimes the appearance of a Mughal hunting party might cause a disobedient or rebellious landholder to back down. An expert on Mughal warfare notes that hunting was "an essential instrument of Mughal government. Under the veil of hunting, the Mughals both rallied and suppressed the enormous military potential of the country surrounding the imperial hunting grounds. Hunting expeditions were often organised to inconspicuously mobilise troops . . . [and] for practising cavalry manoeuvres . . . hunting remained one of the cornerstones of sixteenth—and seventeenth-century Mughal rule."[41]

When Jahangir, as Prince Salim, sentenced to death a servant who made noise and scared away prey during a royal hunt, his act was not the rash behavior of an out-of-control autocrat, but the enforcement of a vital institution, albeit in a startling way. When Jahangir meticulously listed in his journal the animals he killed—in one stretch of 1616, the take was 1 cheetah, 1 lynx, 15 tigers, 33 gazelles, 53 nilgai (large antelopes), 80 boars, 90 antelopes, and 340 waterfowl—he was asserting his majesty. And when he wrote rapturously about Nur's hunting, he was asserting hers.

On April 16, 1617, Nur Jahan set out on elephant-back to hunt in Malwa using the "battue" method of stalking, a regular practice among the Mughals. With the help of dogs, four tigers spotted by scouts were surrounded by beaters, men who pounded the bushes with sticks in order to drive the game into a small, open area. The empress fired six shots and bagged all four tigers.

Jahangir was hugely impressed. "Until now, such shooting was never seen, that from the top of an elephant and inside of a howdah (*'amari*) six shots should be made and not one miss, so that the four beasts found no opportunity to spring or move." In sheer delight, the emperor scattered coins over Nur Jahan. Impromptu, a poet recited this couplet

> *Though Nur Jahan be in form a woman*
> *In the ranks of men she's a tiger-slayer.*[42]

That a woman could aim and shoot with such accuracy stunned this poet. He was not alone in his awe.

TEN

Wonder of the Age

As the Camp of Good Fortune moved through western India to the north and south of Agra, Nur Jahan's dominance was on the upswing. She was involved with Jahangir and his inner circle in ongoing deliberations about the campaign in the Deccan, and in assessing requests from foreign diplomats for trading privileges with India. Her husband sought her counsel when he honored and increased the ranks of deserving officials and noblemen and gave directives for local administration. Nur was making decisions having to do with her *jagir* at Ramsar, about commerce and taxes, and the concerns of her poor subjects. She intervened, for example, to protect peasants from harassment or overtaxation by provincial authorities. The empress also supervised the care of little Shuja, the epileptic son of Khurram and Arjumand, who was pregnant for the fifth time. And Nur was beginning to think over Ladli's marriage prospects, an issue of great political as well as personal import. An alliance that strengthened Khurram's claim on succession would be best.

Nur and Jahangir engaged in standard courtly activities, recreational and official. The emperor wrote busily through this period, about his intense conversations with the ascetic Jadrup and the splendid buildings of Mandu. In March 1617 he issued an order, prompted by a similar ban in Iran, that no one in his realm was to smoke tobacco, because of its ill effects and the possibility of addiction.

In July of 1617, the summer after the tiger hunt that made Nur's reputation as an extraordinary markswoman, an emissary from Khurram arrived at the Camp of Good Fortune, which was pitched near Mandu. The Deccan campaign was going well. Several leaders of the Deccan region had surrendered, turning over to the Mughals the keys to their strongholds. Imperial forces had captured the Ahmadnagar fortress, which had changed hands several times since Akbar first conquered it. The only troubling note: Malik Ambar hadn't yet surrendered.

Nur brought the encouraging news to Jahangir, who wrote in his journal, "Thanks be to Allah that a territory that had passed out of [our] hand has come back into possession of the servants of the victorious State, and that the seditious . . . [have] become deliverers of properties and payers of tribute."[1] If all went according to plan, the Deccan could become the crowning glory of the empire.

As a reward for bringing him the felicitous news of Khurram's victories, Jahangir gave Nur another *jagir*, a tract of land in Ajmer province called Toda, which included several villages and at least one large town.[2] Over time, revenue from Toda would earn Nur a great deal of money.[3] Ramsar, her other estate, was also profitable, thanks in part to Nur's share of the duty collected on merchandise brought into the area.[4]

When the monsoon came to Malwa in late July, buildings collapsed under the powerful winds and old men said they'd never seen such downpours in their lives. Nevertheless, Jahangir wrote, "it is not known if in the inhabited world there exists another place as Mandu for sweetness of air and for the pleasantness of the locality . . . especially in the rainy season."[5] Perhaps Khurram's victories had so buoyed his spirits that he wasn't troubled by the deluge.

Jahangir and Nur visited the courts and buildings of the Shankar Tank, a large, impressive reservoir built by the rulers of Malwa. The rains lessened in August, and soon it was time for the feast of the Shab-i barat, the commemoration of the first revelation of the Quran. The stars had aligned in such a way that this year the holy day was also the anniversary of Jahangir's accession, as well as the Rakhi festival when Hindu women tied threads around the wrists of their brothers or elder men to symbolize the strength of their bonds. To celebrate the three coinciding holidays, the empress arranged a feast at the lakeside mansion on her Ramsar estate. Male guests were fed and entertained first at the lavish event, which honored the emperor and confirmed Nur's social primacy. Increasingly she was at the center of state and private ceremonies—the ritual weighings, holiday celebrations, seasonal festivals, imperial bazaars, weddings. She would preside over some and give gifts at many; always, family and courtiers would pay their respects to her.

At this triple-holiday party, each guest sat according to his rank and station, served by footmen who offered fruit, roasted meats, and various intoxicating drinks. As evening fell, servants lit lanterns and lamps around the reservoir and nearby buildings. "The lanterns and lamps cast their reflection on the water, and it appeared as if the whole surface of the tank was a plain of fire . . ." Jahangir wrote. "Drinkers of cups drank more cups than they could carry." The entertainment went late into the night, and then the men left. After that, royal women joined the merriment until only three hours of the night remained.[6]

Jahangir grew impatient for news from the Deccan; a month had passed since Khurram's emissary had reported imperial victories. Nur and Jahangir knew the danger that Ambar posed. The emperor's anxiety was palpable as he wrote about "the ill-starred Ambar," "the rebel Ambar," "Ambar, the dark face," "that disastrous man."

Jahangir knew that in the time of the Abbasid caliphs, famed rulers of Baghdad from the eighth to the thirteenth century, pigeons were trained to fly long distances carrying messages. He already had royal pigeon keepers in his employ; when he was a boy, his father had kept pigeons that did flying tricks, and Jahangir, too, kept a flock. The emperor instructed his pigeon keepers to teach carrier pigeons to fly in the early morning from Mandu to Burhanpur, in the Deccan, with messages. If the weather was clear, the birds reached that distance of one hundred miles away in three hours; if it was raining, the trip took up to seven and a half hours.

On August 14, perhaps a few weeks after the pigeons took the imperial message to Burhanpur, the birds brought back promising news. Though Ambar hadn't yet been defeated, Khurram had gathered plenty of local support. He had assigned lands to loyal and reliable men of the Deccan, and made arrangements for local administration. The prince requested permission to appoint the governors of various Deccan provinces, and said that he'd soon be traveling north.

Leaving 30,000 cavalry and 7,000 infantry musketeers in the occupied territories, the prince departed, accompanied by 25,000 cavalry and 2,000 musketeers. Asaf Khan hosted a celebration as he awaited the return of Khurram, his triumphant son-in-law. During the party at Asaf's area of the tented camp in Mandu, shaded by verdant mango trees and overlooking waterfalls, intimates and courtiers raised many a glass to the absent hero.[7]

Khurram arrived in Mandu on October 1, 1617; he had been gone eleven months. His new daughter with Arjumand was nearly a month old when he returned. Malik Ambar still commanded strategic forts and was recruiting other chieftains as new allies, but overall Jahangir still considered the Deccan project a great success.[8] There was much jubilation when Khurram kissed the imperial ground of the Camp of Good Fortune. Jahangir summoned his treasured son up to the *jharokha*, the imperial balcony of the tent-palace, then rose and embraced him. Khurram presented thousands of coins as an offering to his father, and gave the same amount in alms. Also among the prince's many gifts to Jahangir was the elephant Sir-nag, the finest beast in the stable of the conquered leader of Bijapur, and a chest of precious stones.

At this victory celebration, Jahangir presented his son with a robe of honor; a gold embroidered jacket edged with pearls on the collar, cuffs, and hem; a jeweled sword; and a jeweled dagger. Then he scattered a tray of gems over his head, just as he showered Nur Jahan with coins when she shot four tigers six months earlier.[9] But perhaps the most potent public demonstration of praise that night was the emperor's giving his son the title Shah Jahan, King of the World, the name by which the world would come to know him. The emperor strongly suggested that he was moving toward what a historian has called "a system of quasi-designated succession," and that Shah Jahan was the anointed one.[10] British Ambassador Thomas Roe, dazzled by the victory celebrations for the prince, wrote that while Jahangir was the emperor, Shah Jahan was the ruler.

Jahangir's acknowledgment of the prince's recent victories was only part of the courtly recognition Khurram, now Shah Jahan, would receive. Of late, every momentous event in the life of the Mughal Empire was heralded by dual recognition—from the emperor and from the empress: two sets of celebrations, independently organized. A week after Jahangir's celebration, she honored Khurram's rise as a brilliant warrior-prince with an event memorialized by an unnamed court artist in a miniature painting, *Jahangir and Prince Khurram Entertained by Nur Jahan*. The empress is dressed in a delicate light-ochre top and mauve trousers, a transparent stole thrown over her shoulders, and she wears pearl-and-ruby earrings, bracelets, and a necklace. She sits across from the emperor, looking directly at him, in an open courtyard lined with carpets into which are woven mythic imagery and decorative motifs of birds, trees, and plants. Khurram, Nur, and Jahangir sit together on a raised carpeted platform with Khurram a bit below his father and stepmother. The prince resembles Jahangir, with the same long sideburns and tapered mustache. He is confident in his posture, yet smaller than the emperor and the empress.[11]

Nur bestowed on Khurram a robe of honor adorned with jeweled flowers and precious pearls, a jeweled turban ornamented with rare gems, a pearled turban, a waistband with pearl beading, a sword with a jeweled scabbard strap, a band of pearls, two horses, one of which had a jeweled saddle, and a royal elephant. She then gave his wives and children gold ornaments and nine pieces of cloth each, and his key officers robes of honor and jeweled daggers.[12] Khurram's mother, Jagat Gosain, wasn't present at Nur's gathering, nor is she known to have hosted her victorious son separately.

Khurram, now Shah Jahan, was aware that although his father had made the final decision about his command of the Deccan campaign, Nur Jahan, along with Ghiyas and Asaf, had been central to orchestrating the plans. Not only that, the prince knew that Nur and her family had ensured that there was no princely machination against him by Khusraw while he was away in the south. In this world of symbolically laden exchanges, Shah Jahan now owed Nur a public show of acknowledgment, as he well understood. Three weeks after his return, following Nur's feast for him, Shah Jahan presented his own offerings, which endorsed Nur's ascendancy. In the courtyard below the royal balcony, he displayed for the emperor gems, jeweled items, fine textiles, 150 elephants and 100 Arabian and Persian horses adorned with gold and silver trappings. Jahangir came down and examined the items with great attention. Among the presents was a ruby that was the heaviest in the emperor's vast collection; a large, valuable sapphire (Jahangir said he'd never seen one of such good color); and the Jamkura Diamond, found, legend said, by royal women in the Deccan state of Berar, resting in the middle of a plant called *sag jamkura*.[13]

Next, the prince displayed his gifts for Nur Jahan, his *valida-i khud*, "his own mother," as Jahangir put it in his journal. The emperor noted that gifts worth 200,000 rupees—an astronomical sum—were given to Nur Jahan alone, followed by 60,000 rupees' worth "to his [Shah Jahan's] other mothers and the Begams."[14] Shah Jahan gave Nur three times what he gave all the other elder women, including his biological mother, combined—a very clear sign of Nur's distinction. "Such offerings had never been made during this dynasty," Jahangir emphasized. By contrast, during Jahangir's reign, harem women received annual cash allowances ranging from about 2,000 rupees to 3,400 rupees, according to a woman's status and her relationship to the emperor.[15]

Courtiers and intimates of the Mughals were certainly aware of Nur's growing role in state decisions, administrative and military. Queen Mother Harkha had every right to be proud of the guidance she'd given her daughter-in-law when Nur first entered the harem. The Mughal princes, especially the ambitious Shah Jahan, felt it was important to forge a strong bond with their influential stepmother. Insiders in the royal retinue such as the longtime courtier Inayat Khan, addicted to alcohol and ailing but considered by the emperor as one of his "closest servants and subjects," knew her eminence. So did Aqa Aqayan, who had been in charge of Jahangir's harem since his youth, and was a member of the party on every royal journey or expedition until her retirement.[16] Dai Dilaram, who would soon take over harem affairs from Aqayan and had known Nur since she was born, must have been delighted by Nur's accomplishments.

Some members of the court, however, took issue with Nur's ascent. As early as 1612, one of Akbar's foster brothers had written a letter to Jahangir condemning his policy of favoring the Indian Muslims and Khurasanis (Iranians from Khurasan) over Hindu Rajputs and Chagatai Muslims from Central Asia. The letter targeted the dominance of Nur and her family.[17] Another person troubled by Nur's rise and her family's high-ranking government positions was Mahabat Khan, a military commander who'd served Jahangir loyally since he was still Prince Salim. He too was uncomfortable with the eminence of the empress and the Iranian faction that had coalesced around her. Mahabat held back his reservations about the empress, but not for long.

In the portable Mughal bazaar, set up at a decorous distance from the entrance to the *lashkar*, the imperial encampment, people spoke— and wrote—about Nur's growing influence at court. One of them was Thomas Roe, the English ambassador, sent by King James I to secure trading rights in India. Roe, a man with a receding hairline, the full mustache of a Rajput warrior, and an incomplete understanding of Mughal culture, was having trouble gaining access to Jahangir and Nur. He decided to tag along with merchants and other followers who erected a tented bazaar near the Camp of Good Fortune wherever Jahangir's traveling court pitched its tents for an extended stay. In the bazaar were barbers, physicians, tailors, launderers, blacksmiths, weapons dealers, musicians, food vendors, tea shops, and tented guesthouses. More distinguished visitors, such as Roe, stayed at inns close to the bazaar or in nearby towns.

Prince Parvez, Jahangir's middle son, had been Roe's first point of contact as he sought an introduction to the court. But Parvez was more interested in alcohol than diplomacy. Evidently Roe wasn't well informed about the workings of the Mughal court. He expected the Great Mughal to be at the helm of affairs. It was months before he understood that he had in fact missed the most crucial connection for acquiring trade privileges: Nur Jahan.[18]

Roe needed someone who could help him reach the empress, and he turned to a fixer and translator in Ajmer whose name, Jadu, literally meant *magic* in Hindi. The magic began to work, according to Roe's journal: "Hee [Jahangir] sent a gentellman for my Commission to show his queene the seale, which he kept one night . . ."[19] But Roe was miffed that his official seal—his diplomatic credential—had been kept overnight and returned without the expected official invitation for an audience, and he blamed Nur for what he considered a disrespectful and arrogant act. Roe wrote disapprovingly of her power:

> At night hee [Jahangir] descends into a court; on a throne hee discourseth and drincketh with much affability. To this place are none admitted but with leave and of eminent quality. This course is infallibly kept, except sickness prevent yt; for which alsoe the people will exact a reason, and endure not long the absence of their king. The rest of this motion is inward amoung woemen, of which sort, though he keepe a thouwsand, yet one governs him, and wynds him up at her pleasure.[20]

The British ambassador also wrote in detail about his face-to-face encounters with Jahangir—but there's no evidence in the Mughal court records that they ever met. The emperor made no mention of Roe in his exhaustively detailed memoir. Furthermore, there's no evidence that Jahangir ever granted the trading privileges to England that Roe would claim to have negotiated. European observers of the Mughal court often embellished (and sometimes invented) stories of their dealings with the emperor.

❧

Nur's next public move suggests that this woman of verve and imagination definitely had state power on her mind: She issued her first royal order. Its vocabulary, and that of the orders that followed, revealed her deep engagement with her sovereignty and her subjects.

In December 1617, the Mughals were considering returning to Agra. But Jahangir decided that since he'd never seen the ocean he would visit the coastal state of Gujarat before heading home to the capital. His mother, and the rest of his traveling harem, "baggage and extra establishment," went on to Agra.[21]

Nur Jahan didn't accompany Jahangir to Gujarat, but she didn't go back to Agra either. Instead, she seems to have gone to Toda, one of her Ajmer estates, to rest, perhaps to hunt, write poetry, and supervise the officers who looked after her properties.[22] The treasurer of the estate, a man named Baroman, was owed money being withheld by an officer of the raja of Bikaner, in India's western desert. On behalf of Baroman, Nur directed the raja to ensure that payment was made immediately. The official order—an irrefutable sign of sovereignty—read:

> The chosen of the peers, worthy of favours and obligations, RAJA SURAT SINGH, hoping for the sublime favours, should know that a sum of money . . . is due, to Kishandas and Baroman his son, the treasurer of Her Majesty . . . he is ordered to pay off the said debts . . . He should not disobey the orders, and should regard it his duty.

Written by a scribe on a paper scroll, the order was crowned by the sacred invocation *Allahu Akbar* in cursive script, and adorned with a beautiful arch-shaped wax seal on which was stamped the following legend: *By the light [nur] of the sun [mihr] of Jahangir—and the Divine Grace the signet of Nurjahan has illumined the world like the moon.*[23]

Another translation has the final clause as "the seal of *Nur Jahan, the Empress of the Age* (*Nur Jahan Padshah Begum*), *has become resplendent like the Moon.*"[24] On the order, the word *nur*, "light"— part of the names of both emperor (Nur ad-Din) and empress (Nur Jahan)—stands out, as does *mihr*, sun, part of Nur's former name. Also worth noting is the clever (and politic) play on the relationship of the sun and the moon—one secondary to the other, but both heavenly eminences.

The Mughals inherited from their Central Asian forebears two terms for edicts issued by women. Orders from a sovereign's mother were called *hukm*, while those from a royal consort, princess, or prince's wife were called *nishan*. An emperor's orders were called *farmans*, and carried the imperial seal and *tughra*, the emperor's calligraphic signature. Jahangir's imperial orders, many of which still exist, covered such issues as instructions to an officer to measure and consolidate lands, military appointments, and the protection of peasants from landlords. *Hukms* and *nishans* were much less authoritative; they covered very small local matters or simply reemphasized an order that had already been issued by the emperor. Mughal women had issued *hukms* at least twice before Nur's time. Jahangir's mother Harkha, and before that, Akbar's mother Hamideh Banu Begum, had issued an order each, both implementing religious and agrarian policies of their reigning sons. Hamideh reiterated her son's declaration that a certain pious man was exempt from taxes and his cows were allowed to graze uninterrupted.[25] Such matriarchs were often consulted for their accumulated wisdom; for example, Emperor Babur wrote in his memoir that "for tactics and strategy there were few women like my grandmother Esan Dawlat Begim. She was very intelligent and a good planner. Most affairs were done by her counsel."[26]

Nur was the first Mughal woman to issue orders in her own right, orders not very different from her husband's *farmans*—about debt and revenue collection, land grants, military matters, criminal cases. She couldn't have done this without some precedents—not just the earlier *hukm* orders of the two queen mothers, but also long-held political traditions of the Mughals and their nomadic Mongol and Turkic ancestors that made a place for female power, at least in principle. Among the Mughals and their nomadic ancestors from the Central Asian steppes, female sovereignty was a theoretical possibility. Since divinity resided in the monarch, and since it could not be transferred except through direct descent, the possibility of a daughter succeeding her father could not be excluded, though it never actually happened in the Mughal world. Still, Nur's advance toward co-sovereignty was groundbreaking: born to foreign parents, she was no daughter of the dynasty, and yet no other woman in Mughal India had embodied power through official signs of sovereignty such as issuing important orders under her own signature.

And that signature speaks volumes. In the past, *hukms* and *nishans* were signed "mother of," "daughter of," or "sister of" the emperor. But Nur signed her own name, and she signed as sovereign: *Nur Jahan Padshah Begum*. Padshah, meaning sovereign or monarch: the same term that appeared alongside Jahangir's name. This signature was a public announcement that she was assuming the role of co-sovereign, with her husband's tacit approval.

Nur issued several edicts. Ten survive in museums, the majority dating from 1622–27, when she was at the height of her power as the de facto ruler of the realm. The imperial orders of Her Majesty, the Empress Nur Jahan were a unique blend: the ornamental signature on the top of Nur's orders identified them as *hukms*, while the body of the text took the form of a *nishan*.[27] Nur drew on traditions of Mughal matriarchy as well as those of royal consorts and princesses in order to create a new form of power, a "third space"—technical proof of her reign, to which even the most diehard jurists would bow.[28]

The mythical Wak-Wak tree first found popularity in *Shahnama*, the Book of Kings, an eleventh-century epic poem by the celebrated Iranian author Firdausi. *A Floral Fantasy of Animals and Birds*, early 1600s. India, Mughal, © The Cleveland Museum of Art.

The fort complex at Agra, built during the reign of Emperor Akbar. Completed in 1573. *Exterior View of the Fort Complex* © Aga Khan Trust for Culture/Michael Peuckert.

Nur Jahan surrounded by harem women, this painting depicts the moment after she came to Agra in 1608. Behind her, the small girl is meant to represent Ladli. The lotus blossom in her right hand is suggestive of longevity. *Chiterin: An Illustration of the Nur Jahan Episode* © Bharatiya Kala Bhavan.

Court painter Abul-Hasan Nadir uz-Zaman's remarkable painting: *Nur Jahan Holding a Musket*, c. seventeenth century CE, courtesy of Rampur Raza Library.

A clear indicator of Nur's sovereignty: a silver rupee bearing Nur Jahan and Jahangir's names.

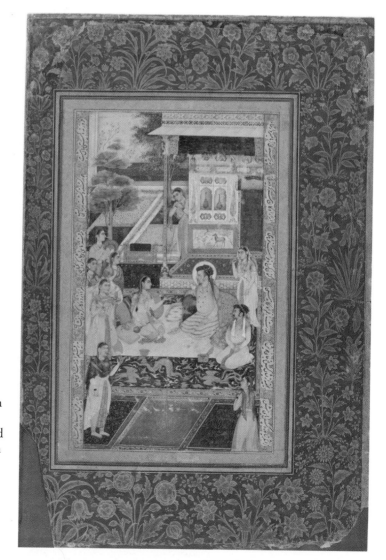

A celebration for Prince Khurram's military successes in the Deccan, hosted by Nur and captured by a court painter in miniature. *Jahangir and Prince Khurram Entertained by Nur Jahan*, Freer Gallery of Art and Arthur M. Sackler Gallery.

Nur Jahan: Portrait to Be Worn As a Jewel, seventeenth century, Harvard Art Museums/Arthur M. Sackler Museum.

Posthumous Portrait of Emperor Jahangir Under a Canopy, c. 1650. India, Mughal, © The Cleveland Museum of Art.

Mausoleum of I'timad ud-Daula, the garden tomb of Ghiyas and Asmat, commissioned by Nur. © Aga Khan Trust for Culture/Samuel Bourne (photographer).

Maqbara-i Jahangir, the Tomb of Jahangir, commissioned by Shah Jahan, but built from Nur's designs, under her supervision. © Aga Khan Trust for Culture.

The Tomb of Nur Jahan at Shahdara. The design echoes Jahangir's tomb, at around half the size. Photo © Guilhem Vellut.

A painting in the Indian and Persian tradition, *Nur Jahan Holding a Portrait of Jahangir,* c. 1627, © The Cleveland Museum of Art.

Mughal Queen Nur Jahan Playing Polo with Other Princesses. Painted by Ustad Haji Muhammad Sharif (1889–1978). The father of traditional miniature painting in Pakistan, Muhammad Sharif was a hereditary court painter from the Patiala family of Muslim painters.

Mughal Brave Queen Nur Jahan with Her Husband King Jahangir after Killing Tiger with Her Spear. Painted by Ustad Haji Muhammad Sharif (1889–1978).

Princess Nur Jahan and Attendants, eighteenth century, the Metropolitan Museum of Art.

Film still from *Noor Jehan*, 1967. Lavish legends of Nur were put on celluloid several times between 1923 and 1967, and most films had the title *Noor Jahan*. Courtesy: The Osian's Archive & Library Collection.

Nur paved the way for later Mughal women to issue wide-ranging orders, though not as co-sovereigns. After her death, a number of orders were issued by her grandniece Jahanara, Arjumand's daughter; and by Nadira Banu, the wife of Nur's grandnephew, in the latter half of the seventeenth century.

Issuing orders was one of the three legally acknowledged privileges of Mughal rulers—the official signs of Islamic sovereignty. The other two were being named in Friday prayers and the striking of coins that bore a monarch's name. In 1617, gold and silver coins began to circulate bearing both Nur and Jahangir's names—the emperor's on the front and the empress's on the reverse. It was the first time that a woman's name had appeared on a Mughal coin; there were even some coins with Nur's name alone. The new power of the empress would be obvious to those in the emperor's household who received these coins as gifts. Ordinary folks would notice too, such as salt makers or cumin traders who brought their products to the Mughal court from far away and received these coins in payment.

Both royal names appeared on a coin marked with the following inscription:

> *By the order of Shah Jahangir*
> *The gold got a hundred honors added to it*
> *By getting impressed on it, the name of Nur Jahan Padshah Begum*

And a half-ounce gold coin, measuring nearly an inch in diameter, now housed in the Lucknow Museum, reads:

> *By order of Shah Jahangir, gained a hundred beauties*
> *Gold by the name of Nur Jahan Padshah Begum*[29]

Numismatists have studied the size, weight, and composition of the eleven existing coins with Nur Jahan's name, held in museums in India and elsewhere.[30] Historians and non-experts are more interested in their symbolic significance. Today, at the Agra fort, both tour guides and local visitors still proudly recall the only moment in Mughal history when coins carried the name of a woman.

Though Jahangir still devoted a great deal of time to state matters, he was increasingly involved in observing nature and pursuing philosophical questions. His entries in the *Jahangirnama* show that he was drawn to anyone or anything that brought him wonder: a conversation with an ascetic; rubies and sapphires; seedless grapes from Kabul; a rare turkey-cock delivered to the emperor by Muqarrab Khan, a surgeon and governor of the Cambay region in western India. On the way back from Gujurat to Agra, Jahangir hunted and stopped with his retinue in the town of Dhar, an ancient city that, he noted, was the home of the great scholar-king Raja Bhoj a thousand years earlier. Jahangir traveled with a pair of domesticated cranes named Layla and Majnun after a pair of famous Persian lovers, and he employed a eunuch who would inform him when the cranes were about to mate. Every day, Jahangir would head out to observe the cranes and make detailed notes. Jahangir had more and more time to indulge his curiosity and his admiration of the natural world as his empress took on more and more matters of governance.

Abul-Hasan, the celebrated court painter and Nur's contemporary who had seen her remarkable life unfold, faced a challenge: how to create a portrait of Empress Nur Jahan that captured her unusual rise to prominence and did justice to her power and presence.

Though Jahangir doesn't mention Hasan in his memoir until 1618, the artist had long been connected with the court. As Prince Salim, he employed Hasan's father, the masterly Iranian painter Aqa Reza, in his atelier. Reza had a strong affinity for the Safavid style of painting, characterized by an emphasis on human figures in natural settings, illumination in the margins or borders of the painting, and a playful approach to lines, shadows, and light. He was adept at classic Persian images—courtiers at leisure, strong natural backdrops, allegorical scenes. Reza also illuminated manuscripts, specializing in border decoration, and was one of the first artists in the Mughal world to blend European and Indian styles of painting. He trained a number of Mughal artists, including a woman, Nadira Banu, and his son, Hasan, a slight young man who started painting in his early teens.[31] One of Hasan's earliest known paintings was a copy of a work by Albrecht Dürer.

Eventually the son surpassed his father in renown and range (and, according to Jahangir, in skill). Hasan developed an eclectic body of work that drew upon a wide range of sources, including European and Persian imagery, and he experimented with color. He understood the expressive potential of drapery—the way carefully rendered folds could bring humans to life as full-bodied individuals rather than flat figures—and he had a gift for capturing with deep perception the essence of his subjects' personalities.[32] He painted sages, pilgrims, and, many times, the emperor himself. Jahangir's first written reference to Hasan marked the artist's presentation of a painting depicting the emperor's accession. That work would eventually serve as the frontispiece of the *Jahangirnama*. In his memoir, Jahangir declared Hasan the *nadir uz-zaman*, Wonder of the Age, the Zenith of the World.

Hasan came from an established artistic tradition in which young Mughal women were regularly presented as stunning, bejeweled beauties in an idealized rather than realistic style, what art historians call the *nayika* mode, after the Hindi word for heroine. Commoners in the court—singers, dancers, servants—were painted in the same way, their faces identical and ritualized. Hasan would also have been familiar with other kinds of portraits in the imperial library. Along with these fanciful depictions of stylized young ladies were more realistic portraits of matriarchs—for example, an aging imperial woman giving advice to her son or brother during his visit to the women's quarters. There were also detailed scenes of the births of Akbar and of Jahangir, and many other paintings of the birth chamber, the post-natal care between mother and infant, the wet nurses at work—all signs celebrating the privileged act of birthing royal children.

Hasan understood that none of these conventions—women as stylized ornaments, as aged advisers, or as vessels of royal birth—would be right for Nur Jahan. The Mughal world had never known a royal woman like her. How could he represent not only Nur's beauty and charisma but also the growing boldness of her leadership, buzzed about in the bazaar and among officials and visiting diplomats? As he launched his daunting work, probably sometime between 1612 and 1617, according to art historians, he knew he would have to experiment.[33]

This was Hasan's challenge: Which of Nur's impressive imperial activities would best represent her in a portrait? Which one spoke to him most? Which might best convey her combination of delicacy and strength?

He decided to present Nur in a way that told her story beautifully without obscuring her accomplishments in conventional stylized notions of glamour. His portrait of her in watercolor and oils was groundbreaking in both style and content.

The empress stands confidently loading a musket. She's dressed in hunting attire—a knee-length tunic tied with a sash, tightly fitting trousers, and the kind of regal turban usually worn by men—and she wears her famous ruby and diamond earrings.[34] Her chin is up, her slender shoulders are back, and her chest is rising slightly. She seems to be focusing on the horizon. She's regal and commanding; the portrait is radiant with energy.

We don't know whether Nur posed for Hasan or he painted the *Portrait of Nur Jahan* from occasional sightings and knowledge of her sterling acts of leadership. What we do know is that the work is unique. The artist played with several Mughal artistic traditions. A new kind of woman required a new kind of portrait.

Hasan honored some conventions of Mughal painting. He worked in a very small space, using just 17 inches by 12 inches of paperboard to present the full figure of the empress and surround her with 14 delicate flowers in red, black, yellow, and blue.[35] But in most other ways, he was daringly experimental, beginning with his decision to represent her as an actor—a doer, a defender, a predator.

Showing Nur loading the musket is a rare example of action in the portrait of female royalty or nobility. Neither of the other two Islamic empires of Nur's time, Safavid Iran and Ottoman Turkey, could boast of such graphic evidence of an empress engaged in intrepid imperial action. Hasan's choice of action says a great deal. Nur's confident stance suggests that she's skilled with this weapon used in hunting and war, that she has technical and military know-how usually reserved for men.[36] The gun is taller than she is, but Nur handles it with ease, tamping down gunpowder with her raised right arm. She looks into the distance "with an appearance of pride, vigor, boldness and freedom," notes Sanam Ali of India's Rampur Raza Library, where the painting is kept.[37] Showing a woman alone and not in a group was another break with tradition. Nur occupies the entire canvas, just as she increasingly filled the canvas of imperial life.

Jahangir once wrote in his memoir "my liking for painting and my practice in judging it have arrived at such a point that when any work is brought before me, either of deceased artists or of those of the present day, without the names being told me, I say on the spur of the moment that it is the work of such and such a man." Chances are that the emperor closely inspected the *Portrait of Nur Jahan*, as he did other works. There was more than one occasion when he showed his great "desire for accuracy in the portraits he commissioned . . ."[38] If there had been anything he didn't like about Hasan's portrait of

Nur, he'd have intervened, as he had done many times before with other artists when he had any misgivings about the execution or appropriateness of a painting. It is a sign of his approval of Hasan's painting of Nur with a musket that in 1618 the emperor not only dubbed him the Wonder of the Age, but also declared his work in general to be "perfect."[39]

Hasan gave to posterity a rare picture of Nur Jahan's power, and he put his name on the painting, unusual for Mughal artists, who didn't always sign their work. The Wonder of the Age validated what everyone was seeing. The remarkable Nur Jahan, a woman who'd only been the emperor's wife since 1611, one of many, was now the empress of Mughal India, a Wonder of the Age herself.

She demonstrated this again in 1618, when she commissioned and designed her first public building, a traveler's inn, the Nur Mahal Serai in Jalandhar, on the Grand Trunk Road between Agra and Lahore. According to one estimate it could hold up to two thousand guests, along with their camels and horses. It had a separate area for the imperial couple—they stayed several times—and its own mosque. On the gateway of the serai, adorned with sculpted animals and mounds of lotus, Nur ordered an inscription in four rhyming verses. The last line was: *This saray was erected by Nur Jahan Begum.*

In commissioning a lodging for male travelers in which international traders would spend time and having her name engraved on its gateway, Nur turned architecture into statecraft, ensuring that visitors would know that she, the empress, was the patron and creator and not just another member of the royal family.[40] Royal women had previously conveyed their ideas about architectural works only by suggesting specific styles and plans. Nur knew that there was a history of overlooked Mughal women: too many names missing from the documents. Her mother-in-law had given the Mughal Empire the precious gift of an emperor, Jahangir, but was left out of the official record. Jahangir never officially noted the name of the concubine who gave birth to his son Prince Shahryar, or mentioned his wife Jagat Gosain in the context of her son's successes. Nur overrode this tradition of silence. In act after act—hunting, advising, issuing imperial orders and coins, designing buildings—she ensured that her name was etched indelibly in public memory and in history.

❊ ELEVEN ❊

Veils of Light

In the autumn of 1618, on the way back to Agra after his first sight of the sea, the emperor rejoined Nur Jahan at her estate in the Malwa region. The empress had been very ill, Jahangir recorded in a November journal entry, though he didn't describe the cause or nature of her distress. "Nur-Jahan Begam had been ailing for some time," he wrote, "and the physicians who had the good fortune to be chosen to attend on her, Musalmans and Hindus, perceived no gain from all the medicines they gave her, and confessed their helplessness in treating her. At this time, Rahim Ruhullah began to wait upon her, and undertook [to find] a remedy. By the aid of God (glory be to his name!), in a short time she quite recovered. In reward for his excellent service I . . . bestowed on the hakim three villages in his native country . . . and an order was given that he should be weighed against silver, which should be given him as a reward."[1] Nur remained grateful to Ruhullah for restoring her health; when she found out later that two of the three awarded villages hadn't been delivered to him, she immediately issued an order directing a Mughal loyalist to make amends.

At the end of December, the Mughal cavalcade reached the out-skirts of Fatehpur-Sikri, twenty miles from Agra. For the third year in a row, an outbreak of bubonic plague had swept through the area, killing up to 100 people a day, but that danger was now over. The emperor's mother, Harkha, came from Agra to greet him; he was shocked at how "decrepit" she seemed.

Though astrologers had established that January 1619 would be the auspicious time for Jahangir and Nur's return to Agra, Jahangir kept the royal party in Fatehpur-Sikri for three months, for reasons unknown. In early April, news came from the capital that Jagat Gos-ain, Shah Jahan's mother, had passed away. Jahangir doesn't record his own response to the death of this senior wife; he writes only that he went to his son's quarters to offer consolation and sympathy and took Shah Jahan back with him to the palace. The next day, the Mughals, including Shah Jahan, entered Agra.

When Nur's health improved, she sat in the *jharokha* so that she could be seen by the people, like a goddess on display. *Darshan*, the traditional practice of viewing Hindu deities and holy people, had been adopted by Jahangir's father Akbar, and adapted to include displaying the person of the monarch. *Nur Jahan: Portrait to Be Worn As a Jewel*, a seventeenth-century image, shows that Nur, too, boldly followed the tradition of *darshan*; her upper body is framed in the window, one arm resting on the sill, a classic posture, in profile.[2] Akbar no doubt believed that to be viewed by the masses was a kingly—that is, male—prerogative, to be kept alive by his succes-sors. He could never have expected that a successor could be kingly and female.

Nur Jahan was now the de facto co-sovereign, the backbone of Mughal government. Mu'tamad Khan, the paymaster who would take over the task of maintaining Jahangir's journal a few years later when the emperor became too ill to do it himself, maintained that Jahangir had granted the rights of sovereignty and government to Nur Jahan. She sat in the *jharokha*, he wrote, while the nobles presented themselves "and listen[ed] to her dictates . . . At last her authority reached such a pass that the King was such only in name. Repeatedly he gave out that he bestowed the sovereignty on Nur Jahan Begam."[3]

Despite the edicts, the coins, the *jharokha*, and the sovereignty her husband publicly bestowed upon her, one technical, legal prerogative of a Mughal ruler eluded Nur: the mention of the monarch's name during the *khutba*, the central sermon of Friday prayers. Yet several court historians noted that even though the *khutba* was not read in her name, it was Nur who directed the affairs of the realm. "Except for the fact that her name was not recited in the sermon, whatever other requisites of kingship there are were performed by her," wrote the historian Bhakkari, an eyewitness to her co-sovereignty.[4] The matter of the sermon wasn't straightforward, anyway; its importance in establishing sovereignty had always been a little ambiguous. As a rebellious young prince, Jahangir had his name read during a *khutba* to challenge his father. In time to come, his son Shah Jahan would revolt in exactly the same way. Nur Jahan wasn't a rebel or a dissenter—and she wasn't a man. She would have accepted that the world she had come to co-rule was an emphatically patriarchal one.

Rather surprisingly, the *ulema*—Muslim theological jurists—of the day didn't object to her increasing power. Technically, the *ulema* were the arbiters of the legitimacy of monarchs, but they never had full control; Mughal sovereignty remained a delicate balance between the ruler and the nobles on the one hand and the jurists on the other. As a prince struggling to win the Mughal throne, Jahangir had bestowed favors on theologians and elite Muslims learned in law in order to earn their support. As emperor, he confirmed all existing religious grants due to the *ulema*. Unlike Akbar, he didn't go so far as to issue an edict publicly declaring himself the ultimate authority in religious matters, but neither did he ask directly for religious intervention or political advice from theologians. In Jahangir's memoir, notes a scholar writing about the emperor, "references to Islam as a driving force behind political thought and action are actually very scarce."[5] The jurists' acceptance of Nur's co-sovereignty had a justification; as early as the twelfth century, the revered Muslim theologian Al-Ghazzali had declared that stable rule was more important than a sovereign's legitimacy.[6] Jurists often cited this maxim: "Sixty years of tyranny are better than an hour of civil strife." Numerous sayings of the Prophet Muhammad and legal judgments that condemned social conflict and disorder suggest that Islam encouraged unconditional obedience to a ruler.[7]

As soon as the royal couple returned to Agra, the emperor began thinking about a pleasure trip to Kashmir, likely as a restorative for Nur and perhaps his mother, Harkha. Jahangir had been there with his father, and he was quite smitten by the place he often described as the garden of eternal spring. We can imagine Jahangir telling Nur about the beauty of Kashmir, its countless waterfalls, the sweet-smelling roses, violets, and narcissi, the views of lofty peaks.

The royal cavalcade set off for Kashmir from Agra in October of 1619. That city on the move included Nur and Jahangir; Queen Mother Harkha and other royal women; Shah Jahan, Ghiyas, Asaf, and their families; nobles, officers, stewards, attendants, servants, and soldiers, all of them on horseback or on elephants. Traveling one stage behind the main convoy was Prince Khusraw, with whom Jahangir had reconciled at the urging of Nur and Harkha; the holy man Jadrup may also have interceded.[8] Shah Jahan would have been watching his older half-brother closely for any sign that he was seriously interested in succeeding to the throne. Mahabat Khan, Jahangir's loyal general, recently appointed governor of Kabul, accompanied the royal cavalcade part of the way to Kashmir. He thought that Khusraw should have been left behind in the capital under the watchful eye of a dependable courtier. Mahabat's opinion carried weight because he'd proved his loyalty to Jahangir in the extreme. A decade earlier, Mahabat's brother had been arrested for his part in the assassination plot against Jahangir planned by supporters of Khusraw. When Mahabat arrived at the spot where his brother was about to be hanged, Jahangir offered him the chance to save his brother's life. But in a show of fealty, Mahabat Khan drew his sword and cut off his brother's head. After that, he became one of Jahangir's closest confidants.[9] Khusraw was for some time in his custody.

Short, stocky Mahabat, a man whose soft facial features belied a sternness of intent and action, found an opportune moment to share his opinion of Khusraw's presence with the emperor, in front of other nobles. He also went on a tirade about the empress, complaining that Nur's control of imperial affairs wasn't an appropriate arrangement. According to the poet and writer Shaikh Abdul-Wahab, often a member of the imperial retinue, Mahabat said to the emperor, "His Majesty must have read . . . the histories of the ancient sovereigns . . . Was there any king so subject to the will of his wife? The world is surprised that such a wise and sensible Emperor as Jahangir should permit a woman to have such great influence over him." For a few days after Mahabat's tirade Jahangir remained reserved toward Nur. But when Mahabat left the cavalcade, the emperor softened. "Nur Jahan Begum had wrought so much upon his mind," wrote Wahab, "that even if two hundred men like Mahabat Khan had advised him . . . their words would have made no permanent impression upon him."[10]

The royals camped first near Mathura, not far from the cave of the ascetic Jadrup, whom Jahangir was keen to meet with again. It was here that villagers entreated the emperor to kill a marauding tiger, and the empress skillfully dispatched the beast, earning the gratitude of her subjects and the admiration of her husband. Then it was north to Delhi for a stopover that lasted two and a half weeks. The royal couple paid their respects at the tombs of Jahangir's grandfather Humayun and a revered thirteenth-century Sufi saint. They visited Aqa Aqayan, the former chief supervisor of the harem, who had retired in Delhi after returning from western India.[11] Aqayan was so weak that she "did not have the power to move about," the emperor wrote. Even so, she was overseeing the construction of a garden, a serai, and a tomb near her home. Jahangir directed the governor of Delhi to serve and guard her "in such a manner that no dust from any road of vexation might settle on the hem of her contentment."[12] Jahangir noted in his journal that at seventy-one, Aqayan was the same age his father would have been had he lived. The Mughal party stopped at various places along the way to Kashmir, visiting the tombs of saints and receiving distinguished nobles. Arjumand gave birth to her seventh child, a boy.[13]

Mughal officers went to great lengths to ensure that the royals found nothing but comfort as the road began to climb through the Himalayas. An officer from Agra went ahead of the cavalcade with a group of stonecutters, carpenters, and shovelers to fix bumps, ruts, and potholes in the roads and make the way easier for wagons and animals carrying loads. Along the way, local grandees extended hospitality. In the first week of March 1620, the cavalcade arrived at Pakhli, the beginning of Kashmir territory. The zamindar, the local landlord, hosted the royal party, proudly commending the breathtaking vista, mighty mountains in every direction.

Advance scouts reported to Jahangir that because Kashmir's harvest of wheat and other grains had been disappointingly meager that year, villages on the road ahead wouldn't be able to supply enough to feed the large train of royal elephants traveling with them. Jahangir noted that he sent all but seven hundred of the animals back to Agra.

Jahangir had larger issues of state power and territorial consolida-

tion to address. Troubles were escalating in the Deccan, where Shah
Jahan had gone to war only three years earlier.[14] Ambar was still resisting Mughal rule. Deliberations on the Deccan problem would have
included Jahangir, Nur, Shah Jahan, Ghiyas, and Asaf, considering
again the steps to be taken, useful tactics, fine details of operations.
Shah Jahan, they decided, would march again to the south.

But the prince agreed to head the military operation only if he
could take along his older brother Khusraw in order to keep an eye
on him. Jahangir acquiesced. Shortly before the royal party reached
Hasan Abdal, Shah Jahan left with his four sons and Khusraw to
gather his troops for a Deccan campaign. On February 22, 1620,
after four months on the road, the royal cavalcade arrived at Hasan
Abdal, where the most treacherous part of the journey began. By
this time, shortages and high prices were making it difficult to feed
not only elephants but humans too—the huge numbers of courtiers,
workmen, servants, and soldiers traveling with the royal party. Jahangir ordered hundreds of people in the retinue, both nobles and servants, to return to the capital. Only those absolutely necessary would
go forward with the royal party.

At a spring and waterfall near Hasan Abdal, they halted for two
days. It was becoming difficult for the entire camp to travel together,
so Jahangir ordered the cavalcade to split up. Harkha, some of the
harem women, and their attendants were to stay on a few days longer
while the rest of the royal party traveled on in smaller groups. An
advance camp—a few nobles, the chief steward and workers—would
cross the mountain passes first, preparing the way. A second set of
imperial nobles would follow, which may have been the group Ghiyas traveled with, followed by the core Mughal camp—Nur, Jahangir,
Asaf, Mu'tamad Khan and some other nobles, a few harem intimates,
servants, and select attendants. Eventually, Harkha and her band
of women caught up with this third group. They stopped in villages
along the way, where subjects paid homage to the emperor. The road

was rocky, the areas surrounding full of langur monkeys, peafowl, and black quail.

Jahangir accompanied some of his men as they cut through a high pass, the Pim Drang, and arrived at a waterfall on the Bahat River, where they drank wine in the shade of the trees. Akbar had built a bridge across this swift and deep waterfall, and a stone hilltop rest house that was still intact. The management of the journey from here on was entrusted to Mu'tamad Khan. The hundreds of elephants still remaining with the cavalcade were most likely sent back to Agra just before Pim Drang; they were too precious to risk on such a dangerous road. The party proceeded on horseback. Mahabat left the group on March 1, heading off to Kabul. Two weeks later, the core party of royals stopped in the village of Bhuliyas. From here on, the passes became even more troublesome. Up ahead loomed the Bhuliyas Pass, one of the toughest and narrowest of the journey. Jahangir gave orders that the camp should split again. Nur, Jahangir, Asaf, and Harkha and the ladies of the harem went on together, with the necessary attendants. The rest, including Mu'tamad and Ghiyas, came one stage behind. Mu'tamad sent some men forward with a message directing his advance men to pitch tents at whatever place they had reached, which they did at the foot of the Bhuliyas Pass.

As the royal contingent, dressed in warm sheepskin coats, neared the pass—the men on horseback, the women carried in palanquins— they ran into a spring snowstorm and sheltered in tents erected by the advance party of Mu'tamad's men. Mu'tamad, in the group one stage behind, hurried to join the emperor. He entered the royal tent, paid obeisance and, worried that he hadn't prepared comfortable enough accommodations, spoke thus:

Your image came to me at midnight.
I offered my soul but I was ashamed
A poor man is embarrassed when a guest arrives unexpectedly.

Calming his fears, Jahangir responded: "What value have the goods of this world in our eyes? We purchase the gem of loyalty at high price."[15] And the arrangements were fine; there were enough tents, warm blankets, cooking utensils—everything the royals required. Nur, Jahangir, and their companions spent a comfortable night in Mu'tamad's quarters. The next morning Mu'tamad received the honor of the gift of the emperor's own cloak, and a rise in numerical ranking.

After traversing passes for four days, the royal retinue came to broad roads leading to the meadows of the Kashmir valley, exuberant with blossoms—roses, sandalwood flowers, violets, hollyhock, narcissus, and unusual flowers like the *bulanik*, which had green leaves growing in the middle of its blooms. Jahangir was ecstatic: "The flowers of Kashmir are beyond counting and calculation. Which shall I write of? And how many can I describe? I have only mentioned the most remarkable."[16]

Once they reached Baramula, a major port on the river Bahat, they were only fifty-six kilometers away from Srinagar, the chief town of Kashmir. It is said that Nur Jahan bathed here before moving on, in a waterfall that Jahangir named Noor-e Chamb—Nur's Waterfall, in the local dialect.[17]

Soon they approached Srinagar, perfumed with the refreshing scent of clover. Peach, almond, pear, and apple trees were beginning to blossom; gateways, walls, courtyards and houses blazed with tulips and jasmine. The trip from Agra had taken 168 days.

Jahangir's father had built a sturdy stone palace-fort in Srinagar on a hill called the Hari Parbat, overlooking the lovely Dal Lake, approximately four miles long and three miles wide, fed by a channel that brought water from the mountains. In the spring of 1620, the royal party settled into the Hari Parbat palace.

Kashmiris traditionally planted tulip bulbs on the roofs of buildings, including garden pavilions. The palace garden was dilapidated, "out of order and ruinous," but tulips flowered luxuriantly on the roofs of its buildings. Mu'tamad immediately began repairs. In a short while, a new charm engulfed Hari Parbat. A lofty three-level platform in the middle of the garden was redecorated. Mughal master painters adorned the buildings with works that "would make the painters of China jealous."[18] Jahangir announced that the restored grounds would be called the *Nurafza bagh*, the Light-Enhancing Garden.

To Jahangir, light was more than a metaphor. The loftiest ambition of a Mughal king was to be seen as the ruler of two worlds: the imperial and the sacred, the visible and the spiritual. Order and harmony, a reflection of divinity—a force of light—resided in the king. When Jahangir gave himself the imperial name Nur ad-Din, the Light of Faith, and when he renamed his new wife, Mihr un-Nisa, the Light of the Palace, then Light of the World, he was participating in this tradition.

The Mughals had long associated themselves with the "great light" of the sun. Jahangir was also drawn to the famous Verse of Light in the Quran cited by many Sufis and Neo-Platonist philosophers, declaring that "God has seven and seventy veils of light. Were these to be stripped from His face, the majesty of His countenance would consume all that He beheld."[19] Even the chosen ones, including sovereigns, were only intermediaries—receiving a touch of the grace of light.

Nur and Jahangir entered into this open philosophical ground, creating a realm of light, even in the names they gave to the gold, silver, and copper coins of various sizes that they struck: Light of Sovereignty, Light of Kingship, Light of the Court, Light of the Sun, Light of the World.[20] The Light-Enhancing Garden of Srinagar became another emblem of the emperor's connection to Nur, a way for Jahangir to honor their common name and joint rule. And the trend would

continue. Already Nur was contemplating the design of another garden in Agra, which she would name the Light-Scattering Garden.

A visit from someone connected to Nur's past continued this link
with light. Twenty-four years earlier, Haidar Malik had served Nur
Jahan in the immediate aftermath of her first husband's murder: She
had spent the forty obligatory days of mourning in his house before
proceeding to Agra. Now living in Kashmir, Malik came to renew his
loyalty to the emperor and empress. The trio went partridge hunting
among the flowing streams and lofty trees near the village of Chahardara, Malik's home, ten miles south of Srinagar. The imperial couple was very pleased with the place. Seized by their delight, or simply
to honor the felicitous moment of their visit to his home, Malik asked
that the name of Chahardara be changed. Jahangir renamed it Nur-
pur, City of Light.

Jahangir wrote with great enthusiasm about the trip to Kashmir with his beloved Nur: where they stopped, the distances they
traveled, the flora and fauna, who came to pay obeisance, the
offerings, his excursions with her, their gardens, the ease of the
times. He mentions honoring Talib Amuli, a Persian poet who
had been a regular presence at gatherings in Ghiyas's home since
Nur's childhood, now one hundred years old and living in Kashmir. Jahangir named him Malik us-Shu'ara, the King of Poets,
and bestowed on him a royal robe. This was a real pleasure trip
after the years the couple had spent in western India, almost like
a much-delayed honeymoon. Present-day tour guides in Kashmir
note that the waters of Dal Lake repeatedly reflected the fantastic
fireworks arranged in Nur and Jahangir's honor, and they recount
the (debunked) legend that Jahangir brought Kashmir's massive,
maple-like Chinar trees from Iran and planted them in Kashmir
to please Nur Jahan.[21]

In September, Jahangir and Nur visited the Vernag springs at the
foot of the mountains southeast of Srinagar, the source of the Bahat

River, which would later play a role in determining the royal couple's fate. Pine trees, Chinars, and aromatic greenery abounded, reflected in the deep green Vernag waters. On visits to Vernag when he was a young prince, Jahangir had ordered the construction of arched walkways around the springs and a pavilion, in front of which a large garden was now nearing completion.

As soon as they arrived, Jahangir instructed that servers fill the wine cups of his attendants. The party drank wine and ate Kabul peaches; later, the men returned drunk to their tents.[22] In these sensuous surroundings Nur may have first read to Jahangir a flirtatious poem attributed to her:

> There is a ruby button on your silken robe
> You have been afflicted by a drop of my blood![23]

Francois Bernier, a French physician and natural philosopher was the first European to visit Kashmir, in 1665. In his *Travels in the Mughal Empire*, he added a legend to Nur and Jahangir's earlier visit. In Vernag, Bernier was especially charmed by one of its ponds, which contained "fish so tame that they approach upon being called, or when pieces of bread are thrown into the water. The largest have gold rings, with inscriptions, through the gills, placed there, it is said, by the celebrated *Nour-Mehalle*, the wife of *Jehan-Guyre* . . ."[24] Perhaps Bernier saw fish with gold rings, or perhaps he intended the tame fish as a metaphor for a compliant emperor.

Little Prince Shuja, the fourth son of Shah Jahan and Arjumand, was a darling of the emperor. One day the boy was playing in a room of the Srinagar palace that had a low door, screened but not shut, facing Dal Lake. When Shuja ran toward the door to look out, he hurtled through it and fell fifteen feet. Luckily, he landed partly on a rug heaped below, and partly on the shoulders of the servant bent to spread it. Shuja's head fell on the carpet and his feet on the shoulders of the man. "God, the Great and Glorious, came to his aid," Jahangir wrote, "and the carpet and the *farrash* [carpet-spreader] became the means of saving his life." When the *farrash* raced inside carrying the little prince, who was weak and not speaking, "my senses forsook me, and for a long time holding him in my affectionate embrace I was distracted with this favor from Allah."[25] Shuja recovered, but a dire prediction by Jotik Rai, the court astrologer, came true. A few months earlier, he'd announced "that one of the chief sitters in the harem of chastity would hasten to the hidden abode of non-existence."[26] Saliha Banu, one of Jahangir's senior wives, passed away. The emperor didn't say in his journal whether she was part of the royal group in Kashmir or back in Agra, but he noted that "the grief for this heart-rending event laid a heavy load on my mind"—more emotion than he recorded at the death of Jagat Gosain. The emperor expressed his sorrow sincerely but briefly. His polygamous household was by this time a somewhat distanced, symbolic presence. Nur was his daily companion.

However pleasing Nur may have found the sojourn in Kashmir, she had a serious matter to deal with, the question that had long weighed on her mind: Which of the Mughal princes should marry her daughter, Ladli Begum? Shah Jahan, Jahangir's favorite and the presumed successor to the Mughal throne, was politically perceptive, accomplished, and fiercely ambitious. Of the four princes, he was most likely to succeed his father. But he was already married to Nur's niece Arjumand and two other women. Nur would certainly have noticed that since his marriage with Arjumand, Shah Jahan had fathered all but one of his children with her; she was his favorite. Ladli would become a subordinate wife.

Furthermore, it had become increasingly clear to Nur that if he were to become emperor, the ambitious Shah Jahan, already looking forward impatiently to claiming his patrimony, might not welcome Nur as any sort of counterpower. With him on the throne, she might have no imperial future at all. Nur's musing on that strong possibility may have accounted for the cooling of her formerly cordial relationship with Shah Jahan. She eventually reached the conclusion, says one modern Mughal scholar, that Shah Jahan "would undermine her power in a post-Jahangir dispensation."[27] She needed to think carefully about choosing a royal husband for Ladli who might become the next emperor instead of Shah Jahan, someone who would preserve something of his mother-in-law's power.

In early October 1620, the imperial banners turned toward Lahore, where the party would stop on the way back to Agra. The return march began from outside the Kashmiri city of Pampur, where as far as the eye could see, there stretched a natural carpet of saffron. Along the way to Lahore, the cavalcade stopped at some of the same spots where they had paused on the journey to Kashmir. As before, the core camp halted at passes that were exceptionally difficult and rough to cross. Jahangir had difficulty breathing.

In early November, the royal party reached Lahore, where they got some good news. Shah Jahan had taken a break from the Deccan campaign to head north and score a victory at Kangra, in the Himalayan foothills; he and his men had taken the fort, subdued a raja fighting Mughal rule, and returned to the Deccan.

In early December, messengers brought news far less cheering. In the Deccan, enemy assailants were destroying fields and pasturelands. Mughal forces had fought a heroic battle, but exhausted and short of resources, they retreated. In early December, Shah Jahan traveled from the Deccan to Lahore for a brief visit, probably a strategy session, with Jahangir, Nur, and their inner circle.

Jahangir's shortness of breath continued to worsen, making the question of Mughal succession seem increasingly urgent. No documentary evidence suggests that Nur ever broached the subject of

Ladli's marriage with either Shah Jahan or Parvez, the alcoholic son on the margins of Mughal political life. Khusraw, the partially blinded prince, wasn't a good prospect either, although the Italian traveler Della Valle, who visited India three years before Jahangir's death, but never met him or Nur, assumed that Khusraw would succeed his father to the throne. In order to "establish herself well," Della Valle wrote in his book *The Travels of Pietro Della Valle in India*, Nur Jahan "frequently offer'd her Daughter [to Khusraw] . . . but he, either for that he had another Wife he lov'd sufficiently and would not wrong her, or because he scorn'd *Nurmahal's* Daughter, would never consent . . ." The fact that Khusraw was in the Deccan during this period suggests that Della Valle was writing from hearsay. Thomas Roe, the British ambassador, speculated similarly about a supposed proposal of Ladli's marriage to Khusraw.[28]

Ultimately, Nur chose Jahangir's youngest son, Shahryar, as her daughter's husband and the potential preserver of her power. He was a long shot to succeed—Jahangir seemed set on Shah Jahan as his heir—but a possibility. Shahryar was known for his good looks, patience, and restraint—and for being easily manipulated.

Mughal princes could be groomed as successors. If the right steps were taken and a prince had enough support, if he skillfully accomplished military and political assignments well, he could become a contender for the throne. Nur decided she would take a chance and campaign for Shahryar as successor to Jahangir, knowing full well that it would be hard to keep Shah Jahan from the throne.

Just before the royal party started the journey from Lahore to Agra, the emperor formally approached Ghiyas. "I asked for the hand of I'timaduddawla's grand-daughter in marriage to my son Shahryar," Jahangir wrote, "and a lac of rupees in cash and goods was sent as a sachiq [a gift sent from the prospective bridegroom's house to the bride's]. Most of the great amirs and important courtiers accompanied the sachiq to I'timaduddawla's quarters, where a large celebration of utmost elaborateness was held. It is hoped the marriage will be blessed."[29] Also attending the celebration at Ghiyas's impressive Lahore residence of the diwan of Punjab—one of Ghiyas's many titles—were Nur, a coterie of royal women, and the newly engaged pair themselves, Ladli and Shahryar.

Once Ladli was engaged to Shahryar, the rift between Nur and Shah Jahan deepened.[30] Shah Jahan knew what Ladli's marriage could mean. He was leaving for the Deccan, the emperor was weakening rapidly—and Empress Nur was at the center of the imperium, now closely tied to another prince who could easily become a contender for the throne. Before Shah Jahan's first expedition to the Deccan, his father, Nur, and others had assured him that his interests could be protected during his absence. As the prince prepared to depart once again for the Deccan this time, his youngest half-brother Shahryar, Nur's new protégé, occupied his mind. On December 16, 1620, Shah Jahan left again for the war in the south, adorned with a robe of honor, a jeweled sword on his waist, mounted on an elephant that Nur had given him—a public acknowledgment, however reluctant, of her power. The royal retinue headed for Agra that same day.

TWELVE

The Light-Scattering Garden

T he empress began overseeing the creation of her Light-Scattering Garden, the Bagh-i Nur Afshan, when she and Jahangir returned to the capital from Kashmir in February 1621. From its ramparts overlooking the Yamuna River, one could see the enormous Agra fort and the spot where the Taj Mahal would one day stand, Shah Jahan's tribute to Arjumand, better known to the world by her imperial name, Mumtaz Mahal. From winter into late spring, the royal family and their court gathered in the Light-Scattering Garden several times for celebrations hosted by Nur in anticipation of the April wedding of Ladli and Shahryar.

During the reign of Jahangir and Nur, and under their direction, palace gardens flowered as a mode of aesthetic and imperial expression. In the Light-Scattering Garden, Nur further advanced the idea of architecture as statecraft, seen in the Nur Mahal Serai on the Grand Trunk Road, and the bold engraving of her name on that large traveler's inn.

A short boat ride from the Agra fort, Nur's garden was built on the site of a much older one established by the first Mughal. Babur, unhappy about the lack of springs and streams in Indian cities, designed a spot that re-created the canals, waterfalls, and pathways found in Persian gardens, which were squares divided into quarters by walkways and waterways to represent the Islamic idea of the shape of Paradise. Babur was temporarily buried here, in the very center, before being entombed in Kabul. In reusing the first Mughal's garden for her own, Nur made an aesthetic link with Jahangir's great-grandfather—a connection between herself and other male emperors.

Nur's plan for the Light-Scattering Garden, today called the Ram Bagh, was less formal and more innovative than a traditional Persian arrangement.[1] She added three descending terraces and walkways along the river, with pavilions, arcades, and walled rooms for shelter and shade—a rhythm of open and closed design that echoed the harem quarters. Beneath the main pavilion were underground rooms, including a *hammam* or bath with a disrobing room, a hot room, and a cool room; and a large hall with pools and waterfalls.[2]

The vaulted ceilings of the pavilions remain impressive, shaped like stars circumscribed by concentric circles and densely painted with winged beings, some carrying parasols; peacocks, birds of prey, ducks, herons, kingfishers, and mythic birds like the simurgh, the representation of the divine in the work of the Persian Sufi poet Attar; and vines and flowering trees, in peacock blue, ochre yellow, wine red. The paint on the ceiling, where still visible, looks newly laid. Fresh air floats in through circular windows shaded by louvered wooden slats.

The gardens lie below riverside walkways. Today, the gardeners of Ram Bagh tend the same varieties of plants that adorned the premises in Nur's time—flowers like jasmine; *raat ki raani*, or queen of the night; and an Agra local, *morpankhi*, peacock flower. Trees, too: lemon, *ashok*, tamarind, guava, orange, almond, pomegranate, and date palm.[3]

In her choice of motifs for her garden too, Nur asserted her co-sovereignty. Large-winged birds had long been part of the decorative repertoire of Islamic rulers; birds and angels also referred to King Solomon, as he appears in the Quran.[4] Contemporary writers often referred to Nur as the Sheba of her age: Bilqis-uz-Zaman, the Powerful Sheba! And as with all the gardens planned and cherished by Nur and Jahangir, she was building a bridge between the whole Mughal past and the dynasty's future.

At the end of March 1621, Nur's brother Asaf invited the young couple, Jahangir, Nur, and other members of the imperial family to a grand entertainment. To mark his niece's wedding, he presented "delicate gems and wonders in cloth, and rare gifts." Jahangir accepted offerings worth 130,000 rupees, but returned the rest as a sign of moderation.[5] Yet again, gifts spoke to the force of the political-personal relationships uniting and binding the Mughals and the clan of Ghiyas Beg. Ladli was the third woman from Ghiyas's family to marry a Mughal prince.[6] Cross-cousin and first-cousin marriages were a norm in elite households, but this was still a somewhat unusual situation. The emperor and empress were giving each other their son and daughter from other relationships to forge a new marital bond.

The wedding took place on April 13, 1621. Jahangir records that his mother, Harkha, Shahryar's grandmother, hosted the henna party before the wedding. Female and male companions led Ladli and Shahryar to separate baths. Then the rituals of decoration with henna began in the men's and women's quarters. Ladli's companions would have drawn delicate henna designs on Ladli's hands and feet; her eyebrows and eyes were painted with kohl. The men were decorated too, but the party in the women's quarters was a more extended and elaborate affair, with music and dancing. Typically, the mother of a Mughal groom readied gems, jewels, gold and silver utensils, brocades, carpets, rugs, canopies, elephants, horses, cash, and more, to give to court servants, princes, harem women, honorable nobles, and relatives. If she was there, Shahryar's unnamed mother no doubt followed protocol. Grandmother Harkha may have joined her in laying out gifts. Shahryar stayed in his quarters, where he had a feast.[7]

The wedding ceremony itself took place in Ghiyas and Asmat's mansion. Mughal princes and senior nobles would have escorted Shahryar from his residence to the palace, where he kissed the ground before his father the emperor, performing *kornish*. Jahangir blessed him and presented him with a robe of honor, a jeweled dagger, sword and strap, a rosary of pearls, horses from the royal stable, and elephants with silver trappings. He then fastened a *sehra* or veil around the prince's head, from which dangled strands of lustrous pearls, rubies, and emeralds.[8] Dignitaries presented gifts to the prince, then helped him mount a horse with a gem-studded saddle and bridle. With some of the men on horseback and others on foot, the entourage set out for Ghiyas's *haveli*, where Ladli waited.[9] At night, the servants lit lamps in the garden below the private hall of the palace. Boats adorned with candles, torches, and lamps lined the river, and fireworks sparked the sky.

No portraits of Ladli survive. I like to envision her as a young version of her parents, with something of the strong will of Nur, and perhaps the courage of her father, Quli, as well as the gentleness and grace of her grandparents. As for Shahryar, a sketch made in preparation for a painting shows the prince on the imperial balcony, his arm leaning on the windowsill. His longish face is delicate, his eyes small, and his gaze tender.[10]

Under ordinary circumstances, as the bride's mother, Nur would have been by Ladli's side during the wedding ceremony. But she was also the Mughal empress. The emperor and the empress likely sat together on a gold-embroidered divan, with Nur on the right, at the helm of the gathering. Hangings embroidered with silken gold threads and strings of pearls surrounded the divan, and Persian carpets cov-

ered the floors. The older women like Harkha and Asmat would have
sat beside Nur. Slightly behind them, on cushioned divans, would
sit Nur's sisters, Khadija and Manija; the wives of her brothers; her
niece Arjumand; and other women of Ghiyas's extended family. And
perhaps in a smaller section, Ladli would be surrounded by women
friends and relatives and Dai Dilaram, tucked away from the public
eye. On Jahangir's side, Shahryar, the princes, Ghiyas, Asaf, foster
brothers, distinguished nobles, and officers would all be positioned
according to rank. Musicians and sweet-voiced reciters performed
wedding poems and songs.[11] The *qazi*, the officiating cleric, finally
pronounced the words of marriage.

A great feast followed the ceremony. Ghiyas Beg bestowed numerous gifts on the wedding party, "rare and choice things from all
countries." A few days after the wedding ceremony, Nur celebrated
the union again, in the Light-Scattering Garden, where she "held
the royal entertainment and presented great offerings" to Shahryar,
showering him with jewels and other precious goods, a worthy ges-
ture for a prince rising in favor.[12]

With two formal rites, a Mughal prince moved to adulthood. The first
was when the emperor gave him an appropriate rank, with or without
a significant administrative-military assignment. The second was the
prince's marriage. But these vital signs of a princely adulthood did
not make him fully independent. He had to work in various offices in
order to establish himself as a holder of power and possible contender
for the throne. So Nur set to work bolstering her new son-in-law's
prospects. She proceeded strategically, building his household and
raising his political profile. Soon after the wedding, Shahryar asked
Nur to appoint a noted loyalist of hers, Sharif ul-Mulk, as a manager
of his household. Sharif continued in this capacity for nearly six years,
a very long stint for someone who was also an imperial officer.[13] The

emperor appointed well-regarded men as paymaster and finance officer to Shahryar's staff.[14] Having key figures working with him would
allow Shahryar to build his resources, and his reputation. Eventually,
Nur hoped, she would maneuver to have him head an important military campaign.

Through messengers and news from his father-in-law Asaf, Shah
Jahan kept abreast of the moves that the empress made in favor
of her young son-in-law, carefully assessing the possibility that his
younger brother could emerge as a major threat to his ambitions.
Among other contemporary courtiers, Bhakkari noted bluntly that a
rift between Nur and Shah Jahan formed not long after Ladli's marriage. Nur Jahan had always, Bhakkari wrote, been in favor of "that
inheritor of the kingdom [Shah Jahan]," but she "gave up (this feeling
of) affection," and began promoting the cause of Shahryar.[15]

While Nur was caught up in building up Shahryar and Jahangir's
health steadily weakened, a letter arrived from the mother of the
Uzbek ruler Imam Quli, the king of Turan, or Transoxiana, the land
beyond the river Oxus. The Turanian king had at some point broken off relations with the Mughals because Jahangir had made jokes
about his inclination to pederasty. This letter of goodwill, accompanied by what Jahangir noted as rarities of Central Asia (most likely
jade, horses, and fruit) was filled with expressions of loyalty and
friendship. Nur Jahan decided to respond immediately in an attempt
to mend relations. The Turanian matriarch extended a hand of peace
and Nur Jahan actively promoted reconciliation.

The friendship proffered by Imam Quli's mother would have been
a relief to Nur. The Safavids of Iran had just begun to mobilize near
Kandahar, and Mughal response was urgently needed.[16] A military
clash was likely, so gaining allies in neighboring kingdoms was critical.
Nur immediately ordered an ambassador sent to Turan, a seasoned
courtier who had served Jahangir since he was a prince, bearing a letter of goodwill from the empress and "choice gifts."[17]

The situation in the Deccan, however, remained uncertain; there was no news of a decisive victory. Jahangir was increasingly agitated by Ambar. The emperor's health deteriorated further. The shortness of breath he'd experienced in Kashmir returned. Hakim Ruhullah applied warm and gentle remedies, but to no avail. Another doctor, Hakim Rukna, was called in. His treatment was more aggressive, including powerful medications blended according to the theories of the second-century Greek physician Claudius Galen, who taught that cures should balance the four natures of the body, warm, dry, cold, and wet. Rukna also tried dosing Jahangir with goat and camel milk, but neither offered relief. He complained that the medications affected his temperament and made his back weak.

The emperor called in a third doctor. Hakim Sadra was formerly the chief physician in Safavid Persia, and had migrated to India in the reign of Jahangir's father, who honored him as "the Messiah of the Age," the *masih uz-zaman*. His treatment failed too. The emperor's deterioration was visible. With no relief in sight, he became malicious: "That ungrateful man [Sadra], in spite of the claims which I had on him, though he saw me in such a state, did not give me medicines or treat me." Everyone, including the emperor himself, knew that the problem was compounded by Jahangir's drinking.

Finally Nur Jahan took over. Once again she reduced Jahangir's intake of wine by degrees and kept him away from unsuitable foods. Jahangir recovered. Nur's "skills and experience," her husband wrote, were "greater than those of the physicians, especially as they are brought to bear through affection and sympathy, [she] endeavored to diminish the number of my cups, and to carry out the remedies that appeared appropriate to the time, and soothing to the condition."[18]

Nur decided to mark his recovery with merriment, even though the improvement was clearly temporary; it was becoming evident that Jahangir's health was beyond repair. At the next solar weighing ceremony in September 1621, she arranged an entertainment that was grander than usual. On that occasion, she paid greater attention than ever to arranging the feast. The servants hovered like moths around the emperor; she honored the attendees with dresses, sword-belts, daggers, horses, elephants, trays full of money. The aging astrologer Jotik Rai had earlier predicted that the emperor would certainly recover. During the weighing ceremony, as usual, Nur Jahan displayed her special offerings for Jahangir, and at the end, astrologer Rai was honored for his optimistic vision. Jahangir was weighed against coins, some of which were distributed to the needy.[19]

Two weeks later, Nur's mother, Asmat Begum, died. The cause of her death is not recorded, but her passing was devastating to all. "What can one write?" mused Jahangir. "Without exaggeration, in purity of disposition and in wisdom and the excellencies that are the ornament of women . . . No Mother of the Age was ever born equal to her . . . I did not value her less than my own mother." No husband, he went on, was equal to Ghiyas in his attachment to his wife. Jahangir went to pay his respects to his grief-stricken wazir and father-in-law. With affection and kindness, he spoke a few words to the old man. It was several days before Ghiyas returned to public gatherings. Outwardly, he was poised and controlled, "yet with regard to his affection for [Asmat]," wrote Jahangir, "what resignation could there be? Ghiyas no longer cared for himself. Although he looked after the affairs of the empire and civil matters, yet in his heart he grieved."[20]

At the end of October, Agra was unseasonably hot. Jahangir was keen to move to more temperate regions, so the imperial camp headed north toward Hardwar, a city revered by Hindus, on the banks of the Ganga River in the Himalayan foothills. If Hardwar wasn't to his liking, he said, the camp would head again toward Kashmir.

With stopovers for hunting and visits to several other places along the way, it was mid-December by the time the royal caravan reached Hardwar, nearly 250 miles from Agra. Here hermits and Brahmins, the declared pundits of Hinduism, thronged to receive alms in silver and gold coins. No suitable place could be found for the imperial tent camp, so the Mughals headed farther north toward Kangra, where Jahangir would celebrate Shah Jahan's recent capture of the region's massive fort from the raja of Kangra. Jahangir's troops had made a previously unsuccessful attempt to take the fort, soon after he ascended to the throne, so this victory was especially satisfying to him.

The core camp was made up of Jahangir, Nur, and Ghiyas, physically weak and in mourning, along with attendants and carriers of goods. As usual, the party on the march hunted, received officers, and granted awards. In the village of Bahlon, Nur Jahan gave robes of honor to "forty-five great amirs and intimate servants." Reports from the Deccan trickled in, including reports that Khusraw was ill. Yearning to tour the fort and hill country of Kangra, Jahangir set off with Nur and a group of chosen courtiers and servants. Ghiyas Beg stayed back in the care of a top officer. They hadn't yet reached Kangra the next day when news arrived that Ghiyas's condition had deteriorated; there was little hope of his survival. Nur was distraught. "I could not bear the agitation of Nur Jahan Begam, and considering the affection I bore towards him [Ghiyas], I returned to the camp," wrote Jahangir.

The dying Ghiyas went in and out of consciousness and lucidity. Once, pointing at Jahangir, Nur Jahan asked her father, "Do you recognize him?"[21] This is the one sentence of Nur Jahan's quoted directly by Jahangir. Ghiyas, it is said, eventually answered his distraught daughter by reciting a verse in praise of the emperor:

> He is (such a) one that even if a person born blind before him
> He would see majesty in his world-adorning forehead.[22]

As the sun set on January 27, 1622, three months and twenty days after his wife's death, one of the most prodigious nobles of the Mughal Empire, on whose shoulders lay, as Jahangir put it, the weight of a great kingdom, passed away. Jahangir offered condolences to Ghiyas's sons and sons-in-law, and presented forty-one of his children, grandchildren, clansmen, and servants with dresses of honor and garments of mourning.[23]

Two weeks later, the emperor declared that everything belonging to Ghiyas Beg's establishment, including all the paraphernalia attached to his government office and household, was to be granted to Nur Jahan Begum—even though Ghiyas's eldest son, Asaf, was alive. The governmental inheritance was the most significant: Jahangir had declared that Nur was, in effect, the oldest son and successor of the Great Wazir—prime minister as well as empress. Jahangir also ordered that drums were to be sounded at Nur's arrival at court, right after the drums of the emperor, exactly the way her father had been announced.

In 1622, Nur ordered the construction of a spectacular garden tomb in honor of Ghiyas and Asmat. It would take nearly six years to complete. Although remembered as I'timad ud-Daula's Tomb, after Ghiyas's title, it houses both his and Asmat's sepulchers. The Jewel Box, as the tour guides of Agra call it today—an exquisite rectangular building made entirely of white marble inlaid with semiprecious stones, colored mosaic tiles, and latticework called *pietra dura*—sits on the banks of the Jamuna, on the other side of the river from the structure that would later echo its architectural form, the Taj Mahal.

Nur built a walled garden, divided into several sections, for her parents' mausoleum. The crypts rest in the center where the pathways cross. In a singular touch, the empress added a pavilion that served as a gate, facing the river. Under an ornamental vault in the central chambers, the grand wazir and his noble wife lie in ochre-colored cenotaphs under a vault richly painted with Persian motifs, such as rose-water vases, wine cups, lilies, and red poppies—a lot of red, red flowers signifying suffering and death, a motif that would appear later in the Taj, built little more than a decade after Ghiyas and Asmat's tomb was completed. Quranic inscriptions decorate the outside walls of the mausoleum.[24]

Nur Jahan built this memorial garden along the classic pattern that Babur had begun: the tomb at the center of the various intersecting paths. But she added her own flourishes—terraces and platforms. The latticed garden plan, says a Mughal garden architecture scholar, with an emphasis on the axis in the center was "a device that would be realized on a grand scale in the Taj Mahal garden," while the marble inlay with multicolored stones on the exterior of this building "anticipates the even more refined inlay of the Taj Mahal."[25]

Josef Tieffenthaler, a multilingual Jesuit missionary and a geographer, who was in Agra in the 1740s, found the tomb of Ghiyas and Asmat more fascinating than the Taj. It surpassed all Agra monuments, he wrote, "if not in size, in art and ornamentation."[26] Though rickshaw pullers and tour guides in Agra today call the tomb the Baby Taj, in truth, the Taj Mahal is the baby of the memorial that Nur Jahan built for her parents.

THIRTEEN

Fitna

The year 1622 started badly and got worse, bringing one disastrous event after another. In January, with the pain of Ghiyas's death still fresh, news came of Prince Khusraw's death in the Deccan. Jahangir's eldest son—once a favorite and an aspirant to the throne but ultimately brokenhearted, half-blind, and fifteen years a prisoner—was thirty-four years old. Shah Jahan had insisted on taking his older brother south with him because he was suspicious of Khusraw's kingly ambitions and persistent appeal among some members of the Mughal family, especially elder royal women. Many in the court's inner circle were certain that Shah Jahan had ordered Khusraw's murder. In his official report, Shah Jahan gave the cause of death as colic—that is, intestinal blockage. Other documents draped Khusraw's death in euphemisms, referring to it as a painful accident.[1] When Khusraw's body was brought back to Agra, crowds flocked to view it, and when it was exhumed and moved to Allahabad in eastern India for final burial, people

lined the streets to pay their respects and installed shrines along
the way.

Nur was caught up in other unfolding troubles. By midwinter, as
Shah Abbas amassed Safavid troops near the Kandahar border, aiming to seize the fort there, the royal couple had to choose a commander
for the imperial forces who could counter this threat; no simple decision. Meanwhile, Nur and the ailing Jahangir were increasingly troubled by Shah Jahan's belligerent behavior toward the empress.

Since Shahryar's marriage to Ladli, Shah Jahan had known that his
powerful stepmother would not back his imperial ambitions. Clearly
her new son-in-law was now the center of her hopes for maintaining
some sovereign power after Jahangir's death. "The elevation of his
younger brother became a source of anxiety and disturbance to [Shah
Jahan]," the emperor wrote in his journal. "Helplessly he sought for
patronage and begged the protection of Nur Jahan Begam, expressing shame and contrition and sought a refuge in her mediation."[2]

Shah Jahan didn't consider his older half-brother Parvez to be a
threat, even though at Nur's urging, Jahangir was considering reconciliation with his least successful son.[3] Nur and Shahryar were the
ones standing in the way of Shah Jahan's succession plans, and he
set about plotting their downfall. From his base in the Deccan, he
ordered a group of his soldiers north to seize properties belonging
to Nur and Shahryar, including the lands and troops of Dholpur,
which had once been owned by Shah Jahan but had been reassigned
by the emperor to Shahryar. The man in command of the Dholpur
garrison fought a brave battle before he was overpowered by Shah
Jahan's army; men died on both sides as the senior prince reclaimed
his lands and soldiers.

Nur was furious; the rift between her and Shah Jahan was now in
the open. Jahangir, heartsore, recognized Shah Jahan's attack as the
first sign of revolt. He knew the omens all too well; he had launched

a similar rebellion against his own father, and Khusraw had launched one against him. He ordered Shah Jahan, still fighting in the Deccan, to restrict himself to the lands he'd been assigned, and to send troops for the looming Kandahar campaign. The prince refused. Jahangir had planned to have Shah Jahan command the Mughal forces against the Safavids in Kandahar, but now that was impossible. Once again seized by debilitating shortness of breath, the emperor was distraught: "Of which of my pains should I write?" Was it really necessary for him to mount a horse and in hot weather gallop "off after such an undutiful son?"[4] He declared that Shah Jahan should be called *bidawlat*, "disgraceful" or "luckless," the opposite of the address he typically expected for the princes: *iqbalmand*, or "favored by fortune."

With Shah Jahan out of favor with the emperor, Nur moved to advance Shahryar's fortunes, proposing him as the commander of Mughal forces in Kandahar. Jahangir agreed, and now it was Shahryar whom he called the fortunate son. Experienced nobles and commanders joined Shahryar's troops. The emperor upped Shahryar's rank and gave more of Shah Jahan's lands to the new favorite. There was more good news: Ladli was pregnant. A potential heir might strengthen Shahryar's claim to the throne. To celebrate the rise of Shahryar, Nur gave the emperor two large Anatolian pearls, subtly underscoring what she knew well—that any future power wielded by the prince would derive from his being the emperor's son, and not from being her son-in-law.[5]

Some members of the court felt that the imminent battle over Kandahar, the insurrection of Shah Jahan, and the subsequent rearrangement of alliances were all Nur's fault—and that she was regularly overriding the emperor's orders. "Not at all under the power and will of his Majesty; everything was contrived and accomplished by the Begam . . . [she] changed everything," wrote Bhakkari. The current conflicts, he declared, were due to the "mischief-making of

Nur Jahan."[6] Bhakkari might praise Nur for her political skills, her artistry, and her generosity—but he still believed a woman should rise only so far.

Nur knew that court alliances and factions could twist, snap, and reconnect in unexpected ways. Without her closest supporters and advisers, Asmat and Ghiyas, by her side, and her brother Asaf's leanings uncertain, the political order Nur had consolidated over the last decade was at risk of fragmenting.

Kandahar, Nur's birthplace, a rich commercial center at the border between Hindustan and Iran, had magnetic appeal for the Mughal emperors. Each in turn had fought for the hereditary kingdom of his ancestors, a major link on the trading routes traveled by merchants, mystics, and those seeking haven in India. The vast northwest territory of Central Asia beyond Kandahar held great dangers. Raiders and conquerors, including his Mughal forefathers, had invaded India from the northwest. Since the 1600s, the Mughals and the Safavids had clashed repeatedly over Kandahar, currently in Mughal hands. Surrounded by Sunni monarchies across Central Asia, the Shi'a Safavids felt vulnerable; the Mughals were unsure of the leanings of the Shi'a rulers in southern India. These skirmishes had so far not flared into outright war, but now the situation was urgent; the troops of the Safavid emperor Shah Abbas seemed poised to attack Kandahar.

Getting the Mughal Army to Kandahar wasn't easy. In winter, snow blocked the southern passes through the Sulaiman Mountains and in summer, sweltering heat and scarce water threatened travelers. Spring was hardly better; torrents often caused mudslides that blocked the narrow passes. Autumn, too, posed logistical problems, since most camel herders headed eastward then, making it hard to hire camels to go westward.

Despite Shah Jahan's rebellion in the south and Shah Abbas's ambitions in the northwest, ceremonial court activities continued, and the emperor and empress went about their engagements. Jahangir appointed men to various postings and promoted favored nobles, including the late Khusraw's son, Dawar Bakhsh, who began to appear frequently in the pages of the emperor's memoir. Within a year, Jahangir would appoint him governor of Gujarat.

Though Nur and Jahangir were much distressed by Shah Jahan's open hostility, Asaf Khan stayed silent. Alarmed by her brother's apparent swing toward favoring the rebellious prince, Nur summoned the noble Mahabat to the capital from Kabul, where he was governor. Though he'd been hostile to Nur's family, the "nucleus of Iranian nobility" at the Mughal court, and he'd spoken out against Nur to Jahangir on the way to Kashmir, Mahabat was also Jahangir's longtime, much-tested supporter.[7] He had begun to turn against Shah Jahan, perhaps over the death of Khusraw, and Nur believed that Mahabat could be convinced to transfer his support to Shahryar. Mahabat wrote back to Nur Jahan that he wouldn't come to Agra if Asaf were there. Mahabat had already suspected Asaf of secretly supporting Shah Jahan. But more than this, he feared that because of his outspoken opposition to the power held by members of Nur's family and other Persians, Asaf had marked him for death.

Mahabat's relations with Jahangir were cordial at this point. He wrote to Nur that he would come to court only if she dispatched her brother to the province of Bengal and punished the paymaster Mu'tamad Khan, who, Mahabat said, was one of a party of nobles conspiring with the rebel prince. Rather then sending Asaf to Bengal, however, Nur ordered him to transport some of the gold and precious jewels in the royal treasury from Agra to Lahore, hoping that his departure would look like fulfillment of Mahabat's request.

Mu'tamad escaped punishment; in fact, the emperor gave his paymaster the esteemed task of continuing to record imperial events in the *Jahangirnama*. Mu'tamad would submit notes for the emperor's

verification and then add the entries to the emperor's memoir. Mahabat, however, came to the court anyway. Perhaps he was satisfied that
Mu'tamad's new job moved him safely away from the center of political machinations. And perhaps the still-close relationship between
the royal couple and Asaf, warm enough that Jahangir conferred on
him a new honorific, Prop of the Sultanate, reassured him. Mahabat may have been convinced that Asaf would do as the emperor
required, and the emperor required that Asaf not harm Mahabat.

Princely rebellions were usually supported by disaffected nobles,
and it wasn't always possible to predict who might be nursing a griev-
ance or how these men of different backgrounds and interests would
affiliate in times of upheaval. Nobles whom Shah Jahan wooed to his
side included Abdur-Rahim, the famed general and mentor of Nur's
first husband, by then seventy years old. Some who had joined Shah
Jahan were already returning to the imperial court after a brief flirta-
tion with insurrection, among them the eunuch Fidai Khan, master
of ceremonies—the courtier in charge of etiquette. Jahangir accepted
Fidai's renewed loyalty.[8]

For over a year, between late 1622 and late 1623, Shah Jahan and
his men fought his father's imperial forces. The prince established
a base in the region of Khandesh, just north of the Deccan, a place
with plentiful supplies of wheat and millet, fertile pasturelands, and
commercial wealth from three critical trade routes: northward toward
Agra, southward toward the Deccan plateau, and westward toward
Gujarat. Shah Jahan left some soldiers behind, but apparently suspended his military campaign in the Deccan against Ambar's troops.
The independent southern states continued to evade Mughal rule.

From Khandesh, Shah Jahan and his forces marched to Agra, hoping to seize the treasury. The assault seemed well timed, since Kandahar preoccupied the imperial forces. But to the prince's chagrin,

the imperial response was swift. When he and his men reached the gates of Fatehpur-Sikri, not far from the capital, they found them shut. Shah Jahan ordered his ally of many years, Sundar Das, who had fought bravely at his side during the Mewar and Kangra campaigns, to take a contingent to Agra and confiscate whatever treasures he could find. Sundar Das and his men entered several houses, seizing money and jewels. But Jahangir's soldiers chased them away and the imperial treasury remained safe.

While the thwarted prince and his forces were regrouping outside the gates of Fatehpur-Sikri, Jahangir dispatched a message to his son saying that he should send a representative to Agra who would outline the terms under which Shah Jahan would call off his rebellion. Shah Jahan's emissary brought the emperor a list of demands. Jahangir, though he didn't record Shah Jahan's exact demands, found them quite unreasonable. Most likely, the prince required restoration of his lands and privileges, and a promise of the throne after his father's death. Jahangir was so enraged by Shah Jahan's requests that he had the prince's representative imprisoned. Shah Jahan retreated to Khandesh to plan his next move.

Though Shah Jahan's rebellion distressed Jahangir, it didn't necessarily disqualify the prince from succession. In the reigns of many of the Great Mughals, princes rebelled against their emperor fathers. It was almost expected, a rite of passage in a way, considered a disruption but not a break in the Mughal world order. In writing of such rebellions, chroniclers often downplayed the role of the princes and blamed individuals within the prince's or the emperor's inner circle. The underlying belief was that the princes were young and impressionable: shortsighted, inexperienced, easily misled, or even simpleminded. Jahangir wrote as though his son's rebellion were in keeping with a Mughal prince's ambition, and an inevitable part of jostling for power. In his memoir, Jahangir called his insurgent son wretch, rash, belligerent, and full of effrontery—but he didn't declare him unfit to rule.

A rebellious prince was forgivable; a noble-led rebellion was not. And it was certainly unacceptable for an empress to drive a prince to rebellion, as several contemporary chroniclers accused. The empress, Bhakkari wrote, had pushed the Mughal world "to tumult and disruption," and thus forced Shah Jahan, a model of sincerity, to defy his father, claiming she "destroyed them in domestic squabbles." Furthermore, Bhakkari said, "the fire (of sedition)" was kindled by Nur Jahan and her allies—Khan-i Jahan Lodi, a noble once out of favor but now restored; Sharif ul-Mulk, who headed Shahryar's household and later would be in charge of the state of Sind; Nur's chief eunuchs Jawahir and Nadim; and perhaps Nur's daughter, Ladli.[9] During his rebellion, Shah Jahan publicly accused Nur of being power hungry and condemned Jahangir for allowing a woman to exercise such authority.[10] Later, official court historians writing during Shah Jahan's reign about the actions of Nur Jahan in the 1620s repeatedly used the word *fitna*—a term in Islamic tradition that describes civil strife so profound that it amounted to cosmic disorder.[11] Nur drove a wedge between the father and the son, they wrote, that forced the prince into rebellion.

Rooted in early conflict among Muslims in Arabia, just after Prophet Muhammad's death, the term *fitna* was first used to describe the actions taken by the Prophet's beloved wife Ayisha. She was the daughter of the first caliph, who opposed the fourth caliph, Ali, her first cousin, the son-in-law of the Prophet, and the first leader of the Shi'a Muslims. She led her forces against his in a seventh-century fight known as the Battle of the Camel, considered to be the first example of Islamic *fitna*—chaos or civil war. Shi'a sources cast Ayisha as the persecutor of Ali, while Sunni canon portrayed her as the champion of the rightful caliph. Ayisha was viewed then in various ways: reviled by some as "mischievous," "worthless," and "ambitious," and hailed by others as a great authority and an impeccable transmitter of the Prophet's traditions.[12] Wounded in battle, the defeated Ayisha was rebuked by the victorious Ali: "Is that what the Messenger of God ordered you to do? Didn't he order you to remain quietly in your house?"[13]

For centuries after the Battle of the Camel, the Islamic world associated *fitna* with what were seen as innately destructive elements in women: Their sexuality was ruinous, their ambition damaging. Women were a source of trouble, turmoil, and temptation.[14] Women's domain was the sacred, inner quarters. What else could follow a transgression of these boundaries but *fitna*? When some women in sixteenth-century Ottoman Turkey became politically prominent, Sunullah Efendi, the foremost guardian of Islamic law there and that empire's highest-ranking cleric, felt compelled to declare publicly that women should have nothing to do with "matters of government and sovereignty." To express his disapproval strongly, he recalled a tradition attributed to Prophet Muhammad about the harmful consequences of women's leadership: "[A] people who entrusts its affairs to a woman will never know prosperity."[15]

Shah Jahan and Mahabat—and many others in the Mughal court—shared such views. Jahangir's assessment was rather different. At the same time that he was invested in Shah Jahan as his successor, he had broadened his vision of his own sovereignty to include Nur Jahan as co-ruler. Perhaps the emperor expected a form of this arrangement to continue after his death, with Shah Jahan ruling the Mughal Empire and Nur serving as his wise adviser and guiding light. There's reason to believe Jahangir had once hoped that someday the empire would rest safely in the hands of his precious son and his beloved empress, to whom he had given the names King of the World and Light of the World, respectively. Jahangir knew, after all, that throughout Mughal history, women had served as counselors and guides, and Nur was far more politically experienced than any of those women had been. The emperor had observed, until their recent rift, the close, admiring, and supportive relationship between Nur and Shah Jahan, an affinity that had been based on their deeply felt sense of imperial responsibility. That Jahangir had once counted on this relationship to survive his demise is not hard to imagine. But by 1622, he would have seen clearly that his wife and son would never share sovereignty in any form. This must have made Shah Jahan's rebellion look even more devastating to the emperor.

Until the break between Nur and Shah Jahan was too obvious to ignore, courtiers and critics had somehow digested the rise of the empress. They accepted her issuing edicts, striking coins, and sitting in the *jharokha*, even as some of them silently lamented her authority. But once she and Shah Jahan were publicly in opposition, condemnatory statements on her character and the dangers of her womanly wiles began to emerge. She had sowed the seeds of dissension within the royal family. What else was this but *fitna*?

The Mughals lost the fort at Kandahar. Official records show that Shah Abbas of Iran personally led the Safavid Army, but Jahangir's memoir is murky when it comes to Shahryar's leadership of the Kandahar campaign. One entry seems to make clear that Shahryar was named commander of the Mughal troops, but another passage suggests that Shahryar traveled only partway to Kandahar and then another commander, Khan-i Abdul Jahan Lodi, actually led the troops into battle.

Nur and Jahangir were unhappy with the loss, though probably not surprised. The Mughals had been forced by circumstances to launch their campaign in the dead of winter. The heavy cannons that would ensure victory needed to be dragged through treacherous passes by thousands of bullocks and several elephants, but that was impossible during the season of snows. The Mughal troops could carry only lighter cannons, which put them at a great disadvantage against the Safavids. The ill-prepared Mughal garrison surrendered, perhaps even before the Mughal reinforcements arrived. Kandahar was no longer under Mughal control; it had become Safavid.

After the confrontation outside the gates of Fatehpur-Sikri and the arrest of his envoy, Shah Jahan retreated with his troops to a series of spots in western and central India. Imperial spies and soldiers followed his movements closely and engaged in occasional skirmishes. Though Jahangir was still in poor health, he insisted on setting out in early February 1623 to confront his son. The imperial retinue stopped in Punjab, where many officers who'd been serving under Shah Jahan in the south came over to Jahangir's side; he promoted many to higher ranks. The emperor was pleased with the expansion of his forces: By late March 1623, some 25,000 men had gathered to fight the prince. Jahangir and his entourage marched with them until Jahangir, exhausted, returned to Agra. He left Mahabat in command.

Shah Jahan's forces and the imperial army came face-to-face near Delhi. Mahabat sent a tactful message to Shah Jahan suggesting that if he'd return to the Deccan, steps would be taken to ensure his landed rights and other privileges. Shah Jahan declined and in the battle that followed, Mahabat drove away Shah Jahan's forces. The prince took shelter in the fort of Mandu, the place in western India from which he had launched his career in the Deccan, and tried to reopen negotiations with Mahabat. But the imperial forces attacked Mandu, and Shah Jahan fled once again. Short of resources and plagued by desertions—like the esteemed elderly general Abdur-Rahim, who had abandoned Shah Jahan and rejoined the imperial troops under Mahabat—the prince next made his way to Asir, a hill fortress outside Khandesh on an important route between Hindustan and the Deccan, where a cousin-in-law of Nur's was in charge. The empress sent orders that the bastion was to be reinforced to keep Shah Jahan out, but Nur's relative surrendered the fortress to the prince without opposition. Yet when Mahabat and the strong imperial forces reached Asir, Shah Jahan once again lost heart and retreated.

In April of 1623, Jahangir received Parvez while the royal retinue was en route to Ajmer, where they would stay for five months. "I took my favored son in the bosom of yearning and affection," Jahangir wrote.[16] At that moment, Jahangir did indeed seem to favor the rather feckless Parvez, not only over Shah Jahan but over Shahryar as well. The next month, Jahangir ordered Parvez to join Mahabat—to whom he'd given the sobriquet "The Trustworthy One of the State"— in leading imperial troops in pursuit of Shah Jahan. The emperor made a list of loyal nobles who were to accompany the two commanders, men to whom the emperor gave robes of honor, royal elephants, horses, and money.

Shah Jahan had several skirmishes with Mahabat and Parvez in various locations, each of them ending with Shah Jahan fleeing and the imperial forces giving chase. By November 1623, the rebellious prince had made his way by a circuitous route to the eastern provinces, Orissa, Bengal, and Bihar, which would become his new base of support, a source of fresh funds, recruits, horses, and artillery. Bengal was particularly profitable, given its abundance of rivers, immense rice-growing capacity, and large supplies of elephants.

In the eastern provinces, Shah Jahan focused on gaining the support of groups that felt alienated from the Mughal center, winning them over by awarding titles, lands, and administrative appointments. He gave offerings to custodians of Muslim shrines, bestowed massive endowments on Sufi families, and visited the tomb of Bahram Sakka, the Sufi saint who was an important influence on Nur when she was a young woman and continued to hold considerable significance for both Nur and Jahangir. He courted local Muslim leaders, praying at the site of a footprint alleged to be that of the Prophet Muhammad.[17]

With money from his eastern supporters, Shah Jahan built up his supplies of gunpowder, lead, iron, stone shot, and corn. The landholding elite of the region furnished more troops; some provided whole armies at short notice.[18] The landlords were also key suppliers of boats, indispensable to any expedition in the riverine provinces. Thanks to a wide network of local pacts, the prince's regional authority grew stronger. He was even able to gain the backing of the Portuguese, who had often tangled with Jahangir over territory on Hindustan's west coast; they ferried supplies for the prince as he advanced westward into Bihar and Allahabad.

In early 1624, Mahabat was in the Deccan drumming up support against Shah Jahan among the very leaders with whom the prince had once fought on behalf of the emperor, the heads of independent states resisting Mughal dominance. He even opened negotiations with the Mughals' enemy Malik Ambar, who offered Mahabat cooperation on the condition that the affairs of his area be left in his charge. Sensing that Ambar had larger ambitions, Mahabat instead chose an alliance with the shah of the state of Bijapur. Then Jahangir sent a message ordering Mahabat north to Allahabad. Shah Jahan had moved up the Ganga and taken the riverside fort of Allahabad and all nearby boats. Mahabat suspended his work in the Deccan, appointing a reliable officer to take charge there, and proceeded immediately to the northeast. Mahabat, Parvez and their troops arrived and camped across the river from Shah Jahan. Nur and Jahangir, who had traveled to Kashmir, followed developments from there.

Several of Shah Jahan's advisers warned him against engaging with the imperial forces, which far outnumbered his. He sent the women of his harem, who'd been traveling with him—always camped a good distance from any battle—to the nearby fortress at Rohtas for extra safety. Then he moved his troops seventy-five miles east to Banaras.

Parvez and Mahabat followed him to the banks of the river Tons.
More men deserted Shah Jahan. The prince's commanders were
divided on the question of fighting the imperial army, now comprising nearly 40,000 skilled horsemen and foot soldiers. The princely
army barely numbered 7,000.

Shah Jahan saw no option but to fight. He arrayed his forces with
himself in the center, as Parvez and Mahabat assembled their troops.
The head of the imperial artillery moved his heavy weapons forward
and fired what sounded like a thousand cannonballs as the imperial
soldiers attacked Shah Jahan's forces from all directions and brought
down the commander at their head. The prince's left wing crumbled.
Shah Jahan and his right wing, no more than 500 horses, pressed
on. Many men were slaughtered on both sides. Imperial commanders presented Parvez with the heads of nobles who supported Shah
Jahan.

A musket ball hit Shah Jahan in the head, but he survived. Carried
back to camp by his men, he sent a message to his trusted lieutenant Abdullah Khan, still fighting with the right flank of the prince's
forces. Shah Jahan wrote to Abdullah that although he and his men
were outnumbered and things looked bad, it was best to put their
trust "in divine grace," and attack the imperial center with the few
forces they had left. "Whatever will be, will be." Abdullah replied that
it was too late for either offense or defense to be of any help, and that
such maneuvers were often counterproductive. It was wiser, he said,
to reassess the situation and retreat from the battlefield.[19] Shah Jahan
seems to have acceded to Abdullah's wishes; the prince's forces, out-
matched and subdued, retreated, and the imperial army entered the
prince's camp. Shah Jahan mounted his horse; a devoted servant held
the reins and led the wounded prince away. Mahabat and Parvez
didn't pursue the defeated rebel—most likely on the emperor's orders.
Though Jahangir was enraged at Shah Jahan, he still wanted his son
alive so that he might come to his senses, repent, and eventually take

the throne. Leaving his favorite wife, Arjumand, and his newly born fifth son in the citadel of Rohtas, Shah Jahan retreated toward the Deccan, beyond imperial control.

In early October 1625, while the royal couple was in Kashmir, Jahangir received a letter from Shah Jahan in the Deccan. Ill and wishing to apologize to his father for past offenses, he expressed his deep regrets and begged forgiveness. The emperor replied that he would forgive Shah Jahan if he surrendered the Rohtas Fort and sent his sons Aurangzeb and Dara Shukoh to live with Jahangir. Shah Jahan agreed.

❧ FOURTEEN ❧

The Rescue

I n the spring of 1626, Jahangir, Nur, and the royal retinue were
back on the road, traveling from Lahore to Kabul. Servants had
raised the colorful tents of the vast imperial camp on both banks
of the Bahat River, now called the Jhelum, wide, swift, and fed by
many tributaries.

On the quiet morning of March 16, the emperor's longtime supporter Mahabat, until then steadfastly loyal, despite his grievances,
entered the lightly guarded imperial compound accompanied by
a large contingent of Rajput warriors. Mahabat burned with rage.
Jahangir, he felt, had behaved in a way that besmirched the honor
of his family. Mahabat and his men passed the harem tents and
approached Jahangir's quarters. At sword-point, Mahabat kidnapped
Jahangir, taking the emperor and a few retainers by elephant to a
bivouac a few miles beyond the royal camp. Then Mahabat ordered
his troops to burn the wide bridge to the other side of the river,
where most of the royal tents were pitched, to thwart any rescue

attempts. The narrow makeshift bridge they erected in its place was closely guarded.

Later that day, two veiled women emerged from the harem and stepped onto the hastily constructed new bridge. The Rajput guards didn't give them a second look, and the pair passed easily to the other side.

After crossing the river undetected, a disguised Nur and her head eunuch, Jawahir Khan, hurried to the tented quarters of her brother Asaf Khan, on the bank opposite Jahangir's pavilion. The empress immediately summoned a council of principal nobles and officers.

Meanwhile, Mahabat, holding the emperor prisoner, realized, as his agitation subsided, that he had neglected to take the empress captive. By the time he became conscious of his folly, it was too late. She had already escaped across the river.

In her brother's tent, Nur rebuked a council of distinguished nobles, declaring that it was through their inattention that the emperor had been kidnapped by Mahabat: "You have been disgraced before God and the people by your own actions. The best tactical plan is to array our forces tomorrow, cross the river . . . overthrow the miscreants, and do ourselves the honor of kissing the ground as slaves of His Majesty."[1] All present agreed with the empress.

The trouble between Mahabat and Emperor Jahangir had begun more than a year earlier, after Jahangir appointed Mahabat the governor of Bengal. Mahabat failed to send the emperor a promised number of elephants captured in Bengal; he also began holding back a huge amount of money from the imperial treasury, the emperor's share of taxes and revenues he'd taken from *jagirdars*, official landowners, whom he now oversaw as governor.

Despite this misbehavior, Jahangir had turned to Mahabat when trouble flared again in the Deccan. Malik Ambar had defeated the combined forces of the Mughals and the Shah of Bijapur, occupying several areas and laying siege to Ahmadnagar and Burhanpur. In late 1625, Jahangir, alarmed, ordered Mahabat and Prince Parvez to head south immediately with a unit of imperial soldiers to relieve the Mughal forces in the Deccan.

While Mahabat was away, Jahangir, already angry about the missing revenues and elephants, was further irked to learn that Mahabat had married his daughter to the descendant of an eminent Sufi without first asking Jahangir for the customary imperial blessing. The emperor sent for the young man; his hands were bound to his neck and he was taken bareheaded—and thus publicly dishonored—to the prison in Lahore. Jahangir directed his master of ceremonies to confiscate whatever gifts and cash Mahabat had given his son-in-law and deposit them in the imperial treasury. Then the emperor ordered Mahabat's daughter to appear in court. Her father, away in the south, knew nothing of these developments.

Jahangir called Mahabat back from the Deccan in early 1626, commanding him to appear at court with the elephants and the taxes he owed. Mahabat replied by messenger that he had already sent the elephants to the court; as to the revenue, he made various excuses for not delivering. Jahangir sent a loyalist, Khan-i Jahan Lodi, to take over from Mahabat as commander of Mughal troops in the Deccan. Parvez was unhappy with the change, and refused the help of Khan-i Jahan Lodi in negotiations with Deccan states. Before he left for the north, Mahabat tried to turn Parvez against the emperor; he "cast a spell and erased the influence of royal command from his heart."[2] We don't know how strong that spell was, or how long it lasted, for Parvez disappears from the record until his death later that year.

Immediately after he summoned Mahabat, Jahangir set off on a journey to Kabul, accompanied by Nur, Asaf, Shahryar, Ladli, the inner circle of nobles and royal women, servants, and soldiers. Mahabat was on his way north from the Deccan to the traveling court when he found out that the emperor had arrested his son-in-law and ordered his daughter to appear in court—acts that he considered a vile attack on his daughter's reputation, and his own. His anger was fed by his profound dislike of Nur Jahan's family, disgust at the extent of their power, and lingering fear of Asaf Khan. Along the route north, he stopped to gather troops in Rajasthan, home of the Rajputs, the valiant warrior class, among whom Mahabat had strong political allies. He was married to an Indian Muslim woman from Mewat, a state bordering Rajasthan that had its own large population of Rajputs. He told the Rajput fighters, known for their strong views on the honor of women, about what had happened to his daughter. "She is our daughter," the Rajputs told Mahabat, and "as long as we live, we do not send her [i.e., to appear before the king]."³ "A large contingent of Rajput soldiers vowed loyalty to Mahabat; of the 6,000 men who eventually went north to the court with him, 4,000 were Rajputs, the rest Indian Muslims, Afghans, and Mughals. Mahabat's brother and his son also joined the troops. Rage had set Mahabat on this course, but it's not clear what he intended to do with this army, or whether he had any coherent plan at first.

Mahabat reached Lahore in the early spring of 1626, not long after the royal party left for Kabul. Nur's brother Asaf further upset Mahabat by sending him a humiliating order to pay the money he owed and produce the missing elephants before he'd be allowed to appear before the emperor at the royal encampment. But humiliating the disloyal commander wasn't all that Asaf had in mind. From allies in Lahore, Mahabat learned that Asaf planned to take Mahabat prisoner when he caught up with the cavalcade.

Mahabat's fury and fear surged. He began to set in motion a plot to kidnap the emperor. He directed one of his trusted lieutenants to move ahead with 1,000 mounted men to protect the bridge over the Bahat, where he knew the royal retinue would camp. As a cover, he sent a message to a court official saying this lieutenant was coming with his men to join the imperial army.

In the royal camp, Asaf had indeed concocted a scheme to capture Mahabat. The commander would be allowed to pay his respects
to Jahangir, after which the emperor would lead him onto the royal
barge, where guards would hold him. Imperial soldiers would then
tear up the bridge so Mahabat's men couldn't rescue him. Believing
that Mahabat didn't represent much of a threat, and certainly not
expecting him to arrive with a large army, Asaf moved his household,
the traveling treasury and armory, and most of the imperial soldiers
to one side of the river and left Jahangir on the other side. A small
number of intimates, dignitaries, eunuchs, and servants stayed on
with Jahangir, and a few guards remained at the entrances and exits
to the camp, the emperor's pavilion, and the harem, which included
Nur's tents.

Mahabat had sent spies ahead to observe the royal camp. When
they reported back that Asaf had moved across the bridge from
Jahangir and left the emperor lightly guarded, Mahabat decided to
act. He rode to the camp with his troops, stationed a large number of
men at the bridge, left others on the perimeter ready for battle, and
marched foot soldiers into the royal camp. Then, accompanied by a
hundred or more Rajput foot soldiers armed with spears and swords,
he rode past the harem to Jahangir's royal pavilion, where he alighted
from his horse.

One of the dignitaries who'd stayed with the emperor, paymaster
Mu'tamad, emerged from the pavilion wearing a sword and warned
Mahabat about the impropriety of approaching the emperor accompanied by soldiers. "*Adab nist?*"[4] he asked in Persian. Where is your
etiquette? He told Mahabat to wait until his presence was announced
to the emperor. Mahabat ignored him and strode to the door of the
private bath where Jahangir usually held secret discussions with special dignitaries. His men began tearing down the boards that the
imperial doorkeepers had put up for security.

Taken aback by Mahabat's audacity, the emperor left the royal pavilion and seated himself on a raised platform, a sort of open-air throne. Mahabat saluted Jahangir, feigning submission and speaking deferentially. Since escaping the deadly malice of Asaf was impossible, he told Jahangir, he was throwing himself on the emperor's mercy. But even as Mahabat spoke, more of his men rode up, fully armed.

Realizing Mahabat's treachery, Jahangir twice placed his hand on his sword as if to draw it, restraining himself on the advice of a noble who said to him in Turkish that the time was not right. Then, openly revealing his true purpose, Mahabat addressed the emperor: "It is time to ride. Mount as usual with this devoted slave next to you so that it will look as though this bold and audacious act was done by me at your command."[5] He offered his own horse to the emperor, but Jahangir refused to ride the horse of a *bidawlat*, a disgraceful one, and ordered his men to bring forward the imperial horse. He rode a distance of two arrow-shots from the imperial pavilion—a few hundred yards—then switched without protest to a waiting elephant, which knelt to accept its passengers.

At some point, paymaster Mu'tamad slipped away, most likely to warn Nur about what was going on. Several retainers stayed close to their monarch. Three trusted Rajput imperial guards took seats surrounding the emperor in the howdah atop the elephant. The celebrated surgeon Muqarrab Khan, who shared Jahangir's interests in the curiosities of the world, was traveling with the royal cavalcade; he too got into the howdah, even though Mahabat tried to chase him away by hitting him on the head with a stick. Jahangir's wine-and-bowl-holder, the noble Khidmatparast Khan, whose name translates as Soaked with Service, began climbing into the howdah as the elephant stood up. Mahabat's soldiers attempted to yank him down but he held on, and the entourage moved forward with Khidmatparast dangling from the elephant until he scrambled behind the howdah. The overseer of the imperial stables followed on another elephant, along with his son, to keep an eye on the monarch. Anyone who saw the emperor in the center of this hastily mustered retinue would think he was heading out to hunt with his inner circle, along with Mahabat and Mahabat's men.

When Mahabat realized his folly in leaving Nur Jahan at liberty, he brought Jahangir and his retainers back to the royal compound, to keep an eye on them while he sought out the empress. But Nur was already safely on the other side of the river, planning her husband's rescue. Mahabat also thought about Shahryar. Letting him stay free would be another great error. A free prince, especially Nur Jahan's son-in-law, could be a big risk. To circumvent trouble, Mahabat led Jahangir to Shahryar's tent, where the emperor spent the night and the next day with his son, under guard.

Perhaps to maintain the appearance of decorum as his hastily crafted kidnapping occurred, Mahabat allowed Jahangir to send Nur two messages. According to the poet Mulla Kami Shirazi, who wrote a fulsome eyewitness account of these events, the first message expressed the emperor's misery at being separated from Nur and asked her to come to him: " . . . without her the flower of my pleasure and delight has fallen down in pieces; and I have stuck to my skirt the thorn of her separation/And if she desires my safety she should start immediately and not quarrel with the circumstances."[6]

Hearing these words, Nur bowed her head as a mark of respect, then told the messenger that she was unyielding in her resolve to conquer the "source of deceit and deception," as she called Mahabat.[7] The second message came after Jahangir somehow learned that Nur and Asaf were preparing to fight. The emperor urged his wife and her brother not to cross the river and provoke a futile and hazardous battle that might endanger them all.[8]

But Nur, Asaf, and the council of nobles proceeded with their plans. They knew that Jahangir was being held in Shahryar's quarters on the far side of the Mughal encampment, now guarded by Maha-

bat's men. Crossing the deep, swift waters of the river in the presence
of Mahabat's soldiers would be a challenge, but the overseer of the
royal barge and inspector of ships concluded that there were sections
of the river shallow enough to ford. Nur and her commanders drew
up detailed plans for carefully distributing their troops, horses, elephants, guns, and cannons.

On March 18, sitting atop a war elephant and armed with a musket, Nur led the Mughal forces into the swiftly moving river.[9] Angry
waves swirled, elephants trumpeted, and royal servants blew bugles.
Mounted on horses and armed with guns and swords, Asaf Khan
and his son, other distinguished nobles, some cavalry, a few camels,
and hundreds of foot soldiers secured the near riverbank opposite
Mahabat's troops, then set out for the far side. But the crossing chosen by the overseer of the royal barge turned out to be a treacherous
part of the churning river, with three or four stretches of deep water.
When the men and animals hit these spots, their orderly advance
turned chaotic. Asaf's son managed to make it to the opposite shore,
where he killed Mahabat's brother. Suddenly Asaf feared that when
Mahabat learned that his brother was dead, he might retaliate by
killing Jahangir. He withdrew from the battle, planning some other
scheme to rescue the emperor.

Nur Jahan, thinking that her brother Asaf was still with her, moved
forward on her elephant, close to the ranks of Mahabat's men: amid "a
tumultuous noise and commotion among the enemies."[10] An account
of the battle by an eighteenth-century courtier named Muhammad
Hadi reported that despite the uproar, while cavalry and foot soldiers,
horses, and camels plunged into the turbulent water, Mu'tamad stood
near a tributary of the river having a philosophical conversation about
fate with another dignitary. The empress's eunuch Nadim approached
him with a reprimand: "Her Majesty wants to know why you have
stopped to contemplate. Be brave, for as soon as you enter the battle,
the foe will be routed . . ."[11] Mu'tamad and his companion rushed

into battle, but the foe stood firm—and Nur's forces were in disarray, struggling to keep from drowning; waterlogged saddles and blankets dragged their horses down. On the opposite bank, Mahabat's troops and elephants guarding the way to the emperor formed a fearsome wall.

Nur drew closer to the riverside lined with Mahabat's men and elephants, shooting continuously as she advanced. Her elephant received two sword wounds on its trunk, and two spears cut gashes in its back. The handler of Nur's elephant urged the injured animal back into the deepest part of the water, and it managed to swim to the safety of their bank. As Nur retreated on the wounded elephant, a band of her followers assembled on the river's edge, shooting to keep the enemy from coming after the empress. Her high-ranking eunuchs Nadim and Jawahir were slain.

Meanwhile, another eunuch, Jahangir's master of ceremonies Fidai Khan, led a group of soldiers across the river toward the emperor. Six men accompanying him perished in the chilly water, and several others returned to the near shore severely wounded. With a gallant effort, Fidai and some soldiers made it to the far shore, fought Mahabat's troops, and got as far as Shahryar's quarters, ringed by Mahabat's men. Fidai fired arrows into Shahryar's encampment. Many of them landed in a private courtyard near where Jahangir was being held, and one accidentally killed a loyal courtier who was shielding the emperor. Fidai's horse was wounded and four men fighting with him died. When it was clear that he couldn't break through to save the emperor, Fidai raced back through the enemy line to the river, and swam to the other side.

Dismounting from her bleeding elephant, the empress walked back to her brother's tented compound. Nur Jahan understood that she would have to join her imprisoned husband on the other side of the river and accept Mahabat's terms—at least temporarily. She needed to come up with a new rescue plan. It would, she knew, take some time to formulate and execute. Her forces had suffered great losses. Scores of officers had been killed; high-ranking nobles had fled.

Asaf, meanwhile, had retreated with his son, 200 horsemen, bearers, and servants, to the fortress at nearby Attock, between the river Indus and the road to Peshawar. From there he too hoped to plan a rescue, and perhaps muster more men.

After watching Nur bravely lead her men into battle, the court poet Shirazi wrote a *masnavi*, a long composition in rhyming couplets, divided into nine chapters, called *Waqi'at uz-zaman* (The events of the time), which he dedicated to the empress. Included in it was a segment entitled "Fathnama-i Nur Jahan Begum" (Chronicle of the victory of Nur Jahan Begum). This account of Nur's victory is the only part of the larger work that survives.

Another eyewitness, paymaster-historian Mu'tamad, who fought on Nur's side, also wrote about the battle of 1626. So did the Mughal chronicler Bhakkari and the eighteenth-century courtier Muhammad Hadi. While these men disagreed on some details, they were unanimous in their conviction that Nur managed and led her men with courage and skill. "Her glory and dignity had captured the world," Shirazi wrote.[12]

None of these chroniclers tells exactly when Nur returned to the far side of the river where Jahangir was being held, or whether she went willingly. After the battle on the river, the next recorded event is the continued journey of the defeated Mughal convoy to Kabul, with Nur and Jahangir at the center, but with Mahabat in charge of the halts, the marches, the order of procession. Fearful and unsure of what might happen next, Mahabat kept up appearances; he remained respectful to Jahangir, careful to avoid any open suggestion that the emperor and empress were captives.

Learning that Asaf and his troops had regrouped in Attock, on the route to Kabul, Mahabat sent a number of men commanded by his son to attack the fortress with the help of local landlords. When the royal cavalcade reached Attock, Mahabat asked permission from the emperor and empress to negotiate Asaf's surrender. Taking him into custody, while promising to spare his life, Mahabat ordered Asaf and his son to join the royal captives on the road to Kabul. At the same time, he meted out severe punishments to some of Asaf's men, executing many. A mullah was chained, and when the loose chains fell off, Mahabat suspected sorcery. The mullah began reciting Quranic verses. Convinced that the cleric was cursing him, Mahabat ordered the man cut to pieces.

Was Mahabat's detention of Jahangir, the first recorded revolt of a noble against a Mughal emperor, simply retaliation for an injured sense of honor? Or was he aspiring to something else? Contemporary and later chroniclers thought Mahabat wanted a central part in Mughal rule. But if his ambition was to control the empire, he'd done little groundwork. For a start, he would need the support of a Mughal prince, and though Mahabat had served with Parvez, who was still in the Deccan, the chances of a successful alliance with him were small.

Those writing in later times about this period say that when Shah Jahan heard what Mahabat had done to his father on the banks of the Bahat, he flew into a rage. Whether because he feared an alliance between Mahabat and Parvez, or because he was eager to assure his father of his renewed allegiance, he decided to go after Mahabat, even with his few troops and limited supplies. In the first week of June 1626, Shah Jahan set out from the south with 1,000 horsemen, hoping to gather more support along the way. In Ajmer, one of his supporters died and his 500-man unit dispersed. With only 500 men left, Shah Jahan abandoned the idea of rescue and returned to the southern provinces.

Mahabat had taken charge of Mughal affairs. He told Jahangir, now a puppet emperor, what to do, and pushed Nur to the sidelines. In April 1626 the Mughals reached Kabul, nearly four hundred miles from the site of the kidnapping and the battle on the Bahat River. Residents gathered to greet the royal couple, who scattered coins as they moved through the marketplace. To the throngs of Jahangir's subjects, this viewing was simply an auspicious moment. They had no idea that the emperor and the empress were in custody.

It was an unusual captivity. Jahangir and Nur were prisoners, but court etiquette and daily proceedings remained intact. The two weren't held at gunpoint. Mahabat kept a close eye on the pair, but left them to their routine activities, such as visits to the tombs of Jahangir's great-grandfather Babur and his great-aunt Gulbadan and excursions to a garden near the Kabul fortress. Nur and Jahangir met with the leader of the Hazara, a local tribal people; Nur gave their leader's son gems and gilded utensils, gifts meant to forge a new alliance. The couple hunted ibexes, mountain rams, bears, and hyenas. As a major *jagirdar*, Nur Jahan was allowed to maintain and regularly parade her small cavalry, a ceremonial event that caused Mahabat no alarm.

A messenger brought Jahangir the news of his enemy Malik Ambar's death—no cause for celebration since there was no real Mughal military presence prepared to take over the Deccan, though Parvez was nominally in charge of a few troops there. Shah Jahan was waiting to see what would happen next in the south before he tried to forge new alliances. All the kingdoms of the Deccan remained intact and independent. Not long after he heard about Ambar's demise, the emperor recieved the troubling news that Prince Parvez was unconscious, seriously ill with an intestinal obstruction, the same malady that allegedly killed his brother Khusraw. Gossip suggested that heavy drinking had contributed to Parvez's decline. At around the same time, the sons of Shah Jahan, sent to the emperor as part of the rebel prince's penance, arrived in Kabul.

Behind the scenes, Nur Jahan was doing more than carrying out her ritual public obligations. She was planning the recovery of Mughal authority, calculating how best to preserve the world she and Jahangir had so carefully built. Her daily schedule allowed her to meet regularly with several intimates and loyalists. With them, she began to formulate her plans, promising the battle-worn warriors still with her that rein-forcements would come. She wooed discontented and resentful nobles back into the imperial camp, allaying the fears of those who remained hesitant, holding out hopes of high offices. According to one account, she spent gold coins worth 300,000 rupees from her own pocket. Through a written order, she instructed her new eunuch, Hoshyar Khan, to begin mustering troops in Lahore. He recruited 2,000 horse-men and 5,000 armed foot soldiers. All this planning took place in secret, unnoticed by Mahabat, while Jahangir pretended friendliness.

One day some of Mahabat's Rajput soldiers left their base camp and rode out to a well-known Kabul hunting ground to let their horses graze. This imperial hunting preserve was entrusted to the care of guards, called *ahadis*, unaffiliated with any commanders or landlords. One of the *ahadis* objected to having the horses graze in the preserve. The exchange turned nasty and the Rajputs hacked him to pieces. When his relatives went to the court and cried out for jus-tice, an official told them that the request would be forwarded to the emperor and an inquest held. Unsatisfied, the *ahadis* returned to the imperial hunting preserve.

Nur Jahan seized the opportunity and sent out instructions that the *ahadis*, expert archers, should move against Mahabat's men. The next morning the *ahadis* attacked the Rajput camp in a narrow valley and killed nearly 900 Rajputs, several of them close associ-ates of Mahabat, whom he was said to love "more than his own offspring."[13] Mahabat set out to join the battle, but changed his mind halfway. Fearing that he might be killed in the fray, he returned to the safety of his compound. The attack shook him, and he became more inclined to follow the emperor's suggestions than to give orders himself.[14]

Following Nur's advice, the emperor worked to calm Mahabat's suspicions. Jahangir showed him special favors, and seemed to take him into confidence, warning him that Nur intended to attack him, and that Asaf's daughter-in-law, the granddaughter of General Rahim, had announced that whenever she had the opportunity, she would shoot Mahabat Khan with a musket.[15] As Jahangir gradually gained his captor's trust, Mahabat became less watchful and reduced the number of men stationed at the traveling palace compound. After the bitter *ahadi*-Rajput combat, there had been no further clashes, no disturbing incidents. But on the banks of the Bahat River, troops loyal to the empress were preparing for battle.

In early August 1626, the royal retinue, still under the ostensible command of Mahabat, left Kabul on the return trip to Lahore, retracing their route. By late September, the imperial cavalcade had nearly covered the four hundred miles back to the Bahat River, where Mahabat had taken the emperor and empress captive. When the cavalcade was two days' ride from the river, Jahangir sent a note to Mahabat saying that he wished to review Nur's cavalry, so it would be best for Mahabat to postpone his own daily parade of troops, lest words should pass between the two parties and lead to strife. Mahabat saw the message as yet another sign of confidence and cooperation on the part of the emperor. What Mahabat didn't know was that the empress was just then adding two thousand men to her cavalry.

Jahangir sent a second message, expressing his wish that Mahabat and his men move on in advance of the royal retinue to the Bahat River, the next big stop on the journey to Lahore. Mahabat agreed— but as insurance against harm, he insisted Asaf travel with him.

Instead of following Mahabat down the road, the royal retinue, including Nur's cavalry and nobles loyal to the emperor, took off at a brisk pace on a parallel route. They didn't stop for the night, and managed to cover two days' journey in one, reaching the river before Mahabat.

Nur, Jahangir, and their party crossed the river by boat. On the other side, Nur's cavalry was joined by several courtiers and the soldiers she'd secretly had them gather.[16] When Mahabat arrived and understood that Jahangir and Nur were now in command of a large number of loyal troops, enough to overpower him and his men, he knew that his imperial design was over. Nur had engineered the final rescue of the emperor and the empire.

Jahangir dispatched an order to Mahabat: He was to return Asaf and two nephews of Nur's who were still with him. Further, the emperor instructed him to leave for the eastern provinces. That Jahangir exiled Mahabat rather than executing him for treason may have been because Shah Jahan's behavior was even more undependable. Despite begging his father's forgiveness and sending his sons to Jahangir as a sign of fealty, Shah Jahan had renewed his rebellion. With 500 men, he was heading to Sind on the border of the Mughal and Safavid empires, in the hopes of eventually getting help from the Safavid shah.

In answer to Jahangir's order, Mahabat sent back one of the royal nephews. Regarding Asaf, he was candid in telling the messenger: "Since I have no assurance of my security from the begam [Nur], I fear that if I give Asaf Khan up, she will send an army down on me. In this case, since I am proud to perform any service to which I am assigned, when I am past Lahore," he added, he would "gladly and willingly" send Asaf Khan to court.[17] Nur flew into a rage over these words, Hadi wrote. She sent the messenger back to Mahabat with a final order. "It is not in your best interests to delay in sending Asaf Khan, and do not allow yourself to think otherwise, for it will result in regret."[18] Mahabat knew that Nur was a force to be reckoned with. He released Asaf immediately, holding on to one nephew for insurance. But he knew that his days of rising ambition and command were over. A few days later he sent the second nephew back to Nur.

Emperor Jahangir and the victorious Empress Nur Jahan returned to Lahore on October 18, 1626. The elite of the city lined the road to the palace. In a few weeks, Nur and Jahangir resumed the regular business of the court—administrative changes, new appointments, the shuffling of provincial governors. Jahangir appointed Asaf imperial deputy and governor of Punjab.

Although the empress had restored the Mughal order, her prominence in strategic and military planning caused much consternation. For many observers, the idea that Nur had fought Mahabat's men, suffered defeat, risen again, strategized, and ultimately rescued the emperor only proved that Nur had brought the Mughal world to chaos—*fitna*—as had happened centuries before when Ayisha fought the Battle of the Camel to protect the Prophet's line of succession. A few, like the poet Shirazi, recognized that Nur had preserved the Mughal dynasty. He wrote in his victory poem,

> *King Jahangir whose abode is exalted and elevated as the sky and who is King through the wise advice of the Queen. . . .*
> *Never was witnessed in the region of my King such a fortified system (refuge) for the kingdom as the Queen.*[19]

FIFTEEN

Angel of Death

At an auspicious hour on March 1, 1627, a departure time determined by the royal astrologers, the imperial cavalcade once again embarked from Lahore for the valley of Kashmir, banners high. Once again, as they did nearly every year, Nur Jahan and Jahangir endured the difficulties of the road to visit the delightful gardens of the north, where the emperor could find relief from his escalating breathlessness and the empress could enjoy a few moments of leisure. Among the royal retinue were Nur's brother Asaf Khan; her son-in-law Shahryar, presumably with her daughter, Ladli; and the late Prince Khusraw's son Dawar Bakhsh, who was under Shahryar's supervision, as ordered by Nur. If there was even a small chance that Dawar's growing popularity among some Mughals could block Shahryar's path to the throne, she wanted him where she could keep an eye on him.

Meanwhile, in the province of Sind, the commander of imperial troops in the town of Thatta, Sharif ul-Mulk—the same man who headed Shahryar's household when the prince married Ladli—

prepared to fight Shah Jahan. He'd gathered 3,000 horsemen and 12,000 foot soldiers, and added more cannons in the Thatta fort. According to partisans of the prince, Shah Jahan forbade his men from storming the fort, to keep them from becoming cannon fodder. A small contingent launched an attack, but advance was impossible. Shah Jahan's official chronicles aren't clear on exactly when Sharif ordered a cannon attack on Shah Jahan's encampment outside the city of Thatta. Firing near the tent of Arjumand, pregnant with her eleventh child, was a "crime of violating the imperial person" that Shah Jahan wouldn't forget.[1] Soon after, Shah Jahan fell ill.

While he was recovering at his camp, Nur Jahan sent Shah Jahan a message reminding the prince that harboring any imperial ambitions would be pointless: He had no backing, no men, no power; she was in charge. "It would be wisest to return to the Deccan and submit to your fate . . ." she wrote.[2] Shah Jahan did as she suggested, and was joined by Mahabat, who realized that after the kidnapping fiasco, his only political option was casting his lot with Shah Jahan, to whom he wrote, "If you will pardon the offenses of this sinful slave, I will turn towards your threshold."[3]

The air of Kashmir seemed to have lost its magic; paradise on earth failed to restore Jahangir's vigor. The emperor wasn't himself. His breathing troubled him and he felt immensely weak. He couldn't ride a horse and had to be carried in a palanquin. By early September 1627, he was gravely ill. The royal physicians offered no hope of recovery.

Breathless and suffering severe chest pains, Jahangir developed an aversion to opium, his drug of choice for forty years.[4] He lost his appetite and would take only a few bowls of grape wine each day. To Nur's alarm, he went in and out of lucidity, sometimes speaking gibberish.

With the emperor failing, Nur's son-in-law, Shahryar, gave her another cause for worry. The prince had developed a severe case of Fox's disease, a kind of leprosy, and was badly disfigured. He lost his hair, beard, eyebrows, and eyelashes. The royal physicians weren't able to help except to suggest that if Shahryar left the cooler temperature of Kashmir and went to warmer Lahore, he might recover. Early in October, Shahryar asked the empress for permission to travel; she immediately agreed. Before leaving for Lahore, presumably with his wife Ladli, he transferred Khusraw's son Dawar Bakhsh to the charge of an imperial officer. For Nur, the outlook was grim. Her husband was dying; the son-in-law she hoped would succeed him was threatened by disease.

Soon after Shahryar's departure, Jahangir also decided to return to Lahore. Perhaps it was Nur's idea. She had good reason to feel that with Parvez gone and Shah Jahan in the Deccan, it was imperative to have Shahryar close to the emperor, whose health was failing. The Mughal cavalcade began the long return journey.

On the way, they stopped at Bahramgalla—a sweet, green spot near a peak with a waterfall called Chitta Pani, or "White Water," a forceful cascade that foamed gloriously.[5] Jahangir had always enjoyed hunting there. For the first time in weeks, the emperor's condition improved a little; he said that he felt like hunting. Preparations began at once. Servants set up a platform at the foot of the mountain, from which Jahangir could shoot with a musket. The plan was that local landlords and soldiers would drive antelopes to the top of the peak. Once they were in sight, the emperor would aim his musket and fire; the antelopes would fall from the pinnacle and hit the ground near the shooting platform.

The hunt began. A soldier chased an antelope toward the summit, but the animal stopped on an outcropping that didn't offer a clear shot to the emperor below. Attempting to get the antelope to move, the soldier stepped onto the ledge and lost his footing; the bush he grabbed for support came out by the roots. The man plummeted to his death. Jahangir, horrified, asked to be taken from the shooting platform. Later, he summoned the soldier's grieving mother to the imperial pavilion and paid her generous compensation, but his distress couldn't be lightened. "It was as though the angel of death had appeared in this guise to the emperor," Mu'tamad noted in his *Iqbalnama*.[6]

As the cavalcade advanced, Jahangir, now sixty, deteriorated. On earlier trips, he'd relished making notes about the changes in customs and terrain he observed as he traveled from Kashmir to lower lands. He customarily stopped near the village of Thana, the place where, Jahangir had recorded in his journal, Kashmiri culture ended: "A great difference was apparent in the climate, the languages, the clothing, the animals, and whatever properly belongs to a warm country . . ."[7]

Late in the day on October 28, as the party set out from the town of Rajaor, modern Rajori, the emperor called for wine. His attendants brought him a cup, but he was unable to swallow. By the time they reached the imperial resting house at Chingiz Hatli, fifteen miles to the south, the emperor's breathing was increasingly ragged.[8] Jahangir had once praised Chingiz Hatli's stone walls carved with floral patterns and its fine terrace, and rewarded a builder named Murad for his excellent work.[9] Now the brick gateway, shielded with weeping grass, gave passage to an emperor clearly failing. The empress, her brother, important nobles, physicians, and servants, gathered around their monarch to wait for the end. At dawn on October 29, 1627, as the light changed, Jahangir died.

In the Mughal camp, still more than a hundred miles from Lahore, the battle for succession began at once. As with other momentous events, Mughal chroniclers have different points of view about exactly what transpired immediately after Jahangir's death. Bhakkari says that Nur Jahan, determined to promote Shahryar as successor, wanted to arrest her brother, Asaf, who favored his own son-in-law, Shah Jahan. No other court historian mentions this episode. The imperial history commissioned by Shah Jahan many years later portrays Nur as "scheming to install her son-in-law Shahryar on the throne" in the aftermath of Jahangir's death.[10] Most accounts, however, agreed on the following events.

Nur Jahan summoned key nobles to a conference. But Asaf Khan, usually discreet and diplomatic, promptly took charge and preempted his sister's command. He came out forcefully in support of his son-in-law Shah Jahan. Asaf sent a man named Banarasi, celebrated as a swift messenger, to deliver the news of Jahangir's death to Shah Jahan in the south. According to the Shah Jahan Nama, the official chronicle of Shah Jahan's reign, Asaf gave the messenger his signet ring and personal seal to convince Shah Jahan that the news was true.

The problem Asaf faced was how to hold the Mughal throne until Shah Jahan arrived. He decided to summon Khusraw's son Dawar Bakhsh, still under the watchful eye of a Mughal officer, and promise the young man that he would be the next king. This was, in the words of the Shah Jahan Nama, "an expedient maneuver" meant to prevent upheaval and thwart the ambitions of Prince Shahryar, who still thought himself the son most suitable for kingship.[11]

Dawar was a pawn in a plot: he would be a placeholder until Shah Jahan returned. Mu'tamad Khan wrote that Dawar had little confidence in Asaf's proposal, and agreed to the offer of the throne only after Asaf professed loyalty to him.

Nur Jahan, mourning her husband and fearing for her position, sent messenger after messenger summoning her brother to meet her, but Asaf made one excuse after another. He isolated her, sending away her eunuchs, companions, and past supporters, and stopped visiting her himself. Court chronicler Farid Bhakkari wrote of Nur's fate: "You shall be treated as you have treated."[12]

Within days of the emperor's death, all the men who had bowed before Nur deserted her. Almost unanimously, the nobles in the imperial camp endorsed Asaf's strategy of using Dawar in order to secure the accession of Shah Jahan. With her husband gone and her brother opposing her, none of Nur's maneuvers was likely to succeed. At a rather astonishing speed, the old order was restored, as if these men had simply been waiting for the emperor's passing so that they could override the empress.

Nur made preparations to send the emperor's body to Lahore, so that he could be buried with full imperial honors. The imperial cavalcade split into three groups. The first carried Jahangir's body, escorted by servants and attendants; the second included Asaf, Dawar, and important nobles and dignitaries; and the third, a day's ride behind the others, was Nur's. She was under Asaf's control: he had carefully chosen the servants now attending her. She followed far behind her husband's body, riding an elephant.

Along the way, funeral rites were performed for the late emperor—his last wash; the removal of the entrails to save the corpse from early decomposition. A man's closest male relatives usually tended to these rites, so Asaf and Dawar may have supervised. In this way the royal body was prepared for burial, which would take place, as the emperor had wished, in a place called the Heart-Contenting Garden, designed by Nur in Shahdara, just outside Lahore.

Meanwhile, a mullah in Punjab read the *khutba* in Dawar's name, officially but not very publicly proclaiming him the Mughal king.

According to Mu'tamad, and later the eighteenth-century historian Hadi, the mourning Nur was unaware of her brother's schemes and still thought that Shahryar could attain the throne.[13] But the *Shah Jahan Nama* tells a different story. In that version, when Nur Jahan learned about Asaf's plans for Dawar—from whom it does not say—she was dumbstruck, then panic-stricken. In a confused state of mind, that royal history says, she forced the three sons of Arjumand and Shah Jahan to join her on the elephant following behind the cortege bearing the emperor's body, their presence ensuring her safety.[14] According to the *Shah Jahan Nama*, she continued to keep

Shah Jahan's young sons with her. "At this point, it was practically impossible to remove the august princes from the confines of the seraglio of Nur Jahan Begam; and moreover, she was already scheming to install her son-in-law Shahryar on the throne."[15]

In Lahore, when Shahryar got the news of his father's death, he raided the treasury and took goods from the imperial workshops, distributing these riches to win supporters. He gathered troops and seized the imperial departments within easy reach—those dealing with elephants, stables, and armory. Mu'tamad Khan notes that Ladli, perhaps thinking of her mother's safety and her husband's fortunes, urged Shahryar to take charge of the empire. Within a week of the emperor's demise, according to Hadi, Shahryar gave large amounts of money to numerous officers and nobles, and promised money and royal appointments to others. A nephew of Jahangir took command of Shahryar's forces.

After the emperor's burial, Asaf and the puppet king Dawar battled Shahryar's men on the outskirts of Lahore, while Shahryar himself remained in the Lahore fort. Mounted on elephants, Asaf and Dawar fought alongside seasoned nobles such as Mu'tamad the paymaster, as well as another of Jahangir's nephews. Shahryar's undisciplined troops soon scattered in all directions. A messenger raced from the battlefield to bring Shahryar the bad news. The next day, Asaf, Dawar, the nobles, and the imperial army entered the Lahore fort. Most of Shahryar's men deserted him and joined Asaf's camp. Shahryar hid in a corner of his late father's harem.

A trusted eunuch brought Shahryar out of the harem, his hands bound with the sash from his waist, and led him to Dawar, who sat on the throne inside the citadel of Lahore, surrounded by courtiers under the control of Asaf. When Shahryar's hands were released, he offered the emperor *taslim*, placing the back of his right hand on the ground, raising it gently as he stood erect, and placing the palm of his hand upon the crown of his head. But the obeisance did Shahryar no good. At Asaf's orders, imperial guards imprisoned the prince in an isolated section of the fort. Two days later he was blinded.

Asaf sent a second message to Shah Jahan, begging him to proceed to Lahore "on wings of haste to rescue the world from fitna."[16] Dawar was doing his job as a stopgap, but, Asaf feared, a shake-up was still possible while Nur Jahan was near and Shah Jahan was absent.

Nur Jahan almost certainly would have prolonged the struggle for the Mughal throne if she could have, but she was left with no options. All the leading nobles and military leaders had joined her brother's camp. There's no record of her whereabouts during Shahryar's uprising, imprisonment, and blinding and Dawar's very short reign. She wasn't in the Lahore fort: more likely, she was a political prisoner in Shahdara, where she would build the tomb of her late husband.

Shah Jahan got the news of his father's death in the third week of November. After four days of mourning and consultations with astrologers, he set out for Agra. On the way he received his father-in-law Asaf's second message telling of Shahryar's defeat and urging Shah Jahan to hurry. The prince sent a reply ordering Asaf to execute his half-brother Shahryar, the pretend king Dawar, the cousin who'd supported Shahryar, and the cousin who'd fought with Asaf—a command his court chroniclers later described as decisive and forceful. Having thus eliminated all other possible contenders for the crown, Shah Jahan marched north in a triumphal procession. Along the way, regional landlords and grandees professed loyalty to the prospective Mughal emperor. In return, he promised new appointments and future honors.

On January 19, 1628, while Shah Jahan was still en route, Asaf consulted with other nobles and had the *khutba* read in Shah Jahan's name in the Hall of Public Audience in Lahore. Dawar, the king with the shortest reign in Mughal history—less than a month—was arrested. He, his brother, Shahryar, and the two cousins Shah Jahan had singled out were executed.

Less than a month later, on February 3, 1628, the day of his accession to the throne, Shah Jahan mounted an elephant and rode through Agra scattering heaps of coins to his right and left. He entered the fort, and sat upon the throne in the Hall of Public Audience. At the same time, he ordered the treasury to strike coins bearing the name of the new emperor of Mughal India.

Shah Jahan rewarded his supporters handsomely. His father-in-law Asaf, the central player in ensuring his accession to the throne, received the highest numerical rank that had ever been given to a noble. In addition to becoming the *wakil*, the highest minister without a specified portfolio, he held the governorships of Lahore and Multan. Shah Jahan bestowed upon him the title Yamin ud-Daula, Right Hand of the State, and he was put in charge of the special imperial seal. Mahabat Khan became the commander-in-chief of the army, and the new emperor replaced several provincial governors with his loyalists.

Besides executing his half-brother and other princes, Shah Jahan ordered the death of Nur's loyalist Sharif ul-Mulk, the defender of Thatta. The new emperor still bore a grudge against the man for once having shot a cannon near the tent of his favorite wife, Arjumand, who was pregnant at the time. Shah Jahan's chroniclers describe these executions as "blessing[s]" rooting out any chance of future "contagion/corruption."[17] Although at the time he rose to power Shah Jahan's attitude toward defeated rivals was harsh, the records show no widespread execution of opposing factions. Like other freshly enthroned Mughal emperors before him, Shah Jahan valued alliance-building with old and new nobles and officers. "The Ancient world turned young again," the chronicler Hadi wrote of the regime change; peace and security prevailed.[18]

In the absence of a man in whose name she could fight, and with no nobles or family members supporting or celebrating her imperial service, Nur could take no further action to retain her position as co-sovereign. Her rise to power had been relatively swift, her fall was even swifter.

The official historians of Shah Jahan's reign deliberately wrote Nur Jahan's merits and accomplishments out of Mughal history. Later records omit all the extraordinary achievements of a twentieth wife who became a co-sovereign, giving audience from the imperial balconies, offering political advice, making laws, shooting a tiger to protect her subjects, commanding a battle on a roaring river, and rescuing a kidnapped emperor. Also effaced from the record is her compassion for the people of the court, the harem, and beyond—the matriarchs she honored, for example, or the orphan girls whose lives she transformed with the marriages she arranged.

When Nur isn't absent from the histories written during the reign of Shah Jahan, she is blamed for the chaos that befell the empire during the final years of Jahangir's reign. A modern scholar who compared two such volumes found that in Mu'tamad Khan's *Iqbalnama* and Kamgar Husaini's *Maathir-i Jahangiri*, descriptions of events related to Mahabat's coup and Shah Jahan's rebellion are exactly the same. He underlines the fact that both these recorders held Nur responsible for the disorder that occurred in the 1620s. This version of events, he writes, "was most probably inserted at the instance of Shah Jahan . . ."[19]

Long before he became emperor, Shah Jahan was obsessed with his "unique place in history."[20] While Jahangir had preferred to write his own straightforward memoir, Shah Jahan was determined to have his royal activities recorded in many volumes by chroniclers writing in the florid and flattering literary style of Abul-Fazl, the author of the *Akbarnama*. These several volumes, known collectively as the *Shah Jahan Nama* or the (Chronicle of the king of the world), were meant not only to highlight Shah Jahan's specialness, but also, in a post-Nur world, reassert the importance of the male line of descent among the Mughals. In the *Shah Jahan Nama*, as in the *Akbarnama*, the genealogical tree began with the Central Asian forefather Timur, also known as Tamerlane—and as "The Lord of the Auspicious Planetary Conjunction." To the string of Shah Jahan's honorifics he added the title Lord of the Auspicious Planetary Conjunction and claimed to be the second Timur. There certainly would be no female co-sovereigns for a second Timur—and no laudatory record of such a woman preceding him.

Shah Jahan may have attempted to erase Nur from history in another way, ambitious but futile. Some scholars have suggested that Shah Jahan withdrew the coins of Nur and Jahangir, "to wipe out all memory of her [Nur Jahan's] erstwhile sway."[21] If such a mandate were indeed issued—though Shahjahani records don't mention it—collecting the coins already in circulation would have been extraordinarily difficult. Even if there were an attempt to withdraw Nur's coins, some survive to this day in museums.[22]

The attempted erasure of Nur Jahan's contributions and accomplishments extended even to Jahangir's tomb. The basic facts about its construction and patronage were hotly contested in the Shahjahani chronicles, and in the public square. In 1660 the writer Muhammad Salih Kanbo described Jahangir's tomb as Shah Jahan's project.[23] The only concession that Kanbo made to Nur Jahan's involvement was a statement that the Heart-Contenting Garden had belonged to the empress, a pleasure garden that she designed and which the couple frequently visited.[24]

Architecture experts and historians, however, have a different view, declaring that Jahangir's tomb was the product of Nur Jahan's vision.[25] Shah Jahan gave the orders for its construction, but the tomb was designed by and built under the supervision of Nur Jahan. It would take her ten years, from 1628 to 1638, to complete this monument to the memory of her husband.

Jahangir, though not a particularly devout Muslim, wanted a tomb that allowed direct connection with the divine. The dilemma for Nur Jahan would have been to reconcile her husband's wish for an uncovered tomb with the requirements of a proper burial. A Mughal architecture expert explains that Nur solved that problem by incorporating some elements of the platform tombs then in fashion. But Jahangir's mausoleum was unique: a "monumental bare plinth," with high minarets at the four corners, open to the sky, the rain, and the clouds, "a symbol of divine mercy."[26] She adds: "The design of Jahangir's tomb was repeated only once, on about half the scale and without corner minarets, in the tomb of Nur Jahan, built by Jahangir's widow herself nearby."[27]

Following Shah Jahan's accession, Nur chose not to stay in the harem, as other elder Mughal women had done. Perhaps if she had, Asaf and Shah Jahan would eventually have turned to her for counsel, as kings and nobles had done with other Mughal matriarchs for generations. Modern biographies of the empress generally conjecture that though she was not in the harem, she lived in strict confinement.

> She had to spend the rest of her life in retirement and seclusion. Shah Jahan fixed an annual pension of rupees two lakhs for her expenses. . . . She spent the rest of her life in Lahore in her personal house near the city. She used to spend lavishly on the needy and the poor. . . . She herself led a very simple life wearing only black garments. She was often seen visiting the grave of her beloved husband accompanied by her . . . attendants.[28]

Yet there is little actual evidence that the eighteen years she lived after Jahangir's death were inactive and empty. Nur's resources as a royal wife and a *nawab*, an aristocratic landowner, were still considerable. An eighteenth-century biographer of Mughal nobles estimated that the estates assigned to her corresponded to a numerical ranking of 30,000 in the *mansab* system devised by Akbar—higher than her father's was.[29] By law, she would have retained these property rights until her death, when they would be returned to the imperial exchequer. And if the records of the British East India Company and other European traders and visitors in India are credible, by 1627 she would have accrued a great deal of profit in commerce. In the event, an aging Nur may well have remained actively engaged in both business and charity.

After Nur passed away, on November 18, 1645, even the *Shah Jahan Nama* acknowledged her greatness:

> In the city of Lahore, the Queen Dowager Nur Jahan Begam—whom it is needless to praise as she had already reached the pinnacle of fame—departed to Paradise in the seventy-second year of her age. . . . The renowned Begam was the chaste daughter of I'timad al-Daula and sister of the late Yamin al-Daula [Asaf Khan]. From the sixth year of the late Emperor's reign, when she was united to him in the bond of matrimony, she gradually acquired such unbounded influence over His Majesty's mind that she seized the reins of government and abrogated to herself the supreme civil and financial administration of the realm, ruling with absolute authority till the conclusion of his reign.[30]

The remarkable fact of Nur Jahan's supremacy emerges undiluted despite the disparaging tone of Shah Jahan's chronicle. In the centuries that followed, the caricature of a besotted, drunken Emperor

Jahangir came to dominate the public imagination as the most likely explanation of Nur's power. And the woman who married Jahangir in her mature years, and ruled with him, was reduced to a paradigm of flighty romantic love. Yet in the Shahjahani histories, in her coins and monuments, in the work of feminist scholars, a much richer and more complete story of Nur's achievements resides. It is as if, no matter what, some people *will* themselves into history.

❧ SIXTEEN ❧

Beyond 1627,
an Epilogue

I slamic history is full of powerful women—Ayisha, wife of the Prophet Muhammad, who fought the Battle of the Camel; Borte, the senior consort of Chingiz Khan; Pari Khanum, the Safavid princess who secured the throne for her brother Isma'il II. Wise matriarchs worked behind the scenes in Mughal India and Ottoman Turkey; so did judicious women counselors in North Africa and the Middle East.[1] Some might say their presence was a central facet of Islam. But faced with the reality of a de facto woman sovereign, most official observers of Nur's achievements, instead of acknowledging that she'd earned her position on the strength of her talents, explained it in terms more palatable (to them) and conceivable (to them): she was a gold-digger and schemer.

Contemporary European observers trapped in their own judgments about feminine power were hardly better. Nur Jahan reminded them of the "overmighty favourites" of the European courts, almost always a man. The European favorite's hold over the monarch was not because of good looks or manners, but rather because he was a "doer," an efficient, effective administrator and political fixer. The favorite often rose because of a "peculiarly lazy" monarch.[2] Until very recently, historians brought a distinct orientalism to bear on the depiction of Jahangir: a drunk, stoned, and oversexed despot, an unexceptional ruler who didn't measure up to his father, Akbar the Great. Several scholars have now taken a hard look at these old-fashioned histories of Jahangir, and reappraised him as a man with diverse talents, an aesthete, nature lover, philosopher open to many doctrines, and curious traveler.

It is fully in keeping with his open-mindedness that having a co-sovereign was no problem for Jahangir. From the moment he became the emperor, he continually challenged limits, including his father Akbar's prescriptions for how an ideal Mughal king should live and be. Drawing upon the wisdom of his early philosophical conversations with the young monk Siddhichandra, Jahangir might well have reminded critics of his co-sovereign that absolutist thinking itself was a heresy.

In a picture likely painted by the brilliant Bishandas, dated 1627, Nur Jahan stands holding a portrait of Jahangir. Standing tall against a forest-green background, she wears a tunic, made of the prized diaphanous muslin that she likely invented, over stylish striped pants. Dark sandalwood paste scents the armpits, and tendrils of wavy hair fall loose down her back.[3]

The painter knew the Indian and Persian literary and painterly tradition of depicting women and men holding portraits.[4] A wife gazes at a portrait of her husband; a princess observes a portrait of herself or of someone else; a lone heroine draws a portrait of her lover or an absent husband.[5] In a Mughal portrait now in the Musée Guimet in Paris, a youngish Jahangir tenderly holds a portrait of his father, Akbar the Great.

Holding: owning, enjoying, viewing, feeling, embracing, continuing, extending.

Jahangir holds his father's image—father to son, ruler to ruler. Nur Jahan holds her husband's portrait, a visual mark of the imperial couple in conversation with each other.

Nur's legacy was furthered in a potent way by Jahanara, the daughter of Arjumand and Shah Jahan. Born in 1614 while her father, then Prince Khurram, was on a campaign against Mewar, young Jahanara accompanied the imperial cavalcade many times. On the road and in court, she could closely observe the activities of Empress Nur, taking them in even if she didn't fully understand their import. Coming of age when her grand-aunt Nur was at the height of her imperial powers, Jahanara would have seen the empress personally supervising the care of young Prince Shuja, discussing family matters with Arjumand, designing buildings, and making vital political decisions with her husband the emperor and her father Ghiyas.

Jahanara was devoted to Sufi practices, but when her mother, Arjumand, by then known as Mumtaz Mahal, died in 1636 giving birth to her fourteenth child, Jahanara took over as the lady of the realm. In that role, she handled imperial duties in place of her mother, enhancing her father's authority and the Islamic face of the empire through her patronage of sacred works, prayer, and pilgrimage, such as the many months she spent in Kashmir with a Sufi spiritual master, Mulla Shah. Her piety is evident in the architectural works she commissioned, such as the Agra mosque and the Mulla Shah mosque in Srinagar, dedicated to her master. According to one art historian, whereas Nur Jahan's constructions were "bold and blunt . . . monumental and exuberant" expressions of her authority, Jahanara's were "sacred commissions," an extension of the "princess's spiritual persona."[6] This scholar is not of the opinion that the architectural works of the "prescient feminist" Nur Jahan were the inspiration for those of the Sufi princess.[7] But Jahanara emulated Nur in an important way. In 1637, a decade after Jahangir's death, and a year after Arjumand's passing, Jahanara asked her father if she could oversee and personally pay for a new mosque being built in Agra on the banks of the Yamuna River, alongside another work in progress—the Taj Mahal, her father's memorial to his late wife, modeled on the tomb Nur had built for her parents.

Jahanara's Agra mosque has a unique feature. Inscriptions frame the main entrance—Persian eulogies praise the detail of the mosque— and its patroness: The mosque was built by Jahanara Begum, who is "Veiled with chastity . . . the pride of her gender. . . . The most honored of the issue of the head of the Faithful [Shah Jahan] . . . "[8]

Only two imperial women had built mosques before Jahanara: Jahangir's mother, Harkha, who had commissioned the Begum Shahi mosque in Lahore in 1611, and Nur, who built the Patthar mosque in Srinagar in 1620. The inscriptions on mosques were usually verses from the Quran, or statements that conveyed a sovereign's policies and attitudes. Jahanara's Persian eulogies had no precedent. But personification of the imperial patroness—inscribing the name of the woman responsible for a remarkable building is exactly the precedent that Nur Jahan had skillfully established. Jahanara, who referred to herself as *faqira* (ascetic) in her Sufi treatises and constantly effaced herself in relation to the divinity she sought, was enchanted by the force of naming. It was there for her to see in everything that her grand-aunt had done.

ACKNOWLEDGMENTS

Writing *Empress* has been a generative and demanding experience. For several years I have been absorbed in trying to understand the gist and consequences of Nur Jahan's sovereignty. We know that she was powerful, yet we didn't know just what that meant. As a historian, the prime irony for me is that the sources that declare Nur Jahan's sovereignty are plentiful, yet no one invoked her as the "Great Mughal Empress." To be able to delve into the politics of how she, as a co-sovereign, was wiped out of the historical and public imagination was the beginning; a great challenge lay in working out what my practice of engaging the plentiful archive would produce. An even bigger task was the form my writing needed to take in order to bring Nur Jahan to the center stage of world history.

This book is what it is because of the remarkable generosity of many individuals and institutions. Lynne Huffer, Leslie Harris, Gyan Pandey, Michael Fisher, Francis Robinson, Colin Johnson, and Narayana Rao read several drafts of this book—and gave sound advice. For suggestions on early drafts, I thank Mary Odem, Rosemary

Magee, Laurie Patton, Wendy Doniger, Rita Gomes, Shalom Gold-man, and Stephen Dale. Allan Sealy, Lois Reitzes, Ralph Gilbert, and Leslee Paul read to see how the historical landscape of India and her history intertwined. Allan suggested that I hold off Jahangir. Thanks to Natasha Trethewey for her interest in my preoccupation with historical evidence. Azra Kidwai, Romila Thapar, Deepa Mehta, Salman Rushdie, Ela Bhatt, Mubarak Ali, Rudrangshu Mukherjee, William Dalrymple, Daren Wang, Namita Gokhale, Meru Gokhale, Shadab Bano, Nadia Maria el-Cheikh, David Page, Susan and Anish Mathai, Mimi Choudhury, Smita Murthy, Steven Hochman, Daniel Weiss, and Elizabeth Hornor have offered unstinting support. Chiki Sarkar first approached me to ask if I would write a "critical biogra-phy" of Nur Jahan: I hope she'll find this book inviting. Allison Busch and Sheldon Pollock gave not only intellectual sustenance, but also their New York home on two occasions. Thanks to Audrey Truschke for the lead on Sanskrit sources, and to Anjali Arondekar, Barbara Ramusack, and Mrinalini Sinha for feminist solidarity.

Sonya Rhea Mace's invitation to join a team of art scholars to study the newly acquired bequest at the Cleveland Museum of Art turned out to be a rewarding experience for me. During the two years when we met on several occasions to absorb the richness of the CMA Mughal collection, I watched closely how art historians touched paintings, how they microscopically looked at every leaf, every bor-der, each feature. A special thanks to Sonya and Marcus Fraser, and to Cathy Bankaim, Pedro Carvalho, and Mohsen Ashtiany. Molly Aitken looked at Nur images repeatedly and shared her ideas. Navina Haidar, Susan Stronge, Catherine Asher, and Robert Skelton have over the years offered valuable insights on art historical materials. Had Walter Melion not been enthralled by *Nur Jahan Loading the Musket*, not just holding it, as he said repeatedly during the Emory faculty trip to China in 2012, I wouldn't have recast a whole chapter around this portrait. I chew on that conversation repeatedly.

Thanks especially to Hossein Samei for help with translating abstruse Persian prose and poetry, and to Devin Stewart and Vincent Cornell, for conversations on Islamic sovereignty. Abdullahi An-Naim of the Emory Law School spent hours discussing the uncertainty around the Friday sermons in parts of the Islamic world. I acknowledge the Emory administration, especially Michael Elliott and Carla Freeman for their support. A fellowship from the Emory Research Council for Arts and Sciences made possible the completion of this book.

August 2016 at the Ring Lake Ranch, Wyoming, was a turning point in the writing of this book. While I couldn't go to Kashmir, I saw the high Alpine appeal that the Mughals would have felt. Special thanks to Andy Blackmun and Amanda Verheul for their hospitality, and for sharing the spectacular hidden history of the Native American petroglyphs. Thanks to Leah for leading us on the long walks through the dizzying mountains. I spent glorious autumn days in September 2017 at the Tool Drop Forge Residency, Hudson, New York, savoring Nur Jahan's spectacular history, doing the final touches. Special thanks to the director, Katharine Daugherty, for her interest in this book.

Parts of this book were presented at a variety of venues. My gratitude to the organizers and the participants: to Sekhar Bandhopadhyay and Michael Gillan and the Australian Association of South Asian Studies, as well as the University of Victoria, Dunedin, and Canterbury (New Zealand); Almut Hoefert and Matthew Mesley, and the University of Zurich; Don Reitzes, the Georgia State University, and Adrian Bailey and Clara Wing-Chung Ho, the Hong Kong Baptist University; Ron Sela, Indiana University; Laurie Patton, Middlebury College; Rudrangshu Mukherjee, Ashoka University; Khushru Irani, the Loft, Pune; Anne Murphy, the University of British Columbia; and Michael Calabria, St. Bonaventure University.

Special thanks to the Emory South Asia librarian, Ellen Ambrosone, for chasing obscure references, and for help with locating images and contacts for permissions. When I couldn't find manuscript reproductions or books, Marie Hansen of Emory Interlibrary Services somehow made them available. The following museums, libraries, and institutions were outstanding in their support and services: the American Institute of Indian Studies (Delhi); the Archaeological Survey of India (Agra); the Aga Khan Foundation (Boston and Geneva); the Cleveland Museum of Art (Cleveland); Harvard Art Museum (Boston); the Victoria & Albert Museum (London); the British Library; the library of the School of Oriental and African Studies (London); and the Rampur Raza Library (Rampur). Thanks also to Aevitas Creative Management, the literary agency that represents my work.

Huge thanks to many colleagues who went out of their way in helping me locate historical materials, and facilitated visits to libraries, museums, and Mughal sites. Rukhsana David put me in touch with Sheikh Mansoor, the grandson of the great painter Haji Muhammad Sharif—the man who in the 1960s painted the empress in her sovereign glory. I am grateful to Rukhsana and to Mr. Mansoor for generously giving me permission to reproduce two paintings. Purnima Mehta, director, AIIS (Delhi), aided my visit to the Rampur Library, and helped with permissions. Mr. R. K. Singh of the Archaeological Survey of India (Agra) arranged several private tours of the Agra Fort, Nur's Ram Bagh, and the Baby Taj. The tour guides in Agra shared heart-gripping stories of Nur Jahan. Thanks to Shahzad Ahmad in Lahore for the interviews; to Anandi Salinas, Juana McGhee, and Tarje Lacy at Emory for technical support; and to Myron McGhee for the author photograph. My undergraduate and graduate students amaze me with their intellectual rigor. I owe thanks for research assistance to Malaika Gutekunst, Sidharth Medakkar, Sayali Bapat, and Faiza Rahman.

Bridget Wagner Matzie is a dream agent. I gave up writing this book at one point, but she didn't let me. I can't thank Bridget enough for her rock-solid support and for her deep care for my intellectual endeavors. As Judy Stone combed through each line of this book, she urged me to ponder over questions that I had overlooked. Carefully and sensitively, she listened to the debates on the lure of the archive, and what constitutes the grounds of history writing. Huge thanks, Judy, for the time and generous attention you gave this project, and for your abiding solidarity. I owe much gratitude to Alane Mason, my editor at Norton, for her wisdom, her faith in me—and for fine-tuning the final work, giving it a refined architecture. Thanks to Ashley Patrick for abundant sustenance that she offered during the production process. She not only helped with permissions but sent scores of email cheer when I was exhausted by the legalities. And what a thoughtful job she did in reading the final manuscript. I am grateful to the Norton production, marketing, and publicity teams, especially to my publicist, Erin Sinesky Lovett.

I acknowledge the affection of my women friends: Lynne Huffer, Leslie Harris, Mary Odem, Rosemary Magee, Maggie Kulyk. My yoga friends, Efrosini (Max) Mandelis, Sue Hunter, Lynda Hill, Atlanta enthusiasts and food activists, formed the Empress Club! I thank them for asking me to read unbaked chapters of this book.

My siblings, parents, partner, and nieces encouraged my preoccupations: I thank Guddan, Reena, Prabhakar—Gyan especially, for sharing many Nur moments—and Fanny, Aashna, and Ananya, superstar nieces, for embracing Nur Jahan.

A particular thanks to my mother, for that delicious storytime, and for long chats across the seas. I hope she—and my father—will be pleased to see *this* Queen of Queens.

Ruby Lal
Atlanta, March 2018

NOTE ON TRANSLITERATION
AND TERMINOLOGY

There is no standard system for transliteration from Persian into English. I have used the modified version of the *IJMES* (*International Journal of Middle East Studies*) system developed and used by Layla S. Diba and Maryam Ekhtiar for their edited volume, *Royal Persian Paintings. The Qajar Epoch, 1785–1925* (New York: I. B. Tauris, 1998). In my narrative I have retained the common English form of all well-known names of persons, places, and Persian texts. Thus: *Baburnama* and *Akbarnama*, rather than *Baburnameh* and *Akbarnameh*; Agra rather than Agreh; and Begum/Beg rather than Bigum/Biyg. Translation of Persian manuscripts and books, unless noted otherwise, is mine.

The original spellings have been retained in quotations. As a result, certain names appear with different spellings in my text, on the one hand, and in some quotations, on the other. In citations throughout the book, all information included in square brackets is mine.

A note on terminology: There are no words in Persian, the chief language of the Mughal court, that translate precisely as "emperor and empress" or "king and queen"; these are titles sometimes used by Europeans in Nur's day to describe Mughal monarchs, by those who later translated Mughal chronicles and court documents, and by modern-day English-speakers. The official titles of the Mughal ruler we'd call emperor or king included a variety of terms in a variety of languages. Jahangir, for example, was called in Persian Padshah (Great King) and Shahanshah (King of Kings), and in Arabic Al-Sultan-al-Azan (The Great Authority). In 1616, Jahangir bestowed on his wife the Persian name Nur Jahan Begum; *begum* was an honorific reserved for eminent wives and respected elder women. Later, Nur would issue imperial edicts as co-sovereign, an unprecedented act for a woman, using the official signature in Persian, *Nur Jahan Padshah Begum*. She was also referred to by the Perso-Arabic term *malika*, or queen. For the purposes of this book, I refer to Nur Jahan as empress.

KEY BIOGRAPHICAL DETAILS

ABDUR-RAHIM KHAN-I KHANAN (D. 1626)*

Translator of the *Baburnama* from Chaghatai Turkish to Persian, versatile Hindi poet and an able general, Abdur-Rahim was the son of Akbar's guardian and mentor, Bairam Khan, and stepson of Salimeh Begum. He employed Sher Afgan, Nur Jahan's first husband, during a campaign in Sind. Nobles whom Shah Jahan wooed to his side during his rebellion included Abdur-Rahim. Eventually that alliance broke and Abdur-Rahim returned to the imperial camp.

ABUL-HASAN, PAINTER (B. 1588–89)

Son of the Persian painter Aqa Riza, Abul-Hasan studied closely with his father, and as a mature painter was most active at the court of the fourth Mughal, Emperor Jahangir. He came in contact with a wide range of artists, played masterfully with ideas of light and composition, and painted some remarkable portraits, including those of the Mughal empress Nur

---

* Only the dates confirmed in the historical records are noted next to each entry. Biographical details of historical figures (such as Asaf Khan) are given only as far as the reigns of Jahangir and Nur Jahan.

Jahan and emperor Jahangir. In 1618, the emperor awarded him the title
Nadir uz-Zaman—Zenith of the World or Wonder of the Age.

AKBAR (1542–1605)

Jalal ad-Din Muhammad Akbar, born in October 1542 in Amarkot (now
in Sindh province, Pakistan) was one of the greatest emperors of India.
Son of Hamideh Banu Begum and the second Mughal king Humayun,
Akbar succeeded to the throne at the age of thirteen. A contemporary of
Elizabeth I, he reigned for four decades, extending Mughal power over the
greater part of India and securing the northwest frontier by recapturing
Kabul and Kandahar. A humanist, he remained dedicated to Islam, and
took an active interest in other religions and denominations. His court
drew world attention and attracted a wave of aristocrats and creative people from Persia, Afghanistan, and Central Asia. At the heart of Akbar's
success was his pluralist outlook.

ARJUMAND BANU (1593–1631)

The niece of Nur Jahan, and the daughter of Nur Jahan's brother Asaf
Khan, Arjumand married the third son of Emperor Jahangir, Mughal
prince Khurram (later known by his regnal name, Shah Jahan). He conferred upon her the title Mumtaz Mahal, the Elect of the Palace. She
bore fourteen children, including Jahanara Begum (Shah Jahan's favorite
daughter). Arjumand died in Burhanpur in the Deccan during the birth of
her fourteenth child. Shah Jahan built the Taj Mahal—meant to represent
her house in paradise—as a mausoleum for her.

ASAF KHAN (1569–1641)

Son of the eminent Mughal courtier, the Persian Ghiyas Beg, he was
named Abul-Hasan at birth. Mughal Emperor Jahangir elevated him as
Asaf Khan, the name by which he is remembered. His younger sister was
Empress Nur Jahan, and his daughter, Arjumand Banu, married Prince
Khurram/Shah Jahan. Asaf Khan held several stellar courtly positions

under Jahangir. After the emperor's demise in 1627, he was instrumental in securing the accession of his son-in-law Shah Jahan.

ASMAT BEGUM (D. 1621)

She was the granddaughter of Aqa Mulla Dawatdar (Ink-Stand Holder) Qazwini, one of the chief courtiers of the Persian monarch Shah Tahmasp. Asmat's family and that of Ghiyas Beg, her husband, had intermarried extensively. In the late 1570s, she accompanied her husband and two sons and a daughter from Iran to India. Pregnant with her fourth child at the time, she gave birth to Mihr un-Nisa, the future Mughal empress Nur Jahan, outside Kandahar. Jahangir records Asmat as a lively and large-spirited woman in his *Jahangirnama*.

BABUR (1483–1556)

The first Mughal king, Babur—poet, wanderer, and the author of the *Baburnama*—descended from Central Asian heroes, Chingiz Khan (1167–1227) on his mother's side, and Timur (1336–1405) on his father's. Babur's paternal grandfather parceled out his empire to his sons. It was over these possessions, provinces controlled by uncles, or cousins of varying degrees, that Babur fought with close and distant relatives for much of his life. During a protracted struggle for the coveted city Samarqand, Timur's capital, Babur lost the territory his father bequeathed to him. By about 1504, he was driven to Kabul, and eventually in 1526 defeated Ibrahim Lodi of Delhi and inaugurated the Mughal rule.

DAI DILARAM

Dilaram nursed Nur Jahan when she was an infant, and stayed with the empress all through her life, becoming prominent as a harem officer. No records give specifics of her life and therefore it cannot be determined with certainty whether she left Iran at the same time as Asmat and Ghiyas and helped with Nur's birth on the way. Dilaram, variously called Dai Dilaram and Dilarani in historical records, became the superintendent of the female servants of the palace during Nur and Jahangir's co-sovereignty, although no date for this appointment is to be found in the records.

DAWAR BAKHSH (1603–1628)

His name means "God Given," and Dawar became famous in Mughal history as the king with the shortest reign, following the death of his grandfather, Jahangir. The eldest son of Prince Khusraw (the eldest son of Jahangir), he became a pawn in the political game around the Mughal throne in 1627. Asaf Khan declared Dawar the emperor, a stopgap arrangement to counter the claims of Nur Jahan, who wanted her son-in-law Shahryar as the king. Asaf thereby ensured the succession of Shah Jahan.

FARID BHAKKARI

He served in several provinces of the Mughal Empire in financial and revenue capacities, as well as a news reporter. He notes being in the retinue of Mughal officers, and in Jahangir's Kashmir camp in 1619. In 1631, he was with Mahabat Khan, and in 1642, he joined the expedition against the chief of the Punjab hills. He was the author of a pioneering biographical dictionary of nobles, scholars, and other influential Mughals. Bhakkari's work, the *Dhakhiratul Khawanin*, completed in 1650, is a rare compilation of non-official facts, and was a major source for the eighteenth-century *Maathir-Ul-Umara*, the biographical dictionary of Mughal nobles.

GHIYAS BEG (D. 1622)

Famous in history as I'timad ud-Daula, the Pillar of the State, an honor conferred upon him by his son-in-law, Jahangir, Ghiyas Beg was one of the most distinguished Persian nobles of the Mughal Empire. Born in Tehran, he belonged to a distinguished family of poets and high officials. After the death of his father in 1576, Ghiyas Beg migrated to India. The third Mughal emperor, Akbar, enrolled Ghiyas into imperial service, and thus began his Indian career. His fortunes increased massively during the reign of Akbar's son and successor Jahangir, who in 1611 married Ghiyas's daughter Nur Jahan and appointed him as his chief minister. Ghiyas Beg died near Kangra in 1622. Nur Jahan commissioned a burial place, unprecedented in style and concept, for Asmat and Ghiyas, on the right bank of the Yamuna River.

GULBADAN BEGUM (1523–1603)

Gulbadan Begum, the daughter of Babur, traveled to Agra from Afghanistan at the age of six and a half, after her father had made substantial conquests in that region. An unusual witness to the emerging Mughal monarchy from its inception in the early conquests of Babur to its majesty in the reign of Akbar, she recorded what she had seen in her memoir, the *Ahval-i Humayun Badshah* (literally, conditions in the time of Humayun Badshah). The *Ahval*, a unique piece of writing, the only example of prose by a Mughal woman, is the best document on Mughal domestic life, and the character of the empire as it was taking shape. As an elderly woman, in 1578, Gulbadan led the senior women of Akbar's harem for a pilgrimage to Mecca, braved the hazards of treacherous seas and unknown territories— including a year at Aden in the Red Sea after their ship was wrecked.

HAMIDEH BANU BEGUM (1527–1604)

It is difficult to precisely chart Hamideh Banu's family tree, but sources suggest that she was a descendent of a renowned saint. Prominent as the revered mother of Emperor Akbar, Hamideh fits well the trajectory of Mughal women who animated the royal circles with their presence, support, and wisdom born of age. She married Humayun, the second Mughal king of India, at Pat in the summer of 1541, and gave birth to Akbar in 1542 while the royals were in exile. Hamideh surfaces frequently in the Mughal sources, especially in the *Akbarnama*. She sought forgiveness on behalf of Prince Salim, future Jahangir. She did not join the party of senior women pilgrims that Gulbadan Begum led, and likely stayed back to support Akbar.

JADRUP

Jadrup was a noted Vaishnavite ascetic of high acclaim. With his guidance, Emperor Jahangir came to believe that the Vedantic philosophy of Hindus and the Sufi thoughts of Muslims were similar. The emperor followed Jadrup and met him whenever he could. Jahangir writes about these meetings in his memoir and gives fascinating details of the space of their gatherings, the discussion, and the decorum. A fine painting from Jahangir's court depicts the meeting between Jadrup and the emperor.

JAGAT GOSAIN (D. 1619)

Wife of the Mughal emperor Jahangir, and the mother of his successor, Shah Jahan, she was a Rajput princess of Marwar (present-day Jodhpur). After submitting to the Mughals, her father decided in 1586 to give Jagat Gosain in marriage to Jahangir, then Prince Salim. Their son was named Khurram ("joyous") by Akbar. Ruqayya Begum, Akbar's childless wife, assumed the primary responsibility for Khurram's upbringing and he grew up under her care. Legends depict immense tension that Jagat Gosain displayed toward her archrival in the imperial harem, Nur Jahan, co-sovereign, indisputably the emperor's favorite wife. Jahangir noted Jagat's passing briefly in his memoir.

JAHANGIR (1569–1627)

Born Prince Salim, Jahangir, Seizer or Conqueror of the World, was a much-coveted son of Akbar the Great. Although he built his rule upon the groundwork established by his father, Jahangir gave it a more intimate and experimental character. He looked up more to his great-grandfather Babur as a model rather than the indomitable Akbar. His memoir, the *Jahangirnama* follows the style of Babur's writing, famous for unusual detail. Among other records, it is in the pages of the *Jahangirnama* that we best meet Nur Jahan, the emperor's last wife, with whom he shared the Mughal imperium and power. Art, especially portraiture and Mughal albums with portraits became a landmark contribution of his reign. The last years of his and Nur's reign were marred by an open crisis when his son, Khurram, fearing that he would be excluded from the throne, rebelled in 1622. The rebellion and court intrigues that followed took a heavy toll on Jahangir's health, and he died in 1627.

KHAFI KHAN (D. ~1732–33)

Muhammad Hashim, also called Hashim Ali Khan, is known as Khafi Khan—Khafi means "concealed"—the chronicler of the Mughal Empire. He worked as a trade agent in Surat, and in the last years of the reign of Mughal emperor Aurangzeb (r. 1658–1689), and into the time of Muhammad Shah (r. 1719–1748), he served in various military capacities. He then served under the first Nizam of Hyderabad, who employed him as a revenue officer. His invaluable work, *Muntakhab-ul Lubab*, details the history of Nur Jahan's birth and life and also records her poems.

KHUSRAW (1587–1622)

A solemn figure in Mughal history, the eldest son of Jahangir and his first wife, Man Bai, Khusraw was a beloved grandson of Akbar, as well as of several imperial women. Deeply disappointed with Jahangir toward the end of his reign, Akbar had wanted Khusraw to succeed as the next ruler. Upon Jahangir's succession, Khusraw went into rebellion. Partially blinded, he was imprisoned in Agra. He remained under the watchful eyes of Asaf Khan, and was later under the similarly watchful eyes of his younger brother, Prince Khurram. He died in the Deccan in 1622.

LADLI BEGUM

The only daughter of Nur Jahan (then Mihr un-Nisa) and her first husband, Sher Afgan, Ladli Begum was born in Burdwan, Bengal. The date of her birth and death is not recorded. She married the Mughal prince Shahryar, according to the wishes of her mother, Nur Jahan. There are stray references to Ladli in the Mughal records. The two descriptions in the memoir of her stepfather, Jahangir, are the lengthiest and detail the moment of her betrothal and wedding with Jahangir's youngest son, Shahryar.

MAHABAT KHAN (D. 1634)

From a family in Shiraz, Zamana Beg (entitled Mahabat Khan by Jahangir) joined the service of Prince Salim as a trooper. When Jahangir became the emperor, impressed with Mahabat's loyalty and service, he repeat-edly increased his ranks and deputed him against the rebellious Prince Khusraw. Mahabat also joined Khurram's campaign against Mewar, and was posted in the Deccan along with other officers. His relations with the family of Nur Jahan were strained. He took Jahangir into custody in 1626. Nur Jahan fought a battle to rescue Jahangir, and initially lost, but was later able to free him. Mahabat was sent to Sind, but he joined Shah Jahan.

NICCOLAO MANUCCI (1638–1720)

Born in Venice, he left for Corfu in 1651. With the help of an English-man, he then went to Persia and on to Delhi in India. Under the tutelage of Jesuit fathers, he learned Persian, and dedicated himself to studying medicine. By 1656, he was employed as an artilleryman in the service of Prince Dara Shukoh, the son of Arjumand and Shah Jahan. At different points he attempted to serve as an intermediary between the Mughals and the Portuguese. From 1707, until his death, he spent time between Madras and Pondicherry. Written in five parts, his work *Storia Do Mogor* was first translated in three volumes by William Irvine of the Indian Civil Service.

MUHAMMAD HADI

Muhammad Hadi Kamwar Khan, an eighteenth-century court historian is well known to modern historians as Muhammad Hadi, the man who added a continuation to Emperor Jahangir's memoir from 1624 (where Mu'tamad Khan stopped; see below) and brought it to the point of Jahangir's death in 1627. Author of several other chronicles, he was a contemporary of the Mughal emperor Aurangzeb, and in the fifty-fourth year of Aurangzeb's reign, he went to Ahmadabad in the company of the paymaster general. Not much is recorded about his life other than the facts associated with his writing.

MULLA KAMI SHIRAZI (D. ~1635–36)

Very little is known about the life of Mulla Kami Shirazi, a Shi'a Muslim from Shiraz, who served the Mughals in various capacities and traveled with the court in 1626 when Jahangir was kidnapped. He lived for some time in Ahmadnagar, then Sind, and Agra during Akbar's reign. Part of the royal retinue, Shirazi saw Nur lead her men into battle in 1626. He wrote a long composition in rhyming couplets called *Waqi'at uz-zaman* (The events of the time), which he dedicated to Nur Jahan. Included in it was a long segment entitled *Fathnama-i Nur Jahan Begum* (Chronicle of the victory of Nur Jahan Begum). Shirazi's account of Nur's victory is the only part of his larger composition that survives. In 1976, an officer of the Archaeological Survey of India located the epitaph that noted his death from a graveyard in Hyderabad, likely where he lived after Jahangir's death.

MU'TAMAD KHAN

He served as the paymaster of troopers before receiving higher offices from Jahangir. His fortune rose when he looked after the Mughals Nur Jahan and Jahangir on their first journey to Kashmir, making arrangements in the midst of a heavy spring snowfall. In 1622, Jahangir instructed him to continue the writing of his memoir because the emperor fell rather ill. Mu'tamad did so, regularly submitting the memoirs to Jahangir for editing and correction until 1624. Mu'tamad Khan wrote another account, called the *Iqbalnama-i Jahangiri*, which drew heavily from the emperor's memoirs. We do not have the precise dates, but Farid Bhakkari notes that Mu'tamad died in the reign of Shah Jahan.

NUR JAHAN (1577–1645)

Daughter of Ghiyas Beg and Asmat Begum, she was born on the road outside Kandahar, as her parents fled Persia. They called her Mihr un-Nisa—Sun of Women. She married Sher Afgan in 1594 and lived in Burdwan in Bengal until 1608, where her only daughter, Ladli, was born. In 1611, Nur married Jahangir, and rose to be an astute politician, governing as co-sovereign along with her husband. She acquired new names symbolic of her rise and shared sovereignty: Nur Mahal upon marriage (Light of the Palace) and Nur Jahan (Light of the World). As co-sovereign Nur issued imperial orders over her signature, coins of the realm bore her name, and she gave audience from an elaborately carved balcony high up in the palace. An ingenious architect, she innovated the use of marble in her parents' tomb, the jewel-box mausoleum on the banks of the Yamuna that inspired her stepson's Taj Mahal. She fought hard to retain her imperial rights after Jahangir's death, but lost to Shah Jahan's faction, whom her brother Asaf Khan backed strongly. She would live to be sixty-eight.

SIR THOMAS ROE (~1580–1644)

Born in Leyton, Thomas Roe entered Magdalen College in Oxford in the early 1590s, eventually becoming an esquire of the Body to Queen Elizabeth. In 1603, he was knighted by James I. Although he became Member of Parliament for Tamworth for the year 1614, his resources were threadbare. He went to India on the *Lion* in February 1615 and reached Ajmer in December 1615, having made acquaintance with Prince Parvez in Burhanpur. He went back to England in February 1619. Later he reentered Parliament for Oxford and served in a variety of other political positions. He wrote an account of his embassy to Mughal India.

RUQAYYA BEGUM (D. 1626)

One of the longest living matriarchs of the Mughal Empire, she was the first wife of Emperor Akbar. She was also the emperor's first cousin, a Mughal princess by birth. She had no children of her own and raised Akbar's grandson, Khurram. As a senior Mughal woman, she was instrumental in forging peace between Akbar and her stepson, Jahangir, paving the way for his accession to the throne. Ruqayya was an important Mughal guide for Mihr un-Nisa when she came to the harem. Jahangir wrote fondly of Ruqayya in his memoirs and recorded her death. Her burial place is in the Garden of Babur (Bagh-e-Babur) in Kabul, Afghanistan.

SALIMEH SULTAN BEGUM (D. 1613)

Salimeh was the granddaughter of Babur. In 1557 she accompanied Gulbadan and Hamideh Banu to Agra and she was married shortly after that to Akbar's regent, Bairam Khan. After Bairam's death in 1561, Salimeh married her first cousin Akbar. A senior wife of Akbar, she was central in pleading forgiveness on behalf of Prince Salim and wielded much influence in his eventual succession to the throne. She was one of the senior women who accompanied Gulbadan on the hajj. Along with Ruqayya, she guided Mihr un-Nisa upon her arrival in Agra. There is some uncertainty about the date of her death. Jahangir records it as 1613 in Agra. Mentioned repeatedly as a cultured and wise woman, Jahangir notes particulars of Salimeh's birth and ancestry, her marriages, and her death.

SHAH JAHAN (1592–1666)

Son of Jahangir and Jagat Gosain, his grandfather Akbar named him Khurram ("joyous"). Khurram emerged as a successful young prince, heading major campaigns in Mewar and the Deccan, outshining his older brothers Khusraw and Parvez. Things turned around when Jahangir married Nur Jahan, a central figure in the empire. The relations between Nur and Khurram were cordial and close by all accounts: both were ambitious and politically astute. They were both part of an intricate family web, given that Khurram married Nur's niece, Arjumand, his second wife. When Nur had her daughter, Ladli, marry the youngest Mughal prince, Khurram, fearing his future was in jeopardy, went into rebellion. Asaf Khan was central in securing Khurram's accession in 1627. Shah Jahan built the Taj Mahal, one of the Seven Wonders of the World.

SHAHRYAR (1605–1628)

Jahangir's youngest son, he was born to a concubine, unnamed in the emperor's memoir or in other records. Nur Jahan arranged his marriage to her daughter, Ladli. In the battle for succession after Jahangir's death, he lost to his elder brother Shah Jahan. At Shah Jahan's orders, along with other princes, he was executed.

SHER AFGAN (D. 1608)

Ali Quli Istajlu, well known by his later name, Sher Afgan, or Tiger Slayer, that Jahangir gave him, was a table attendant of Shah Isma'il II of Iran (1576–78). He fled Iran when the shah was murdered at the end of his brief reign. Abdur-Rahim, who commanded the Mughal army in Sind, employed Quli and later recommended him for a position at the Mughal court. He married Mihr un-Nisa and lived with her in Burdwan till 1608. They had a daughter named Ladli. Implicated in a plot against Jahangir, he was killed in a brawl with the Mughal governor in 1608. His tomb is in Burdwan.

NOTES ON SOURCES

My work as a feminist historian has focused on two interrelated questions: First, how can I best tell the stories of women and girls, which are largely missing from the precolonial and colonial history of South Asia? Then, what counts as evidence, and therefore as history?

One answer to both questions has involved using sources that other historians have ignored. In my first book, *Domesticity and Power in the Early Mughal World*, I delved deeply into the memoir of the elderly sixteenth-century Mughal princess Gulbadan Banu Begum—Princess Rosebody—daughter of Babur, the first Mughal. Scholars have long been aware of the memoir, written when Gulbadan was seventy at the behest of her nephew Akbar (and translated into English in 1902), but had used it only peripherally. I decided to read it line by line in the original Persian, and found it to be a treasure, an astute and detailed account of the daily lives of women in the Mughal court, yielding information otherwise effaced from the official record. In my second book, *Coming of Age in Nineteenth-Century India: The Girl-Child and the Art of Playfulness*, my aim once more was to illuminate a feminine world missing from the record, again using sources, some untranslated and some unknown or disregarded by earlier historians, which provided depictions of domestic spaces in fiction, textbooks, ethical treatises, and oral histories.

In writing this book, I revisited Gulbadan's rarely consulted memoir for insights into the world that Nur Jahan and Jahangir inherited and inhabited. In order to advance our knowledge about the women of the Mughal harem and their essential role in politics and empire formation, I had to challenge a commonly held belief summed up by a male colleague: "How are you going to write a history of Mughal women, their relationship with the court and empire?" he asked me. "There are no sources for it!" It was to counter that belief that I returned to Gulbadan. What she wrote wasn't a standard encomium; it doesn't fit into any recognized genre of her time. Her memoir covers Mughal women's multifarious concerns and negotiations: the difficulties of childbirth, unfulfilled desires, anticipation, marriages, love and death, war and peace, ritual and celebration. This compelling piece of writing helped bring to view a polychromatic women's world. Momentously, in the light of her memoir, the standard, dry Mughal chronicles appeared multidimensional. Events that earned only a single line in official (male) records sometimes acquired a different significance thanks to Gulbadan's wide-ranging discussions of exactly the same occasions.

I also turned to other primary sources in Persian, foremost among them Jahangir's memoir, the *Jahangirnama*, which he wrote himself between 1605 and 1622, then turned over to a trusted noble when he fell ill. In Jahangir's accounts, Nur Jahan emerges as a sensitive consort, a skilled politician, and a talented woman. The emperor made his first entry about Nur Jahan in 1614, and over the years he included more than thirty discussions of the empress that include praise of her many talents and descriptions of personal moments—a vivid record depicting an outstanding royal woman and her actions.

Mu'tamad Khan, who took over Jahangir's memoir when the emperor became ill and wrote it until 1624, also composed the *Iqbalnama-i Jahangiri*, a history of Jahangir's reign, drawing heavily from the emperor's memoirs. In the eighteenth century a court historian named Muhammad Hadi added a continuation of the *Jahangirnama* from 1624 to the point of Jahangir's death in 1627. The *Jahangirnama* of Jahangir—and to a certain extent the *Iqbalnama* of Mu'tamad Khan—are, in a sense, the only "official" history of Jahangir's reign. Jahangir did not commission professional chroniclers to record the events of his rule, but did so himself. A fascinating change, given that his father, Akbar the Great, had initiated the imperial practice of recording the life and history of his empire: commissioning official histories, gazetteers, and innumerable other reports and accounts of the empire, including the first Mughal painting atelier.

Nur Jahan herself left no memoir or diary. But ten of her imperial orders survive, and so do several lines of her poetry. Artists painted her portrait; curious observers, diplomats, court visitors, tradesmen, chroniclers, and critics of the empire wrote zealously about her; each, of course, observing and assessing through his—it was always a he—own cultural lens. Mulla Kami Shirazi, who served the Mughals in various capacities and traveled with the court in 1626 when Jahangir was kidnapped by a disaffected noble, wrote a lavishly laudatory *fathnama*—a proclamation of victory—about Nur soon after her rescue of her husband. Persian writers documented Nur Jahan's achievements in the form of biographical entries in encyclopedic works. Notable among these is one transcribed in 1650, in which the author discusses 368 Mughal male nobles and only *one* distinguished woman—Nur Jahan. Carefully read and interpreted from a feminist viewpoint, these sources—only a handful of examples of the wide range of the archives I've used for this book—yielded provocative and extensive evidence of the forces that formed Nur and allowed her to flourish, and allowed me to fill in the daily details of her private and public life.

I dived deeply into the Persian court records. Nur is there, it turns out; all we have to do is to look for her, which sometimes entails peering around the towering figures of men. For example, to tell the story of Nur's parents' migration from Iran to India during the time of Akbar the Great, her father's employment at the court, and Nur's upbringing, I've used a number of Akbari court chronicles, and a three-volume history written in secret by a severe critic of Akbar's policies. To re-create the details of her girlhood, I looked into conduct books—guides to childrearing in the Islamic world that were used at the time she was growing up.

I also consulted later court histories, written after Nur's death in 1645, which often conflated the historical and the legendary. In the eighteenth century, for instance, Khafi Khan, an agile writer who served the last grand Mughal, Aurangzeb, drew inspiration from works written during the reign of Jahangir and his successor, Shah Jahan. Khafi Khan embellished Nur's history, shaping the most magical legends of Nur Jahan's birth and life. It was he who first published the story of the infant Nur's abandonment by her parents. He also sketches an intense rivalry between Nur and another of Jahangir's wives, complete with detailed scenes worthy of *Real Housewives of the Harem.*

Did these things actually happen? I can't say for certain. For a feminist historian, the most useful thing about the legends is what they reveal about the cultural and political forces that made them necessary or influenced their details. Though not entirely factual, these legends and others are fact-adjacent; they tell us about what the public believed, what persisted, what people thought about the role and character of women. At the very least, they tell us what a man writing in eighteenth-century India thought about a remarkable seventeenth-century woman.

Writing the history of Nur Jahan has posed another challenge for me, aside from the question of the archive and the politics of claiming history. Often, I've had to roll up my sleeves and work out specifics that are treacherous. For instance: What was the precise character of political and economic events in the eastern provinces where Nur lived after her first wedding? There are no details in the record of her life per se, but we have enough indication of the tension between the capital and the provinces, and about Bengali life at the time, to fill in some blanks. Another example: The seventeenth-century names of many towns, rivers, and mountains are not to be found on the modern map. This has meant studying closely the landscape and geography of that region in order to establish the location of the particular villages and towns.

Regarding the travels of the Mughals: Medieval European monarchs left formal itineraries available to scholars; the Mughals did not. Charting the whereabouts of the Mughals is possible, especially for Emperor Jahangir, who wrote copiously about his every move until 1624, though the task is time-consuming because his stream-of-consciousness journal can be confusing. In the matter of travel as in all other aspects of Mughal life, the record offers clues for the careful, crafty, and patient scholar. If God is in the details, then writing this book has meant reaching for the godly by constantly poring over the worldly.

NOTES

There is a great deal of fine writing on Mughal history and the wider Islamic world in the sixteenth and seventeenth centuries. I have opted not to give an exhaustive bibliography. The following notes provide details of archives and books that are central to the life and times of the Mughal empress Nur Jahan.

ONE: QUEEN OF QUEENS, AN INTRODUCTION

1. For detailed discussion of the royal hunt, and its use, especially in cavalry, Jos Gommans, *Mughal Warfare: Indian Frontiers and High Roads to Empire, 1500–1700* (London and New York: Routledge, 2003), 110–11.
2. Augustin Hiriart about Jahangir's court, cited in Ibid., 99.
3. *Portrait of Nur Jahan*, the Rampur Raza Library, India. Milo Cleveland Beach suggested the date of composition between 1612 and 1615 in *The Grand Mogul: Imperial Painting in India, 1600–1660* (Williamstown, MA, 1978), 90. In the catalogue of the Rampur Raza Library, it is dated 1617, in English, as part of the exhibit where it was included. In the most recent edition by Milo C. Beach, Eberhard

Fischer, and B. N. Goswamy (ed.), *Masters of Indian Painting* (Artibus Asiae Publishers, 2011), Nur's portrait is entitled *Portrait of Nur Jahan* and the date ascribed is 1612–13. Sanam Ali Khan provided the details used above from the Rampur Raza Library conservation lab's treatment records, letter dated November 24, 2013, 2–3.

4. On Mathura and its environs, scattered comments are found in Jahangir's memoir. For a fuller description of Mathura, F. S. Growse, *Mathura: A District Memoir* (1st ed, 1882; New Delhi: Asian Educational Services, 1993 repr.), especially 21, 27, 32–38, and chapter 4.

5. Alexander Rogers and Henry Beveridge (eds.), *Tuzuk-i Jahangiri or Memoirs of Jahangir*, 2 vols. (London: The Royal Asiatic Society, 1909), cited as *Tuzuk; Tuzuk*, 2:104–5. For the Persian edition, Muhammad Hashim (ed.), *Jahangirnamah, Tuzuk-i Jahangiri* (Tehran: Intisharat-i Bunyad-i Farhang-i Iran, 1980). For a more reader-friendly translation, W. M. Thackston, *The Jahangirnama: Memoirs of Jahangir, Emperor of India* (New York: Oxford University Press, 1999). Thackston's translation covers the eighteenth-century account of Muhammad Hadi. Hadi advanced Mu'tamad's account, added a continuation from 1624, and brought his chronicle to the point of Jahangir's death in 1627.

6. Mu'tamad Khan, *The Iqbalnama-i Jahangiri* (Calcutta: The Asiatic Society of Bengal, 1865); English translation of some sections of this text are available in H. M. Elliott and John Dowson, *The History of India as Told by Its Own Historians*, 6 vols. (Allahabad: Kitab Mahal Pvt. Ltd. 1964, 1st Indian ed.); *Iqbalnama-i Jahangiri*, 405. Among others who noted similar comments about Nur Jahan were Farid Bhakkari: Z. A. Desai (tr.), *Nobility Under the Great Mughals: Based on Dhakhiratul Khawanin of Shaikh Farid Bhakkari*, Parts 1–3 (New Delhi: Sundeep Prakashan, 2003), 14; Muhammad Hadi in the eighteenth century: *Tatimma-i Vaqi'at-I Jahangiri*, in Elliott and Dowson, *The History of India*, 6:398–99. And in an invaluable biographical dictionary of Mughal nobles compiled in alphabetical order, from the time of the first Mughal to the eighth decade of the eighteenth century: Desai. H. Beveridge (tr.) and Baini Prashad (compiled and annotated), Shah Nawaz Khan and Abdul Hayy, *The Maathir-Ul-Umara*, 3 vols. (Patna: Janaki Prakashan, 1979), 2:1077.

7. *Iqbalnama-i Jahangiri*, 405.

8. F. Hill Rivington, [*Nur Jahan.*] *Grieve Not for Me.* [*Song.*] *From the Opera Nur Jahan. Words and Music by F. H. Rivington* (London: Weekes & Co, 1925); T. B. Krishnaswami, *Nur Jehan: a Play in Five Acts* (Madras: Modern Print Works, 1918); Mirza Qalic Beg, *Nur Jahan 'ain Jahangir nataku: hikro tankhi nataku/joriyalu* (Sakhar: Harīsinghu Penshinaru ain Tājir Kutub, 1900; historical drama in Sindhi); Guru Bhakta Simha, *Nur Jahan* (Ballia: n.p., 1935); Mathura-prasada, *Nur Jahan Begam* (Lucknow: n.p., 1905); Jogendra Singh, *Nur Jahan: The Romance of an Indian Queen* (London: James Nisbet, 1909); G. Devasher, *The Otto of Roses. A Romance of Nur Jahan's Times* (Bombay: Orient Longmans, 1969); Hoticandu Mulicandu Gurbakhshaṇi, *Nur Jahanu, Chapo biyo* (Karachi: Tarachand Mang-hanmal, 1930); Jethanad Lalvani, *Maharaṇi Nurjahan: Zabardast Tavarikhi Navil*, 2nd ed. (Bombay: Bharat Jivan Navil Malha, 1964); Dwijendra Lal Roy, *Nurajahaṃ: Naṭaka*, 12th ed. (Bombay: Hindi-grantha-Ratnakara Karyalaya, 1951); Saadat Hasan Manto, *Nur Jahan: Sarur-i Jahan* (Lahore: Makhtabah-yi Shiro Adab, 1975); Pa. Tavutsa, *Nurjahan* (Cennai: Tarul Islam Apis, 1927).

9. Muhammad Husain Azad, *Darbar-i Akbari* (Lahore. n.p., 1888), 187–88. The pigeon story is also found in: Abdul Latif Siddiqi, *Sawanih-Umri Noor Jahan Begum*, (Delhi: n.p., 1918), 9, 13. Other Urdu biographies that use the pigeon story include Khwaja Muhammad Shafi Dihlavi, *Ishq-i Jahangir* (Lahore: n.p., 1957, 1968). Nawab Imad Nawaz Jung of Hyderabad compiled a biography of Nur Jahan titled *Hayat-i Noor Jahan.* He describes the pigeon incident and the romantic meetings of Nur and Jahangir. This book is out of print. For further references to the pigeon legend, see Mohammad and Razia Shujauddin, *The Life and Times of Noor Jahan* (Lahore: The Caravan Book House, 1967), 4–11.

10. William Foster (ed.), *The Embassy of Sir Thomas Roe to India, 1616–19* (Delhi: Munshiram Manoharlal Publishers, 1990, 1st Indian ed.), 89, 337.

11. Sir Richard Carnac Temple (ed.), *The Travels of Peter Mundy in Europe and Asia* (London: The Hakluyt Society, 1914), 2:206.

12. Alexander Dow, *The History of Hindostan* (London: J. Walker, 1812), 3:20–28; Mountstuart Elphinstone, *The History of India: The Hindu*

and Mahometan Periods (London: John Murray, 1857, 4th ed.), 483–84; James Mill, *The History of British India*, ed. Horace Hayman Wilson, 2 vols. (London: James Madden, 1858, 5th ed.), 1: 303, 309, 313.

13. The most useful Mughal women's biographical accounts, aimed at "bringing women to life," were never thought of as serious mainstream histories. These biographies existed in a separate sphere, all its own. At best they came to be seen as mild correctives: there were women too, some of them quite talented! While these studies of Mughal women opened up a neglected area of investigation, the women biographers themselves excluded the possibility of raising new questions about the accepted boundaries of family and household, public and private spheres, gender relations and political power. Rekha Misra, *Women in Mughal India 1526–1748* (New Delhi: Munshiram Monoharlal, 1967); Chandra Pant, *Nur Jahan and Her Family* (Allahabad: Dandewal Publishing, 1978); Renuka Nath, *Notable Mughal and Hindu Women in the 16th and 17th Centuries A.D.* (New Delhi: Inter-India Publications, 1990).

14. Ellison Banks Findly, *Nur Jahan: Empress of Mughal India* (New York: Oxford University Press, 1993), 89, 115, 126.

15. I spent a lot of time researching whether Ghiyas Beg and his family were Shi'a or Sunni, a question I was asked repeatedly. The problem is that the strict boundaries of religious identity that we ascribe to individuals in the modern world is not the way denizens of the premodern worlds lived. Their confessional identities were much more open than we imagine. There is quite a lot of information about Ghiyas Beg's ancestors. The family can be traced back to the Timurid period, when they were part of the urban nobility of Rayy (Tehran close by), which was mostly Shi'ite. The choice of the names that the family members took suggests that they were "culturally" Shi'a with no clearly pronounced strong religious ties. My conversations with several scholars confirmed that even if the family started as Sunnis, they must have converted to Shi'ism under the Safavids, but there was no sign of fervent religiosity. Nur Jahan's first husband, Ali Quli Khan Istalju, or Sher Afgan Khan, was in the service of Safavid king, Ismai'il II. His name, Ali, being from the

Istalju tribe (one of the ten Qizilbash tribes that helped Safavids to power), and serving a king may be some, but not enough, evidence of being Shi'a. On the tomb of Nur Jahan's parents that she built, we find verses from the Quran: from chapters 48 and 73. There is no allusion in these verses that they had anything to do with Shi'a polemical texts. Neither are the first three companions of the Prophet mentioned. Lack of reference to the caliphs says nothing about the confessional identity of the dweller of the tomb. I am grateful to Mohsen Ashtiany, Hossein Semei, Devin Stewart, and Yusuf Anal for conversations on this issue.

16. *Embassy of Sir Thomas Roe*, 89, 337.

TWO: MIRACLE GIRL

The Persian sources that I have consulted for the wider socio-cultural context and the birth of Nur Jahan are as follows: Annette Susannah Beveridge (tr.), *Babur-nama (Memoirs of Babur) of Zahiru'd-din Muham-mad Babur Padshah Ghazi* (1921; reprint, Delhi, 1997); W. M. Thackston (tr. and ed.), *Zahiruddin Muhammad Babur Mirza: Baburnama*, Parts 1–3, Turkish transcription, Persian edition, and English translation (Cambridge, MA: Harvard University Dept. of Near Eastern Studies, 1993); Gulbadan Banu Begum, *Ahval-i Humayun Badshah*, British Library Ms. Or.166; Henry Beveridge (tr.), *The Akbar Nama of Abu-l-Fazl*, 3 vols. (1902–39; reprint Delhi: Low Price Publications, 1993); Maulawi Abdur-Rahim (ed.), *Akbarnamah by Abu-l Fazl I Mubarak I 'Allāmi*, Persian text, 3 vols. (Calcutta: Asiatic Society of Bengal, 1873–1886); Henry Bloch-mann (ed.) and H. S. Jarrett (tr.), *The Ain-i Akbari*, 3 vols. (1873, 1894; reprint Calcutta: Royal Asiatic Society, 1993), Persian text, 3 vols. (Calcutta, 1872–1877); Kabiruddin Ahmad (ed.), Muhmmad Hashim Khafi Khan, *Muntakhab-ul-Lubab*, 2 vols. (Calcutta: Bibliotheca Indica, The Asiatic Society of Bengal, 1869).

1. *Akbar Nama*, 3:311–17; Shireen Moosvi, "Science and Superstition Under Akbar and Jahangir: The Observation of Astronomical Phe-nomenon," in Irfan Habib (ed.), *Akbar and His India* (Delhi: OUP, 1997), 109–20; David A. J. Seargent, *The Greatest Comets in His-*

tory: *Broom Stars and Celestial Scimitars* (New York: Springer, 2009); Arthur Koestler, *The Sleepwalkers: A History of Man's Changing Vision of the Universe* (New York: Penguin, 1990).

2. There is no historical record of the itinerary or the schedule that Asmat and Ghiyas followed in their passage from Persia to the land of the river Indus or Hind-Hindustan, as the northern region along the rivers Ganges and Brahmaputra, under the sway of the Mughals, was called then. But hints in the historical records provide clues and outlines of the likely route. The first Mughal (itinerant) king Babur, and later travelers, sketch evocatively the travel routes, geography, layout, flora and fauna, and pleasures and difficulties of voyages in these regions, which Ghiyas and Asmat were to navigate. Details of references follow below. For the part of the journey that would take Asmat and Ghiyas to the border of Persia, it was logical that they would first follow the popular (and the most direct) ancient route from Khurasan, along the southern slopes of the mountains that constituted the northern limit of the Iranian plateau.

3. Records mention the celebration of Ghiyas's fortieth birthday in 1595. The translator of the Mughal gazetteer of Akbar's reign mentions that a brother of Ghiyas Beg accompanied them as well. In the biographical notices of the grandees of Akbar's empire, appended to the translation of the *Ain-i Akbari*, Jarrett notes that Jafar Beg arrived in India in 1578. No other source discusses this. *Ain-i Akbari*, 1:451. *Rijal* or the biographical literature of the seventeenth-century Mughal nobles, as well as court histories of this and later times give extensive details of Ghiyas Beg's family background and the historical Iranian social and political milieu that may have driven him to India. A rare set of biographical sketches, striking for "non-official" facts, were put together by Shaikh Farid Bhakkari, a contemporary witness of the reign of Jahangir and Nur Jahan, and then of Shah Jahan. It is supposed to have been transcribed soon after its complication in 1650. The *Maathir-Ul-Umara*, an invaluable biographical dictionary of Mughal nobles compiled in alphabetical order, from the time of the first Mughal to the eighth decade of the eighteenth century. Compiled between 1741 and 1780, and drawn on Shaikh Farid above, the history of the production of this compilation is variegated

and complex. The details are available in the Preface of the first volume of the translation, as well as in the introduction by Desai. H. Beveridge (tr.) and Baini Prashad (compiled and annotated), Shah Nawaz Khan and Abdul Hayy, *The Maathir-Ul-Umara*, 3 vols. (Patna: Janaki Prakashan, 1979); Amin Razi, *Haft Iqlim* (Aligarh: Qutbuddin Collections, MS. Persian 100/20). For references to Ghiyas Beg in the context of the discussion of Nur Jahan, see also, *The Iqbalnama-i Jahangiri*, and the *Ain-i Akbari*. Most modern histories refer to the context of Ghiyas Beg's early career and family, as well as the later placement of various family members among Mughal ranks. Among others, Beni Prasad, *History of Jahangir* (Allahabad: The Indian Press Publications Private Ltd., 1962), especially chapter 7; Irfan Habib, "The Family of Nur Jahan During Jahangir's Reign," in *Medieval India: A Miscellany* (Delhi: I.M.H. Press for Aligarh Muslim University, 1969); 1:74–95.

4. Khafi Khan, *Muntakhab-ul-Lubab*, 1:263.
5. Isma'il was announced as a descendent of Twelver Imams. Twelver Shiism forms the principal branch of Shiite Islam, and describes the followers of the twelve imams they consider to be the only rightful successors of Prophet Muhammad. The Shi'a/Sunni distinction is indispensable to the story of Muslim societies and politics the world over. The Prophet Muhammad died in 632 without naming an heir. With his ascension, the question, what it meant to be a Muslim came to be tied to the grave issue of leadership. In the Sunni tradition, the caliph was a substitute for Muhammad, in whose selection skill or merits mattered most. For the Shi'a, a distinct genealogical connection, an imam chosen from among the Prophet's descendants was most appropriate. Writings on Shi'a/Sunni differences are vast. For an excellent introduction: Jonathan Berky, *The Formation of Islam: Religion and Society in the Near East, 600–1800* (Cambridge and New York: Cambridge University Press, 2003), 70–71, 86–87; Annemarie Schimmel, *Islam: An Introduction* (Albany: State University of New York Press, 1992); For Safavid political history and its historical wider context: Peter Jackson (ed.), *The Cambridge History of Iran: The Timurid and Safavid Periods*, 6 vols. (Cambridge: Cambridge University Press, 1986); Marshall G. S. Hodgson, *The Venture of Islam: Conscience and*

History in a World Civilization, 3 vols. (Chicago and London: The University of Chicago Press, 1974); Kathryn Babayan, *Mystics, Monarchs, and Messiahs: Cultural Landscapes of Early Modern Iran* (Cambridge, MA.: Harvard University Press, 202); Kathryn Babayan, "The Safavid Synthesis: From Qizilbash Islam to Imamite Shi'ism," *Iranian Studies* 27, no. 1/4 (1994): 135–61; Stephen F. Dale, *The Muslim Empires of the Ottomans, Safavids, and Mughals* (Cambridge: Cambridge University Press, 2010); and more recently, A. Azfar Moin, *The Millennial Sovereign: Sacred Kingship and Sainthood in Islam* (New York: Columbia University Press, 2012).

6. Kathryn Babayan, "The 'Aqa'id al-Nisa: A Glimpse at Safavid Women in Local Isfahani Culture" in Gavin R. G. Hambly (ed.), *Women in the Medieval Islamic World: Power, Patronage, and Piety* (New York: St. Martin's Press, 1998), 359.

7. Karim Najafi Barzegar, *Mughal-Iranian Relations During Sixteenth Century* (Delhi: Indian Bibliographies Bureau, 2001), 170.

8. For details of migration to India and the wider political culture of the time: Ali Anooshahr, "Shirazi Scholars and the Political Culture of the Sixteenth-Century Indo-Persian World," *The Indian Economic and Social History Review* 51, no. 3 (2014): 331–52; Masahi Haneda, "Emigration of Iranian Elites to India During the 16th–18th Centuries," in Maria Szuppe (ed.), *L'heritage timouride: Iran—Asie Centrale—Inde, XVe-XVIIIe siècles*, special number of *Cahiers d'Asie Centrale*, 3–4, 1997, 129–40. Indian ports in Bengal in southwest India and Gujarat in western India were emporia for sea-borne trade between China, Southeast Asia, and the Middle East, as well as locations for the export of Indian raw materials and manufactured goods. Increasingly, the Portuguese, Dutch, French, and English were getting embroiled in the waters of the Indian subcontinent, which would bring a new dynamic to trade relations.

9. Muzaffar Alam, *The Languages of Political Islam in India, c. 1200–1800* (New Delhi: Permanent Black, 2004), 124–25.

10. This was a powerful contest of Irano-centrism, a rejoinder to the claim of those Iranians who looked down upon the Indian style of Persian poetry, or the so-called Sabk-i Hindi. Muzaffar Alam and Sanjay Subrahmanyam, *Indo-Persian Travels in the Age of Discoveries,*

1400–1800 (Cambridge and New York: Cambridge University Press, 2007), 177.

11. Beveridge, *Babur-nama*, 202, 338–39. Details of caravans and caravanserai are drawn from Edward Grey (ed.), *The Travels of Pietro Della Valle in India: From the English Translation of 1664, by G. Havers: In Two Volumes* (London: Printed for the Hakluyt Society, 1892); William Irvine (tr.), *Storia Do Mogor or Mogul India 1653–1708 by Niccolao Manucci Venetian*, 4 vols. (London: Murray, 1907); E. Denison Ross and Eileen Power (eds.), *Jahangir and the Jesuits: With an Account of the Travels of Benedict Goes and the Mission to Pegu* (New York: Robert M. McBride and Co., 1930).

12. Bento de Goes, a Jesuit missionary of the Society of Jesus who traveled through northern Afghanistan and Central Asia in the first quarter of the sixteenth century, was robbed more than once as he passed through upper northwest Afghanistan. Ross and Power, *Jahangir and the Jesuits*, 145–46, 151–52. In the 1630s, an Iranian poet 'Abdullah Sani traveled through the same parts as Ghiyas and Asmat. His caravan was robbed just beyond Qandahar; Alam and Subrahmanyam, *Indo-Persian Travels*, 224. The next two paragraphs that follow are based upon these texts.

13. Henri Masse, *Persian Beliefs and Customs* (New Haven: Behavior Science Translations, 1954), 7, 12. Details of the rituals of birth on 13–14.

14. *Storia Do Mogor*, 1:159. Starting as an artilleryman in Mughal prince Dara's services, Niccolao Manucci (1639–1717), subsequently succeeded in attaching himself in disguise to the army of the last grand Mughal, Aurangzeb. He then became a physician to a provincial governor, and afterward a plenipotentiary of a Portuguese viceroy. Manucci gained fame as a (quack) "doctor," and also worked as a foreign correspondent to a British governor at Madras. Eventually he began writing, and the product in 1705 was the *Storia Do Mogor* (The first English translations of this work appeared as early as 1708 and 1722).

15. Susan Stronge, *Painting for the Mughal Emperor: The Art of the Book, 1560–1660* (London: V&A Publications, 2002), 137.

16. Khafi Khan, *Muntakhab-ul-Lubab*, 1:264. Only the dates of his death are available, 1732 or 1733.

17. Willem G. J. Kuiters, "Dow, Alexander (1735/6–1779)," *Oxford Dictionary of National Biography* (Oxford: OUP, 2004); online edition, January 2008, http://www.oxfordnb.com/view/article/7957, 1–2.

18. Alexander Dow, *The History of Hindostan* (London: J. Walker, 1812), 3:19–20 (1735–1779). The work was written between 1768 and 1772.

THREE: AL-HIND

1. Anonymous, *Nushka-i Jahangiri* (Mss. no. 831, Patna University), mentions October 1578 as their date of arrival. In addition to the texts and manuscripts cited in chapter 1, here I have consulted the following records. *Akbar Nama*, cited in chapter 2; *Tarikh-i-Khandan-i Timuriyyan*, manuscript of the Khuda Baksh Oriental Public Library, Patna, India; Muhammad Arif Qandahari, *Tarikh-i Akbari*, eds. Muin ud-Din Nadwi, Azhar Ali Dihlawi, and Imtiyaz Ali Arshi (Rampur: Rampur Raza Library, 1962); Chandarbhan Brahman, *Chahar Chaman*, British Library, Persian Ms. Add. 16863; And, George S. A. Ranking, W. H. Lowe, and Sir Wolseley Haig (trs. and eds.), *Muntakhabu-t-tawarikh*, 3 vols. (1884–1925; reprint Delhi, 1986).

    For the architectural, social, and economic history of Akbar and his capital city, Fatehpur-Sikri: S.A.A. Rizvi and V.J.A. Flynn, *Fathpur-Sikri* (Bombay: D. B. Taraporevala Sons Pvt. Ltd., 1975); Michael Brand and Glenn D. Lowry, *Akbar's India: Art from the Mughal City of Victory* (New York: The Asia Society Galleries, 1986); Michael Brand and Glenn D. Lowry (eds.), *Fatehpur-Sikri* (Bombay: Marg Publications, 1987). For scholarly sketches, among others, Alam, *Languages of Political Islam*; Iqtidar Alam Khan (ed.), *Akbar and His Age* (New Delhi: Northern Book Center, 1999); Ruby Lal, *Domesticity and Power in the Early Mughal World* (Cambridge: Cambridge University Press, 2005), chapter 6.

2. For historical details of Lahore, see, M. Baqir, *Lahore: Past and Present* (Delhi: Low Price Publications, reprint 1996), 309, 363, 364.

3. Such a sense of shared community and spaces is brought out in the memoir of the Jain merchant Banarasi, written in 1641 during the reign of Jahangir, the fourth Mughal. For the Hindi text and transla-

tion, Mukund Lath, *The Ardhkathank: Half a Tale* (New Delhi: Rupa and Co. 2005).

4. Masud and Murtaza are figures exclusive to Khafi Khan's history, the first narrator of Mihr's abandonment on the road.

5. *A'in-i Akbari*, cited in chapter 2, 2:317.

6. Alam, *Languages of Political Islam*, 123.

7. Ibid., 121, 123, and 135.

8. *Akbar Nama*, 2:503, 530.

9. Brand and Lowry, *Akbar's India*, 44.

10. For *jharokha darshan*, see, *A'in-i Akbari*, 1:165; Brand and Lowry, *Akbar's India*, 47–48; Glenn D. Lowry, "Urban Structures and Functions," in *Fatehpur-Sikri*, 48.

11. One of the descriptions of the *darshan* comes from the records of Akbar's grandson Shah Jahan, who aspired a great deal after the emperor. The way the majesty of the moment was captured would be accurate for both Akbar and Shah Jahan. Brahman, *Chahar Chaman*, folio 20a–21a.

12. Akbar's court physician, accompanying the imperial camp in Punjab at one time, wrote a letter to a friend who was looking for a job, suggesting that he make his way straight to Fatehpur-Sikri. "If you have the ambition of seeking His Majesty's service, you will—God Willing!—be appointed to a distinguished position; if you wish for *madad-i ma'ash* [revenue-free grant of land], that too is procurable; and if you are inclined towards commerce (*tijarat*) that too is better pursued at Fatehpur-Sikri . . ." Irfan Habib, "The Economic and Social Setting," in *Fatehpur-Sikri*, 78. In 1574, Mulla Badauni, the emperor's future critic, and a little later Abul-Fazl, were introduced. S.A.A. Rizvi, "Philosophical Traditions at Akbar's Court," in *Fatehpur-Sikri*, 190.

13. *A'in-i Akbari*, 1:166

14. Khafi Khan, *Muntakhab-ul-Lubab*, 1:264–65.

15. Confirmed details of Ghiyas Beg's first encounter with Akbar: that it occurred at some point between late 1578 and early 1579, and that following the audience he was given employment in the service of the Grand Mughal. For a detailed record of *mansab* holders and their evolution in the ranks of the nobility, M. Athar Ali, *The Apparatus of Empire: Awards of Ranks, Offices and Titles to the Mughal Nobility,*

1574–1658 (Delhi: Oxford University Press, 1985). For the information on Ghiyas's ranks, see xii, 19, 25, 42. It is unlikely that he received an audience with Akbar in Lahore. Akbar held two public meetings in the Hall of Audiences of the Lahore fort. The first, ten years after Ghiyas and Asmat were in Lahore; and the second, ten years later, following the repairs of the hall that had been damaged in a fire. By the latter date, Ghiyas Beg was a well-placed noble in the Mughal Empire.

16. Abul-Fazl, who wrote about Akbar's daily meetings, describing the conventions of such gatherings for posterity, does not mention Ghiyas Beg. Ghiyas's introductory rank (*mansab*) in Mughal service is unrecorded. This may have to do with gaps in the main document from Akbar's reign that gives us a list of *mansab* holders of 200 and above. Abul-Fazl's voluminous gazetteer of Akbar's empire, the *A'in-i Akbari*, does not include names of *mansab* holders who died before the system was instituted in 1575. The list also does not include a number of persons granted a *mansab* before 1596. For Ghiyas Beg's titles and ranks, Ali, *The Apparatus of Empire*, xii, 19, 25, 42.

FOUR: THE CUPOLAS OF CHASTITY AND THE PERFECT MAN

1. For a detailed discussion of Gulbadan's hajj, Lal, *Domesticity and Power*, cited in chapter 3, 208–13; also, *Akbar Nama*, cited in chapter 2, 3:205; *Muntakhabu-t-tawarikh*, 2:216, 320.

2. For Akbar's marriages and sources for Mughal marital alliances, Lal, *Domesticity and Power*, 166–75.

3. Allison Busch, "Hidden in Plain View: Brajbhasha Poets at the Mughal Court," *Modern Asian Studies* 44, no. 2 (2010), 271.

4. Kishori Lal (ed.), *Acharya Keshav Das, Jahangir Jas-Chandrika* (Allahabad: Sahitya Bhavan Pvt. Ltd., 1998, 1st ed.), 11–12. The raja referred to is Raja Indrajit.

5. Scholarly writings on Akbar's religious and ethical life are extensive. See, as examples, S.A.A Rizvi, "Dimensions of Sulh-I Kul (Universal Peace) in Akbar's Reign and the Sufi Theory of Perfect Man," in Alam, *Akbar and His Age*, cited in chapter 3, 17; Irfan Habib, "Commemorating Akbar," in Alam, *Akbar and His Age*, xii, xiiii, xiv;

S.A.A. Rizvi, *Religious and Intellectual History of the Muslims in Akbar's Reign* (New Delhi, 1975); Muzaffar Alam et al. (eds.), *The Making of Indo-Persian Culture: Indian and French Studies* (New Delhi, 2000); more recently, Anooshahr, "Shirazi Scholars and the Political Culture of the Sixteenth-Century Indo-Persian World," cited in chapter 2, 342–43.

6. Widely in circulation was also Firdausi's twelfth-century *Shahnama*, the *Book of Kings*, which referred to the "Sun of Iran" and the "Moon of Turan"—highlighting different principles for cycles of time. Zodiacal signs, astrological symbols, the sun on a lion's back were signs of a prosperous kingship. For an excellent discussion of the themes of time and the millenarian philosophy of Akbar, Moin, *The Millennial Sovereign,* cited in chapter 2.

7. Michael Brand, "The City as Artistic Center," in *Fatehpur-Sikri*, cited in chapter 3, 98, and fn. 41.

8. *Muntakhabu-t-Tawarikh*, cited in chapter 3, 2:253.

9. John F. Richards, *The Mughal Empire* (Cambridge: Cambridge University Press, 1993), 40; S. Nurul Hasan, Religion, *State and Society in Medieval India*, ed. Satish Chandra (Delhi: OUP, 2005).

10. Moin, *Millennial Sovereign*, 9.

11. What a modern historian describes as his "autocratic centralism." Richards, *The Mughal Empire*, chapter 3, with the title above.

FIVE: THE WAK-WAK TREE

1. Asmat gave birth to two more children, a boy and a girl. There is no information on the place or time of the births or the age difference between them. Muhammad Sharif, the eldest boy; the second, Abul-Hasan (the future Asaf Khan); and Manija, the eldest daughter, were born in Iran. Little companions of their parents on that arduous journey from Iran to India, they had witnessed the birth of their little sister Mihr on the road near Kandahar. Khadija, the youngest girl, and Ibrahim Khan, the youngest boy, were born in India. Mirza Abul-Hasan came to be referred to as Asaf Khan in most histories. In 1611, he was given the title Itiqad Khan, and in 1614, Asaf Khan, the name by which he is remembered. Ibrahim

Khan Fath-jang was given the title Itiqad Khan sometime before 1615. For biographical details and titles, *A'in-i Akbari*, cited in chapter 2, 1:575–76; *Dhakhiratul Khawanin*, cited in chapter 1, 9–14, and 68–69; *Maathir-ul-Umara*, cited in chapter 2, 1:287–95 and 657–59. P. N. Ojha discusses the ranks and titles of Ghiyas's sons; *Asaf Khan and His Times* (Patna: K. P. Jayaswal Research Institute, 1986), 31–35.

2. Mohammad Yasin, *A Social History of Islamic India, 1605–1748* (New Delhi: Munshiram Manoharlal, 1974, 2nd ed.) 61, 62.

3. *Maathir-ul-Umara*, 2 (2):1077.

4. *Akbar Nama*, cited in chapter 2, 3:614–15.

5. Yasin, *Social History*, 48, fn. 2.

6. Simon Digby, *Wonder-Tales of South Asia: Translated from Hindi, Urdu, Nepali and Persian* (New Delhi: OUP, 2006), 286.

7. For an excellent discussion and detailed references to artistic productions of the Wak-Wak tree, Marcus Fraser, *Deccan and Mughal Paintings: The Collection of Catherine Glynn Benkaim and Ralph Benkaim* 2 vols. (England: Pureprint; Private Research Document, undated). These volumes are a private gift to me.

8. G. M. Wickens (trans. and ed.), *The Nasirean Ethics* (London: George Allen and Unwin Ltd., 1964), 167–68.

9. *Tuzuk*, cited in chapter 1, 2:117–18.

10. Shaykh Mushrifuddin Sa'di of Shiraz; Wheeler M. Thackston (tr.), *The Gulistan (Rose Garden of Sa'di): Bilingual English and Persian Edition with Vocabulary* (Maryland: Ibex Publishers, 2008).

11. *Nasirean Ethics*, 173.

12. Reuben Levy (tr.), *A Mirror of Princes: The Qabus Nama by Kai Ka'us Ibn Iskandar* (New York: E. Dutton and Co., 1951), 119–25.

13. The literature on women's literacy in the Islamic societies is extensive. The following books are good examples: Hambly (ed.), *Women in the Medieval Islamic World*, cited in chapter 2; D. Fairchild Ruggels (ed.), *Women, Patronage, and Self-Representation in Islamic Societies* (Albany: State University of New York Press, 2000); and more recently, collected essays on women's education in the Muslim world, especially Nadia Maria el-Cheikh, "Observations on Women's Education in Medieval Islamic Societies," in Francois Georgeon and Klaus Krreiser (eds.), *Enfance Et Jeunesse Dans le Monde*

Musulman: Childhood and Youth in the Muslim World (Paris: Maison-neuve and Larose, 2007): 57–72.

14. *Nasirean Ethics*, 169–70.

15. K. M. Asharf, *Life and Conditions of the People of Hindustan* (New Delhi: Munshiram Manoharlal Pvt. Ltd., 1988, 3rd ed.), 269.

16. *A'in-i Akbari*, 1:287.

17. *Maathir-ul-Umara*, 2(1):497.

SIX: THE MIRROR OF HAPPINESS

1. Gulbadan, *Ahval*, cited in chapter 2, folio 28b; Masse, cited in chapter 2, *Persian Beliefs and Customs*, 46–47.

2. For wedding clothes and jewelry, see Gulbadan, *Ahval*, folio 28b; *A'in-i Akbari*, cited in chapter 2, 1:96.

3. For wedding descriptions, Gulbadan, *Ahval*; Masse, *Persian Beliefs and Customs*, 42–56. For the above quotation, Masse, *Persian Beliefs and Customs*, 45. Descriptions of weddings among aristocratic household are often noted in tales that are grounded in the oral Indic renditions, such as Inshallah Khan's Hindi-Urdu story of 1801, *Rani Ketki ki Kahani*; Ruby Lal, *Coming of Age in Nineteenth Century India: The Girl-Child and the Art of Playfulness* (New York: Cambridge University Press, 2013), ch. 2.

4. Although Mu'tamad Khan, the compiler of *Maathir-Ul-Umara*, and Hadi note that Mihr and Quli's wedding took place immediately after the victory over Sind in 1593, the location of the wedding is not discussed. Since Ghiyas Beg became the diwan of Kabul in 1595, it is likely that the wedding did not take place there.

5. For details of various kinds of Muslim marriage legal arrangements and practices, John L. Esposito, *Women in Muslim Family Law* (Syracuse: Syracuse University Press, 1982), 24–26.

6. Beni Prasad, cited in chapter 2, *History of Jahangir*, 160.

7. For Abdur Rahim Khan-i Khanan and the capture of Sind, see *Maathir-ul-Umara*, cited in chapter 2, 1:50–53, 62.

8. For a sketch of Ali Quli, and Abdur Rahim's help to him, *Maathir-ul-Umara*, 2(2): 837–39.

9. Among others, *Dhakhiratul Khawanin*, cited in chapter 2, (2):83–85; *Maathir-ul-Umara* 2(2):837–38. References to Quli from 1605 until

his death are available in Jahangir's memoir, the *Tuzuk-i Jahangiri* and several other Jahangiri sources cited in chapter 1.

10. Masse, *Persian Beliefs and Customs*, 46.

11. Ibid., 51.

12. L. Tessitori, "A Progress Report on the Work Done During the Year 1917 in Connection with the Bardic and Historical Survey of Rajputana," *Journal and Proceedings of the Asiatic Society of Bengal*, New Series, 15 (1919), 58.

13. Khafi Khan, *Muntakhab-ul-Lubab,* cited in chapter 2, 1:265–67.

14. Dow, *The History of Hindostan*, cited in chapter 2, 3:20–22.

15. Azad, *Darbar-i Akbari*, cited in chapter 1, 187–88.

16. Syed Muhammad Latif, *History of the Panjab: From the Remotest Antiquity to the Present Time* (1889; New Delhi: Eurasia Publishing House, reprint 1964), 154–56. Several editions of this book are available in print and online. The author's first name is variously spelled: Syad, Syed, Saiyid.

17. For charting the travel route from Agra to Bengal, I use the writings of Sebastien Manrique; C. Eckford Luard (tr.) and Father H. Hosten (assisted), *Travels of Fray Sebastien Manrique, 1629–1643*, 2 vols. (Oxford: The Hakluyt Society, 1927), 125–243. For the quotation, 135. And of Jean-Baptiste Tavernier, William Crooke (ed.), *Travels in India by Jean-Baptiste Tavernier* (London: Oxford University Press, 1925; 2nd ed.), especially 92–115; Mirza Nathan, a Mughal general who took a leading role in campaigns in Bengal and Assam— and collaborated with Emperor Jahangir's son Shah Jahan when he was based in Bengal as an insurgent prince; M. I. Borah (trans.), *Baharistan-i-Ghayabi: A History of Mughal Wars in Assam, Cooch Behar, Bengal, Bihar and Orissa During the Reigns of Jahangir and Shah Jahan by Mirza Nathan*, 2 vols. (Guwahati: Pratilipi Printers, reprint 1992), (2):711.

18. John R. McLane, *Land and Local Kinship in Eighteenth-Century Bengal* (New York: Cambridge University Press, 1993), 127.

19. Ibid., 129; Tapan Raychaudhuri, *Bengal Under Akbar and Jahangir: An Introductory Study in Social History* (Delhi: Munshiram Manohar Lal, 1969, rpt.), 176.

20. Raychaudhuri, *Bengal Under Akbar and Jahangir*, 226.

21. For information on Mughal Bengal, I rely on the definitive work by Raychaudhuri, *Bengal Under Akbar and Jahangir*. For a description of Mughal Burdwan, McLane, *Land and Local Kinship*, chapter 6. For the quotation, Raychaudhuri, *Bengal Under Akbar and Jahangir*, 85. Mirza Nathan boasted of his ruthless exploits. During a campaign in southeast of Burdwan, his brother captured 4,000 women, old and young, and stripped them of their clothes. At the same time, Nathan had sent 42,000 rupees to the court in anticipation of a promotion.

22. Raychaudhuri, *Bengal Under Akbar and Jahangir*, 193.

23. Ibid., 169, 171–73, 175.

24. Ibid., 148.

25. An eyewitness of a dramatic moment of Mihr's last years as Empress Nur Jahan notes her daughter's name as Bahu Begum. This may well have been an honorific, "the honorable bride," given to her in the aftermath of her marriage to a Mughal prince. Mulla Kami Shirazi, *Waqa-i-uz-Zaman*, ed. W. H. Siddiqi. (Rampur: Rampur Raza Library, 2003), 12, 196. I have also consulted the Aligarh copy, *Fathnama-i Nur Jahan Begum*, Center for Advanced Study Library, Aligarh Muslim University, Rotograph 10. References to the wedding of Ladli and Shahryar are to be found in Jahangir's memoir. Ladli's absence in the historical record is immense. No details, no sense of her person, only stray references. This is glaring namelessness compared to other women of the time, who somehow crawl into the records. Even when Ladli appears in the historical record, she is noted as her mother's daughter.

26. Raychaudhuri, *Bengal Under Akbar and Jahangir*, 173, 213, 198. I construct the landscape of Ladli's childhood on the basis of the information on 206–20.

27. M. N. Pearson, "Recreation in Mughal India," *The British Journal of Sports History* 1, no. 3 (1984): 335–50.

SEVEN: GRAVE MATTERS

I use the following documents to chart Khusraw's rebellion: Hindi text and translation: Mukund Lath, *The Ardhkathank*, cited in chapter 3; the *Akbar Nama*, cited in chapter 2; the *Tuzuk-i Jahangiri*, cited in chapter 1; the *Dhakhiratul Khawanin and the Maathir-ul-Umara*, cited in chapter 2; *Muntakhab-ul Lubab*, cited in chapter 2; Ni'matullah Khan Harvi, *Tarikh-i-Khan Jahani wa Makhzan-i Afghani*, ed. S. M. Imam-ud-Din, 2 vols. (Dhaka: Asiatic Society of Pakistan, 1960); and Hyder Malik Chadurah, *Tarikh-i Haidar Malik*, Razia Banu (ed.), *History of Kashmir* (Delhi: Bhavna Prakashan, 1991)

1. Munis D. Faruqui, *The Princes of the Mughal Empire, 1504–1719* (Cambridge: Cambridge University Press, 2012), 31.
2. *Tuzuk*, (1):113–14.
3. When the news of this event reached Akbar, he "uttered a cry and became insensible. After a long time, he recovered. For several days in succession he had moist eyes and a sorrowful countenance because of the sacrifice of that excellent companion, that prince of loyalty, that interlocutor or lofty intellect, that friend of the private meeting and that faithful confidant and counseller." *Akbar Nama*, 3:1219.
4. *Tuzuk*, 1:114
5. Faruqui, *Princes*, 161.
6. *Akbar Nama*, 3:1217.
7. Ibid.
8. Faruqui, *Princes*, 33.
9. *Ardhkathank*, 165.
10. Ibid.
11. Michael H. Fisher, *A Short History of the Mughal Empire* (London: I. B. Tauris, 2016), 149.
12. *Tuzuk*, 1:114.
13. Ibid., 113.
14. Fisher, *Mughal Empire*, 150.
15. *Akbar Nama*, 1:129.
16. Faruqui, *Princes*, 223. W. H. Moreland and Peter Geyl (eds.), *Jahangir's India: The Remonstrantie of Francisco Pelsaert* (Cambridge: W. Heffer and Sons Ltd., 1925), 36.
17. *Tuzuk*, 1:53; Thackston, *Jahangirnama*, cited in chapter 1, 49; Harvi, *Tarikh-i Khan Jahani*, 674.
18. Richards, *Mughal Empire*, cited in chapter 4, 94.
19. *Tuzuk*, 1:51.
20. Faruqui, *Princes*, 224.
21. *Tuzuk*, 1:54, 55–56, 122.

22. Ibid., 57.

23. Jahangir nowhere says that Khusraw was blinded, but his memoir from a few years after these events indicates that something was done to Khusraw's eyes. According to a later entry in the *Jahangirnama*, an impostor created a lot of disturbance in Patna, claiming that he was Khusraw. In proof of his identity, he showed marks around his eyes, which he said had been caused by the application of a hot bowl to them. It is clear that Khusraw's eyes were tampered with in some way, and that he was partially blinded.

24. *Tuzuk*, 1:65.

25. Ibid., 114.

26. *Tarikh-i Haidar Malik*, 96.

27. *Tuzuk*, 1:114–15.

28. Maulawi Abdul-Wali, "The Antiquities of Burdwan," *Journal and Proceedings of the Asiatic Society of Bengal* 13 (1917), 185.

29. Latif, *History of the Panjab,* cited in chapter 6, 154–56.

30. At the commencement of Jahangir's reign, Yusuf Khan Kashmiri, in charge of the rural areas of Bukyanah and Duabah in Kashmir, was invited to join the new emperor's services. Malik was Yusuf's trusted *faujdar.* When Sher Afgan rebelled, Yusuf Khan was assigned to the province of Bengal. Malik accompanied him, and along with Yusuf was in the retinue of the murdered governor of Bengal in 1608.

31. *Tarikh-i Haidar Malik*, 95–96.

EIGHT: A KEY FOR CLOSED DOORS

1. Pelsaert, *Jahangir's India,* cited in chapter 7, 2. To understand the philosophy and planning behind the architectural spaces in Agra, I have drawn a great deal from the writing of Ebba Koch, especially her *Mughal Art and Imperial Ideology: Collected Essays* (New Delhi: OUP, 2001); *The Complete Taj Mahal and the Riverfront Gardens of Agra* (New Delhi: Bookwise India Pvt. Ltd., 2006); Milo Cleveland Beach and Ebba Koch (new translation by Wheeler Thackston), *King of the World: The Padshahnama, An Imperial Mughal Manuscript from the Royal Library, Windsor Castle* (London: Azimuth Editions Ltd., 1997), among other writings listed in chapter 3.

2. On Aqa Aqayan, cf. chapter 10, note 16; and *Tuzuk*, cited in chapter 1, 2:110.

3. *Tuzuk*, 1:325–26; *Tuzuk*, 2:86, 159–60; *Ain-i Akbari*, cited in chapter 2, 1:323, 533n, 686.

4. For an excellent discussion of princely households, see Faruqui, *Princes*, cited in chapter 7, ch. 3.

5. The *Tuzuk*, the *Dhakhiratul Khawanin*, and the *Iqbalnama-i Jahangiri*, for example, suggest it was Ruqayya, whereas the *Maathir-Ul-Umara* suggests it was Salimeh Sultan Begum.

6. For a brief biography of Salimeh, see Annette S. Beveridge, *The History of Humayun*, *Humayun-Nama* (New Delhi: Munshiram Manoharlal Publishers Pvt. Ltd., 2001 rpt. Originally published in 1902), 276–80.

7. Foster, *Embassy of Sir Thomas Roe*, cited in chapter 1, 270.

8. Edward Terry, *A Voyage to East India* (London: J. Wilkie, rpt. from 1655 edition), 406.

9. Clements R. Markham (ed.), *The Hawkins Voyages During the Reigns of Henry VIII, Queen Elizabeth, and James I* (New York: Burt Franklin Publisher, n.d.; reprint from Hakluyt Society Series), 421.

10. R. Nath, *Private Life of the Mughals 1526–1803 A. D.* (Rupa Publications, India, 2004), 15, 17. A fiction writer gives nineteen as the number of the emperor's women: Mihr becomes his twentieth wife; Indu Sundaresan, *The Twentieth Wife: A Novel* (Penguin Books, India, 2002).

11. From his account, and a variety of other sources, we may glean the order of some of his marriages. Tuzuk, 1:18–20; *Ain-i Akbari* 1:323, 533n, 686; *Akbar Nama*, cited in chapter 2, 3:561; Markham, *The Hawkins Voyages*, 399–440 (names spread across discussion of events). Aside from the wives discussed above, here are the details of other wives of Jahangir: In 1592, Jahangir had also married the daughter of Ali Rai, ruler of Tibet. Jahangir notes his marriages to several other women. Malika Jahan, the daughter of Raja Kalyan of Jaisalmer, a Rajput chieftain whose family had maintained a strong alliance with the Mughals, was wedded to him while he was still a prince (before 1605). Nur un-Nisa Begam, sister of Mirza Muzaffar Husain (married to Jahangir's sister) also married the emperor, an exchange of sisters on both sides. Saliha Banu, another wife, the

sister of a man named Abdur Rahim (titled Tarbiyat Khan), was said to be from a house that had served the Mughal court for generations. Jahangir's other wives were: the daughter of Mubarak Chak of Kashmir; the daughter of Husain Chak of Kashmir; the daughter of Raja Ali Khan, king of Khandesh; the daughter of Khwaja-i Jahan of Kabul; the daughter of Mirza Sanjar and granddaughter of Khizr Khan Hazara (Khizr Khan was married to princess memoirist Gulbadan, Jahangir's great-aunt, so this wife would be Jahangir's second cousin); the daughter of Rai Singh of Bikaner; and the daughter of Said Khan Ghakkar. A possible daughter of this union, 'Iffat Banu, is mentioned.

12. *Tuzuk*, 1:56. Man Bai and Raja Man Singh (sister and brother) were (*Tuzuk*, 1:15–16) children of Raja Bhagwan Das (their grandfather was Raja Bihari Mal). Man Bai, Jahangir's first wife, was also his first cousin. Jahangir was a grandson of Raja Bihari Mal through his mother Maryam-uz-zamani, sister of Raja Bhagwan Das.

13. *Tuzuk*, 1:19.

14. *Ain-i Akbari*, 1:323.

15. *Tuzuk*, 1:18–20.

16. Ibid., 144, 145, 160; *Ain-i Akbari*, 1:323.

17. Jahangir notes Ladli's betrothal to Shahryar and mentions that the wedding took place from her grandfather Ghiyas Beg's house. I discuss Ladli's wedding later in the book.

18. Though five hundred years divide Mihr's sensibility from ours, a painting comes in handy in conveying the spirit of this time. *Chiterin* (Lady artist and her model), a painting included in this book's photo gallery and housed in Bharat Kala Bhavan of the Banaras Hindu University, is drawn in subtle tones. The foreground of the painting has four women and a small girl seated on the floor of a terrace in front of a palace-apartment. A handsome lady artist is seated on the left with her sketchboard resting on her right knee, painting in the tradition of Mughal artists. Behind the artist sits an attendant: the artist's elegant clothes and confident demeanor show the difference from her escort. In front of the artist is a young woman (seated in the center). Her head, the lower half of her face, and the rest of her body is covered in an *orhani* (a long cloak or veil). Behind her is a small girl with a lotus blossom in her right hand, and behind the girl, an older woman,

seated, watching the painting session. On the extreme right of the terrace, a maid stands at a half-open door, looking out on the ongoing scene. For a reproduction and discussion of the painting, Vijay Krishna, "Chiterin (Lady-Artist and Her Model): Identified as an Illustration of the Nurjahan Episode," in *Journal of the Indian Society of Oriental Art*, New Series, 10, (1978–79): 60–63.

19. *Tuzuk*, 1:118, 119, 120.
20. Ibid., 132.
21. Ibid., 197, 199, 200. For the details of the presents sent by Shah Abbas, Thackston, *Jahangirnama*, cited in chapter 1, 121–22, note 2.
22. For an extended discussion of the year 1611, *Tuzuk*, 1:191 onward.
23. *Jahangirnama*, B. M. Ms. Or. 3276, folio 314.
24. Hadi, *Tatimma-i Vaqi'at-i Jahangiri*, cited in chapter 1, 398.

NINE: ASCENT

1. For a chart that shows the imperial camp and its layout, see, *Ain-i Akbari*, cited in chapter 2, 1:48, on the plate facing this page. And for a discussion of Mughal tent cities, Stephen Blake, *Shahjahanabad: The Sovereign City in Mughal India* (Cambridge: Cambridge University Press, 1993), especially, 83–99. For a discussion of the architecture and meanings attached to tents in Central Asia, Afghanistan, and Iran, past and present, Peter Alford Andrews, *Nomad Tent Types in the Middle East* (Wiesbaden, 1997), 13.
2. *Jahangir Receives Khurram on His Return from the Mewar Campaign*, by painter Balchand. *The Windsor Castle Padshahnama*, folio 43b, ca. 1635.
3. *Tuzuk*, cited in chapter 1, 1:277, 278.
4. *Dhakhiratul Khawanin*, cited in chapter 2, 15; See also, *Iqbalnama-i Jahangiri*, cited in chapter 2, 405.
5. *Dhakhiratul Khawanin*, 15.
6. *Tuzuk*, 1:266–67.
7. Irfan Habib, "The Family of Nur Jahan During Jahangir's Reign," in *Medieval India: A Miscellany* (Delhi: I.M.H. Press for Aligarh Muslim University, 1969), 78.
8. For the evolution in the ranks of the nobility of Nur Jahan's fam-

ily, Ali, *The Apparatus of Empire*, cited in chapter 3, and Habib, "The Family of Nur Jahan," 78, fn. 22 and 79.

9. *Ain-i Akbari*, 1:276–77 and note 1 and 2; *Tuzuk*, 1:239.

10. *Tuzuk*, 2:214–15.

11. She was born in 1539. There is some uncertainty about the month of her death. According to the authors of a couple of other chronicles, she died in January 1613. *Tuzuk*, 1:232, fn. 2, for a discussion of the death of Salimeh. See also, Annette Beveridge, *The History of Humayun*, cited in chapter 8, 276–80.

12. Jahangir wrote about Asmat's invention of the rose perfume in 1614. Clearly, Asmat had found the rose scent when Salimeh was alive. *Tuzuk*, 1:270–71.

13. Ibid.

14.

گشاد غنچه اگر از نسیم گلزار است
کلید قفل در ام تبسم رای است
نه لگ شناسد و نه رنگ و نه وب و نه عراض و زلف
دل کس کی هک هب حسن و ادا گرفتار است

Nur Jahan's poems are reproduced in Khafi Khan's *Muntakhab-ul-Lubab*, cited in chapter 2, 1:270–71. A Mughal officer in Bengal, Shir Khan Lodi completed a short *tezkerah* or a memorial of poets compiled in the form of a biographical anthology in which he listed Nur Jahan, who used the popular pseudonym Makhfi (The Hidden One). The first monumental *tezkerah*, Valeh Dhagestani's *Riaz al-sho'ara*, compiled around 1747 with 2,500 entries, included Nur Jahan's name. For Valeh, a successful female poet was one who wrote like a man. In his compilation, Nur's poetry was subsumed within the frame of Jahangir's entry. Azar Begeli's *Atashkhand*, completed in 1760–61 in Iran included Nur Jahan. For a history of these compilations, see, Sunil Sharma, "From A'esha to Nur Jahan: The Shaping of a Classical Persian Poetic Canon of Women," *Journal of Persianate Studies* 2 (2009): 148–64.

15. Beveridge, *Humayun*, 130–31; Gulbadan, *Ahval*, cited in chapter 2, folio 30a–30b.

16. Khafi Khan, *Muntakhab-ul-Lubab*, 1:289–90.

17. Noted in Shujauddin and Shujauddin, *The Life and Times of Noor Jahan*, cited in chapter 1, 95.

18. Thackston, *Jahangirnama*, cited in chapter 1, xxiii.

19. *Tuzuk*, 1:309; for the above details, *Tuzuk*, 1:307–9, and fn. 3.

20. Beveridge, *Humayun*, 130–31; Gulbadan, *Ahval*, folio 30a–30b.

21. *Tuzuk*, 1:48, 49.

22. *Tuzuk*, 2:214.

23. Manucci, *Storia Do Mogor*, cited in chapter 2, 1:158.

24. Ibid., 2:35.

25. Brij Narain and Sri Ram Sharma (trans. and ed.), *A Contemporary Dutch Chronicle of Mughal India* (Calcutta: Sisil Gupta Ltd., 1957), 5, 91–92.

26. Corinne Lefevre, "Recovering a Missing Voice from Mughal India: The Imperial Discourse of Jahangir (r. 1605–1627)," *Journal of the Economic and Social History of the Orient* 50, no. 4 (2007), 469.

27. Mohan Lal Dalichand Desai, *Bhanucandra Carita: By His Pupil Gani Siddhichadra Upadhyaya* (Ahmedabad-Calcutta: The Sanchalaka-Singhi Jaina Granthamala, 1941), 56. I am grateful to Audrey Truschke for bringing this text to my attention and for sending me the Sanskrit text as well as her writings on Siddhichandra. Siddhichandra, a Jain monk, and his guru Bhanuchandra spent twenty-three years at the courts of Akbar and Jahangir. Siddhichandra's account *Bhanuchandra Carita* is a biography of his guru, but toward the end he also writes a fair bit about himself. The episode seems to have taken place, according to Desai, 52, between 1611 and 1616. According to Truschke, the exchange took place just before 1616; Truschke, *Culture of Encounters: Sanskrit at the Mughal Court* (New Delhi: Penguin, 2016).

28. Nur ad-Din Muhammad Jahangir, *Tuzuk-i Jahangiri* (Tehran: Buni adi Farhangi Iran, 1980); citation in Lisa Balabanlilar, *Imperial Identity in the Mughal Empire: Memory and Dynastic Politics in Early Modern South and Central Asia* (New York: I. B. Tauris, 2012), 56.

29. Gommans, *Mughal Warfare*, cited in chapter 1, 109.

30. *Tuzuk*, 1:239, 241.

31. Ibid., 318–19.

32. *Akbar Nama*, cited in chapter 2, 2:86; Maulawi, *Akbarnamah*, cited in chapter 2, 2:54–57. Nizam al-Din Ahmad records the same event, and uses the following expressions: "Khalifa-i Ilahi" for Akbar, "Pavilion of Chastity" for women, and so on. See B. De and Baini Prasad

(trans.), *The Tabaqat-i Akbari of Khwajah Nizammudin Ahmad*, 3 vols. (1936; rpt Delhi, 1992), 2:222. For a detailed discussion of practices of naming among Mughals, Lal, *Domesticity and Power*, cited in chapter 3, ch. 8.

33. For a detailed discussion of the titles of the Mughal emperors, W. E. Begley and Z. A. Desai (ed. and comp.), *The Shah Jahan Nama of 'Inayat Khan* (Delhi: OUP, 1990), 3–4.

34. *Tuzuk*, 1:319–20.

35. Foster, *Embassy of Sir Thomas Roe*, cited in chapter 1, 256.

36. Faruqui, *Princes*, cited in chapter 7, 35.

37. *Tuzuk*, 1:341–42.

38. Ibid., 355–56.

39. Alam, *Languages of Political Islam*, cited in chapter 3, 95; on Jadrup and other ascetics and Jahangir, apart from the *Tuzuk-i Jahangiri*, see also, Nazr Ashraf (ed.), *Dabistan-i Mazahib* (Calcutta, 1809); David Shea and Anthony Troyer (trans.), *Oriental Literature or the Dabistan* (New York: Tudor Publishing Co., 1937).

40. Balabanlilar, *Imperial Identity*, 84–85.

41. Gommans, *Mughal Warfare*, 110–11.

42. *Tuzuk*, 1:375 and n1.

TEN: WONDER OF THE AGE

1. *Tuzuk*, cited in chapter 1, 1:380.

2. Its size then was 443,028 bighas: 1 bigha was five-eighths of an acre, so in acres it was 276,892.5. The revenue that came from Toda in Akbar's time was 5,859,006 dam: a dam was one-fortieth of a rupee, so the total revenue amount would be Rs. 146, 475. *Ain-i Akbari*, cited in chapter 2, 1:280. Computation of modern numbers based upon equivalents given by Thackston, *Jahangirnama*, cited in chapter 1, Appendix A, 473–74.

3. *Tuzuk*, 1:380.

4. S. A. I. Tirmizi, *Edicts from the Mughal Harem* (New Delhi: Idarah-I Adabiyat-I Delli, reprint 2009), xii.

5. *Tuzuk*, 1:383.

6. Ibid., 385–86.

7. Ibid., 388.

8. The final victory over the Deccan wouldn't take place until later, during the reign of Shah Jahan.

9. *Tuzuk*, 1:394, 395.

10. Faruqui, *Princes*, cited in chapter 7, 34.

11. Most art historians agree on this one painting as portraying the "real" Nur Jahan, chiefly because the depiction directly illustrates an event recorded in the *Jahangirnama*. Copies of *Jahangir and Prince Khurram Entertained by Nur Jahan* is held at the following locations: the Freer Gallery of Art, Smithsonian Institution, Washington, DC, 07.258; the Victoria & Albert Museum, London, I.M. 115–1921; and the Maharaja Sawai Man Singh II Museum, City Palace, Jaipur, A G 823. Among others, the following scholars have discussed this painting: Juan R. Cole, "The Imagined Embrace: Gender, Identity and Iranian Ethnicity in Jahangiri Paintings," in Michel Mazzaoui (ed.), *Safavid Iran and Her Neighbors* (Salt Lake City: The University of Utah Press, 2003): 49–61; Ellison Banks Findly, "The Pleasure of Women: Nur Jahan and Mughal Painting," *Asian Art* (Spring 1993): 67–86.

12. *Tuzuk*, 1:394, 395.

13. Ibid., 400.

14. Ibid., 399–401.

15. Ibid., 401; Tirmizi, *Edicts from the Mughal Harem*, xi.

16. *Tuzuk*, 2:110. In 1619, Jahangir noted Aqayan's "hereditary attachment to this illustrious family," and her placement by Akbar in Jahangir's harem at the time of the latter's marriage in 1585. "It is 33 years from that date that she has been in my service, and I esteem her greatly, for she has served me with sincerity." However, as she grew older, Aqa Aqayan requested Jahangir to allow her to remain in Delhi. Her induction into Jahangir's harem in 1585 and the note about her thirty-three years of service helps us to establish that she would have left the imperial service in 1618, perhaps just after the Mughal cavalcade returned from Malwa and Gujarat. Perhaps it was in 1618 then that Dai Dilaram was appointed as the harem-in-charge. Her appointment is noted in Mughal biographies and other chronicles.

17. Tirmizi, *Edicts from the Mughal Harem*, xxxiv.

18. Foster, *Embassy of Sir Thomas Roe*, cited in chapter 1, 70, 71, 88.

19. Ibid., 88.

20. Ibid., 270.

21. *Tuzuk*, 1:401.

22. The reference to Nur Jahan's *vakils* in made by Jahangir. *Tuzuk*, 2:192.

23. N. R. Khadgawat, *A Descriptive List of Farmans, Manshurs and Nishans addressed by the Imperial Mughals to the Princes of Rajasthan* (Bikaner: Directorate of the Archives, Govt. of Rajasthan, 1962), 38. Also, Tirmizi, *Edicts from the Mughal Harem*, Appendix I, 116. "As the aforesaid Rathor is in Surat Singh's service, the latter is ordered to pay off the said debts, from his own estate, to their people (Kisandas and Baroman) and to deduct the same from his (Rathore's) salary . . . He should not disobey the orders and should regard it his duty."

24. *Ain-i Akbari*, 1:212. By the 1580s, Akbar had ordered that Allah-u-Akbar be employed as invocation on all his documents.

25. For the Persian text and other details of these orders, Tirmizi, *Edicts from the Mughal Harem*, 4–16.

26. Beveridge, *Babur-nama*, cited in chapter 2, 43; Thackston, cited in chapter 2, *Baburnama*, 49.

27. Tirmizi, *Edicts from the Mughal Harem*, xvii–xviii.

28. I take this concept following Gloria Anzaldúa's *Borderlands*, in which she reflects on the possibiites that arise out of contradictory human conditions that help enunciate a complex view of social self. Anzaldúa, *Borderlands: La Frontera, The New Mestiza* (San Francisco: Aunt Lute Books, 2012, 4th ed.), 9, and also the entire introduction.

29. The location of this coin (that bears the first verse above) is not given by Shujauddin and Shujauddin, *The Life and Times of Noor Jahan*, cited in chapter 1, 100. The first verse documented by Shujauddin and Shujauddin is close in character to the second. For the latter, see, M. K. Hussain, *Catalogue of Coins of the Mughal Emperors* (Bombay: Department of Archaeology, Government of Maharashtra, 1968), 10.

30. As examples, see, R. B. Whitehead, "The Mint Towns of the Mughal Emperors of India," *Journal and Proceedings of the Asiatic Society of Bengal*, New Series, 8 (1912): 425–531; R. B. Whitehead, First Supplement to "The Mint Towns of the Mughal Emperors of India," *Journal of the Asiatic Society of Bengal*, Numismatic Supplement 25 (July and August 1915); C. R. Singhal, *Mint-Towns of the Mughal*

Emperors of India (Bombay: The Numismatic Society of India, 1953), 33–35.

31. For a discussion of Reza, Nadira, and Hasan, see Priscilla Soucek, "Persian Artists in Mughal India: Influences and Transformations," *Muqarnas* 4 (1987): 166–81.

32. Beach, Fischer, and Goswamy, *Masters of Indian Painting*, cited in chapter 1, 228.

33. Milo Cleveland Beach suggested the date of composition between 1612 and 1615 in *The Grand Mogul,* cited in chapter 1, 90. The title he used was: *Portrait of a Lady with a Rifle.* In the catalogue of the Rampur Raza Library, where this painting is held, it is dated 1617, in English, as part of the exhibits where it was included. For a reproduction and the English inscription, see Barbara Schmitz and Ziyaud-Din A. Desai, *Mughal and Persian Paintings and Illustrated Manuscripts in The Raza Library, Rampur* (New Delhi: Aryan Books International, 2006). The title for Hasan's painting varies in the writings of art historians: *Portrait of Nur Jahan Holding a Musket; Nur Jahan in Hunting Attire.* In the most recent edition by Beach et al., *Masters of Indian Painting,* Nur's portrait is entitled *Portrait of Nur Jahan* and the date ascribed is 1612–13. Cf. 214.

34. Sanam Ali Khan provided these details from the Rampur Raza Library conservation lab's treatment records. The director of the library sent me a letter with these details, dated November 24, 2013, 2–3.

35. On the right side of the portrait of Nur is that of Jahangir. Schmidt and Desai consider the latter figure to be a Mughal prince. According to Sanam Ali Khan of the Rampur Raza Library (India), where this painting is held, and according to the Rampur library catalogues, the portrait adjacent to Nur is that of Jahangir. Schmitz and Desai, *Mughal and Persian Paintings,* 49.

36. I am grateful to Jos Gommans for looking at this painting, and for his comments on the kind of musket Nur Jahan holds.

37. Sanam Ali, letter to the author, 2.

38. Stronge, *Painting for the Mughal Emperor,* cited in chapter 2, 133.

39. Both citations by Jahangir in this paragraph are from the *Tuzuk,* 2:20.

40. The construction of this inn is discussed in Ellison Banks Findly, "Women's Wealth and Styles of Giving: Perspectives from Mughal,

Jain, and Buddhist Sites," in Fairchild Ruggles (ed.), *Women, Patronage, and Self-Representation in Islamic Societies*, cited in chapter 5, 109–12; also, Afshan Bokhari, *Gendered Landscapes: Jahan Ara Begum's (1614–1681) Patronage, Piety and Self Representation in Mughal India* (D.Phil. Dissertation, University of Vienna), 230–33.

ELEVEN: VEILS OF LIGHT

1. *Tuzuk*, cited in chapter 1, 2:53.
2. *Iqbalnama-i Jahangiri*, cited in chapter 2, 405; *Dhakhiratul Khawanin*, cited in chapter 2, 14. The small seventeenth-century portrait, attributed to Abul-Hasan, *Nur Jahan: Portrait to Be Worn as a Jewel*, is held at the Harvard Art Museum. It is reproduced in Thackston, *Jahangirnama*, cited in chapter 1, 368, as well as in this book. The Harvard museum has more recently expressed some doubt about the exact date, authorship, and subject of the painting. A second 1840–50 painting of Nur Jahan in a *jharokha* is held at the National Museum, New Delhi, entitled, *Nur Jahan*. Ebba Koch notes that the *jharokha* scenes from Jahangir's time were rare, and when they did appear, they tended to repeat the characteristics of the *jharokha* paintings from late Akbari period: canopied platform or throne in which the emperor was surrounded by nobles. For a discussion of the development and formalization of the *jharokha* under Shah Jahan, see Koch, *Mughal Art and Imperial Ideology*, cited in chapter 8, 133–45.
3. *Iqbalnama-i Jahangiri*, 405.
4. *Dhakhiratul Khawanin*, 14. Other documents where we note the issue of *khutba* are: Hadi, *Tatimma-i Vaqi'at-I Jahangiri*, cited in chapter 1, 398; *Maathir-Ul-Umara*, cited in chapter 2, 1077.
5. For an extended discussion of Jahangir's interest in naturalism and its relation to power, see Lefevre, "Recovering a Missing Voice from Mughal India," cited in chapter 9, 452–89.
6. Al-Ghazzali, in his major work, *Revival of Religious Sciences*, a treatise on Sufism, speaks about the ultimate goal of politics, which is to provide well-being for humans in this world and the other world. He has also a book in Persian, called *Naṣihat al-molūk* (Counsel for kings), which belongs to the literary genre of "mirrors for princes," in which he explains the beliefs and principles on which a ruler should act, as

well as counsels according to which a ruler should administer his charge. In both these books, he outlines the significant issue of stability.

7. Faruqui, *Princes*, cited in chapter 7, 184–85.

8. Alam, *Languages of Political Islam*, cited in chapter 3, 95; Faruqui, *Princes*, 35; *Tuzuk*, 2:107.

9. Afzal Husain, *The Nobility Under Akbar and Jahangir: A Study of Family Groups* (New Delhi: Manohar Publishers, 1999), 166.

10. *Intekhab-i Jahangir Shahi*, B.M. Or. 1648, folios 320–22. Elliott and Dowson discuss the identity of the author and have some passages and translations included in their *History of India As Told by Its Own Historians*, cited in chapter 1, 6:446–52.

11. As noted earlier, Jahangir wrote of her attachment to his family. Her date of induction into Jahangir's harem in 1585 and the note about her thirty-three years of service by the emperor establishes that she left the imperial service in 1618, perhaps just after the Mughal cavalcade returned from Malwa and Gujarat. *Tuzuk*, 2:110–111; *Maathir-Ul-Umara*, 1078; *Tatimma-i Vaqi'at-i Jahangiri*, 308.

12. *Tuzuk*, 2:110–11.

13. It is not clear whether Arjumand accompanied the royals and her husband, Shah Jahan, to Kashmir. *Tuzuk*, 2:112, 113; In the *Padshahnama*, the epic history of Shah Jahan's reign, the birth of this prince is recorded on December 18, just before Shah Jahan's departure with his father, which is noted to be in February 1620; Begley and Desai, *Shah Jahan Nama*, cited in chapter 9, 8.

14. *Tuzuk*, 2:155–56.

15. I have used Thackston's translation of the lines cited above, which is more in keeping with the feel in Persian, and less Victorian as in Beveridge's rendering of these particular lines. Thackston, *Jahangirnama*, 327.

16. *Tuzuk*, 2:134.

17. Sabir Hussain, "A Road Less Travelled," *The Hindu*, July 14, 2014, http://www.hindu.com/a-road-less-travelled.

18. The citation is from Thackston, *Jahangirnama*, 335; cf. *Tuzuk*, 2:145, 150–51.

19. For a discussion of this verse and also Subrawardi's principles of illumination, see, William C. Chittick, *The Sufi Path of Knowledge: Ibn al-*

'Arabi's Metaphysics of Imagination (Albany: State University of New York, 1989), 401, *n*19; Mehdi Aminrazavi, *Suhrawardi and the School of Illumination* (New York: Routledge, 2013), 111.

20. *Tuzuk*, 1:3, 10–11: *nur-shahi* (light of sovereignty), *nur-sultani* (light of kingship), *nur-daulat* (light of the court), *nur-mihr* (light of the sun), and *nur-jahani* (light of the world).

21. Shujauddin and Shujauddin, *The Life and Times of Nur Jahan*, cited in chapter 1, 40.

22. *Tuzuk*, 2:174.

23. Khafi Khan's *Muntakhab-ul-Lubab*, cited in chapter 2, 1, 270.

تارت ز دمکه لعل است رب قابی حریر

شده است قطره خون منت گری ابانگری

24. Archibald Constable (ed.), Francois Bernier, *Travels in the Mogul Empire, AD 1636–1668* (New Delhi: S. Chand and Co., 1968, rpt.), 413, *n*2, 414.

25. *Tuzuk*, 2:152.

26. Ibid., 160.

27. Faruqui, *Princes*, cited in chapter 7, 35.

28. Grey, *Travels of Pietro Della Valle*, cited in chapter 2, 1:55–56; Foster, *Embassy of Sir Thomas Roe*, cited in chapter 1, 369.

29. Thackston, *Jahangirnama*, 353. Thackston's translation here reads more appropriately compared to the cumbersome tone of Rogers and Beveridge; cf. *Tuzuk*, 2:186.

30. *Dhakhiratul Khawanin*, 19.

TWELVE: THE LIGHT-SCATTERING GARDEN

1. The Jats renamed it Ram Bagh upon capturing Agra in the last quarter of the eighteenth century, tradition goes. Ebba Koch, "Notes on the Painted and Sculpted Decoration of Nur Jahan's Pavilions in the Ram Bagh (Bagh-i Nur Afshan) at Agra," in *Facets of Indian Art: A Symposium Held at the Victoria and Albert Museum* (London: The Victoria & Albert Museum, 1986), 53.

2. Koch, *Taj Mahal*, cited in chapter 8, 30, 38, 39.

3. The description of Ram Bagh is based upon my visit in January 2016, with the support of the Archaeological Survey of India team led by

Mr. R. K. Singh. Jahangir had been there twice before the celebration of Ladli's betrothal, after the victory of Kangra in March 1621, and then again, Nur Jahan held celebrations marking the sixteenth year of their reign in 1621.

4. Ebba Koch, an expert who has studied the ceilings of Nur's garden pavilions says, they draw an "implicit parallel between the Mughal emperor and his wife and Solomon and his consort Bilqis [Sheba]." Koch, "Ram Bagh," 59.

5. *Tuzuk*, 2:200.

6. Shahryar was born in 1605, the same year that his father ascended the throne. Nur's first marriage took place in 1594 and in all probability, Ladli was born before 1605. No record mentions her date of birth, but most note that she was a little girl when she came to Agra along with her mother. She is represented as a small child in *Chiterin* (Lady artist and her model), a painting housed in Bhartiya Kala Bhavan of the Banaras Hindu University.

7. For rituals of henna, see Masse, *Persian Beliefs and Customs*, cited in chapter 2, 52–53.

8. It was such a veil that Jahangir had put on Shah Jahan's head, which the latter gave his son. Beach and Koch, *King of the World*, cited in chapter 8, 66.

9. Spectacular visual images of the weddings of princes, roughly a decade later, allow us to picture the scene of Ladli and Shahryar's wedding. Beach and Koch, *King of the World*. Folios and texts used for the discussion in this paragraph are: "The Presentation of Dara-Shikoh's Wedding Gifts," "The Delivery of Presents for Dara-Shikoh's Wedding," "The Wedding Procession of Prince Dara-Shikoh," "Shah Jahan Honoring Prince Awrangzeb at Agra Before His Wedding," "Shah Jahan Honoring Prince Awrangzeb at His Wedding," 46, 60, 61, 104, 108.

10. *Single Leaf Portrait of Shahryar*, the Walters Art Gallery, Baltimore. Shelf mark: W. 697.

11. The best descriptions of the codes and decorum around Mughal marriages come from Gulbadan Banu Begum. On the seating arrangements in times of feasts and weddings, notably at the time of the marriage of the Mughal prince Hindal, Gulbadan, *Ahval*, cited in chapter 2, folio 24b–29a.

12. Tuzuk, 2:199–200.
13. Faruqui, *Princes*, 85, 86, 109.
14. *Tuzuk*, 2:205.
15. *Dhakhiratul Khawanin*, 19.
16. Richard C. Foltz, *Mughal India and Central Asia* (Karachi: OUP, 1998), 132; M. Athar Ali, "Jahangir and the Uzbeks," *Proceedings of the 26th Indian History Congress* (1964), 111.
17. *Tuzuk*, 2:205.
18. Ibid., 212–14.
19. Ibid., 214–15.
20. Ibid., 216–17.
21. Ibid., 222.
22. Ibid. This episode is also reproduced in *Dhakhiratul Khawanin*, 4; and *Maathir-Ul-Umara*, 2(2): 1076.
23. *Tuzuk*, 2:222–23.
24. An inscription on the southwest wall bears the date 1626/27 and the name of the calligrapher, 'Abd-un-Nabi al-Qarshi. Mason marks or signatures, such as a *tota*, or parrot, appear on the floors outside, in letters and images.
25. Koch, *Taj Mahal*, 49, 51, 52.
26. Cited in Ibid., 52.

THIRTEEN: *FITNA*

1. Ghulam Yazdani (ed.), *Muhammad Salih Kanbo, 'Amal-i Salih* (Lahore: n.p., 1967–72), 1:133–34.
2. *Tuzuk*, cited in chapter 1, 2:289.
3. Seen to be destabilizing imperial expansionist plans, Parvez had been dismissed from his Deccan responsibilities in 1616. Instead, Shah Jahan was given the charge, a campaign that became his crowning glory. Parvez was packed off to Allahabad and was barred from court appearance for three years. When Jahangir met the ascetic Jadrup in 1619, the emperor had a change of heart. Nur Jahan had already been facilitating a resolution of sorts between Parvez and his father.
4. Thackston, *Jahangirnama*, cited in chapter 1, 387. This translation captures beautifully the emotive quality of Jahangir's lament. Cf., Tuzuk, 2:248.

5. Irfan Habib, "The Family of Nur Jahan During Jahangir's Reign," cited in chapter 2, 77. For the events sketched in this paragraph, I have drawn information from the following chronicles: *Jahangirnama*; *Iqbalnama-i Jahangiri*, cited in chapter 2; *Dhakhiratul Khawanin*, cited in chapter 2; *Maathir-Ul-Umara*, cited in chapter 2; *'Amal-i Salih*; and Borah, *Baharistan-i Ghaybi*, cited in chapter 6. For recent, excellent writing on the subject of princely rebellions, Faruqui, *Princes*, cited in chapter 7. Specific references to these texts and to other scholarly literature covering these events are below. *Dhakhiratul Khawanin*, 19–20.

6. *Dhakhiratul Khawanin*, 20.

7. Afzal Husain, *Nobility Under Akbar and Jahangir*, cited in chapter 11, 165.

8. *Tuzuk* 2:250. Rahim's career in the Deccan had begun as early as Akbar's reign. Later, while working in prince Parvez's command there, he had requested additional enforcements from Jahangir on several occasions. Rahim repeatedly sent petitions for help and even threatened to immolate himself along with his family if help was not sent. There was a section of the nobility, opposed to Rahim that had convinced Jahangir that he was in league with the influential forces in the south and that he had deliberately surrendered conquered regions to them. Mahabat went to make an inquiry, and he was asked to bring Rahim back to the court. Parvez was recalled. It was then that the campaign was handed over to Shah Jahan in 1617. Rahim stayed on in the Deccan and came to some understanding with Shah Jahan. For further details, Afzal Husain, *Nobility Under Akbar and Jahangir*, 37–39, 40.

9. *Dhakhiratul Khawanin*, 20.

10. Faruqui, *Princes*, 207.

11. The chronicles composed in Shah Jahan's time used the word *fitna*, notably, Kamgar Husaini, *Ma'asir-i Jahangiri*, ed. Azra Alvi (Bombay, 1978); Begley and Desai, *Shah Jahan Nama*, cited in chapter 9; and the *Dhakhiratul Khawanin*; *Maathir-Ul-Umara*; and *Iqbalnama-i Jahangiri*, noted above. For a discussion of *fitna* and the princely rebellion, Faruqui, *Princes*, 188–190.

12. D. A. Spellberg, *Politics, Gender, and the Islamic Past: The Legacy of*

A'isha Bint Abi Bakr (New York: Columbia University Press, 1994), 118.

13. Fatima Mernissi, *The Forgotten Queens of Islam* (Minneapolis: University of Minnesota Press, 1993), 66–67.

14. Spellberg discusses how the idea of *fitna* comes to be configured around Ayisha. Spellberg, *Politics, Gender, and the Islamic Past*, especially, 107, 109, 111, 118, 141.

15. Leslie Peirce, *The Imperial Harem: Women and Sovereignty in the Ottoman Empire* (New York: Oxford University Press, 1993), vii, 267.

16. Thackston, *Jahangirnama*, 395.

17. On details of Shah Jahan's alliances, Faruqui, *Princes*, 208–21.

18. Borah, *Baharistan-i Ghaybi*, 417.

19. The time of Shah Jahan's arrival in Allahabad and Banaras and the details of the Battle of Tons in 1624 are from the eighteenth-century account of Muhammad Hadi. Thackston, *Jahangirnama*, 425–27; citations on 426.

FOURTEEN: THE RESCUE

1. The events of 1626–27 are based upon the encyclopedic bibliographical work of Farid Bhakkari, *Dhakhiratul Khawanin*, Mu'tamad Khan's *Iqbalnama-i Jahangiri*, and the account of Muhammad Hadi, all cited in chapter 2. For the above citation, Thackston, *Jahangirnama*, cited in chapter 1, 441. In addition, Shirazi, *Waqa-i-uz-Zaman*, cited in chapter 6. I have also consulted the Aligarh copy, Rotograph 10, *Fathnama-i Nur Jahan Begum*. Most citations are from the Siddiqi edition.

2. *Fathnama-i Nur Jahan Begum*, 102.

3. *Dhakhiratul Khawanin*, 42.

4. *Fathnama-i Nur Jahan Begum*, 128.

5. Thackston, *Jahangirnama*, 440.

6. *Fathnama-i Nur Jahan Begum*, 132.

7. Ibid., 132, 134, 136.

8. *Dhakhiratul Khawanin*, 20; Hadi and Mu'tamad Khan both make note of a similar message.

9. The dates differ. Bhakkari notes March 28 and Hadi has March 18.

Shirazi does not give the date, but is clear about the year and general time, spring 1626.

10. It is Shirazi who points out candidly that Asaf withdrew upon the killing of Mahabat's brother. *Fathnama-i Nur Jahan Begum*, 154.

11. Thackston, *Jahangirnama*, 442.

12. *Fathnama-i Nur Jahan Begum*, 148.

13. *Dhakhiratul Khawanin*, 17.

14. Thackston, *Jahangirnama*, 447.

15. Ibid.

16. According to Hadi's account, Buland Khan carried Nur's message to Mahabat: "Today the Begam will hold a review of troops for His Majesty. It would be better to hold in abeyance the ceremonies for the beginning of the day lest an argument ensue and battle break out." Thackston, *Jahangirnama*, 447. On the heels of the first messenger, she sent another person to convince Mahabat of the reasonableness of obeying her order. Who sent these messages to Mahabat varies according to who records the history of these times. For Mu'tamad, while the empress was fully in charge, Jahangir was working behind the scenes. Indeed, the two messengers who carried the message to Mahabat were Jahangir's. It was the emperor who was building grounds of trust with Mahabat, not Nur Jahan.

17. Thackston, *Jahangirnama*, 447.

18. Ibid.

19. *Fathnama-i Nur Jahan Begum*, 256.

FIFTEEN: ANGEL OF DEATH

1. Faruqui, *Princes*, cited in chapter 7, 254.

2. Thackston, *Jahangirnama*, cited in chapter 1, 450.

3. Ibid., 453.

4. Ibid., 456.

5. For a rich description of areas that the Mughal retinue went by at this time, parts that Sir Richard Temple would describe later, see, Richard Temple, *Hyderabad, Kashmir, Sikkim and Nepal Vol. II* (London: Allen and Co., 1887), 19 for the Chitta Pani waterfall. Temple's description

comes close to Jahangir's, in that the latter notes briefly the beauty of the waterfall in 1620. *Tuzuk*, cited in chapter 1, 2:179.

6. *Iqbalnama-i Jahangiri*, cited in chapter 2, 435; Hadi makes exactly the same statement, see Thackston, *Jahangirnama*, cited in chapter 1, 456.

7. *Tuzuk*, 2:180.

8. Khafi Khan does not refer to Chingiz Hatli at all: *Muntakhab-ul-Lubab*, cited in chapter 2, 1:338. The *Iqbalnama-i Jahangiri*, cited in chapter 2, and the "Maasir-i Jahangiri" note the emperor's death here, as does Hadi, but he calls it Chakkar Hatli. H. M. Elliott and John Dowson, "Maasir-i Jahangiri of Kamgar Khan," in Elliott and Dowson (eds.), *The History of India*, cited in chapter 1.

9. *Tuzuk*, 2:181.

10. Begley and Desai, *Shah Jahan Nama*, cited in chapter 9, 12.

11. Ibid.

12. *Dhakhiratul Khawanin*, 21.

13. Thackston, *Jahangirnama*, 457; also noted in *Iqbalnama-i Jahangiri*, 436.

14. Begley and Desai, *Shah Jahan Nama*, 12–13.

15. Ibid., 12.

16. Thackston, *Jahangirnama*, 458.

17. Faruqui, *Princes*, 252.

18. Thackston, *Jahangirnama*, 460.

19. *Fathnama-i Nur Jahan Begum*, cited in chapter 6, ii, and viii. We get a further evidence of Shah Jahan's involvement in the production of these texts from another translation. Elliott and Dowson suggest that Husaini noted at one point that it was as a result of the incomplete character of Jahangir's memoir that "he had long contemplated supplying its deficiencies [sic] by writing a complete life himself; when he was at last induced to undertake it at the instigation of the Emperor Shah Jahan in the third year of his reign [1630–31]." Elliott and Dowson, "Maasir-i Jahangiri of Kamgar Khan," 439.

20. Begley and Desai, *Shah Jahan Nama*, xiii.

21. Prasad, *History of Jahangir*, cited in chapter 2, 403; Shujauddin and Shujauddin, *The Life and Times of Noor Jahan*, cited in chapter 1, 99–100.

22. R. B. Whitehead, "The Mint Towns of the Mughal Emperors of India," *Journal and Proceedings of the Asiatic Society of Bengal*, New Series, 8 (1912): 425–531; R. B. Whitehead, First Supplement to "The Mint Towns of the Mughal Emperors of India," *Journal of the Asiatic Society of Bengal*, Numismatic Supplement 25 (July and August 1915); Singhal, *Mint-Towns of the Mughal Emperors of India*, cited in chapter 10, 33–35.

23. Kanbo, *'Amal e Salih*, cited in chapter 13, 1:13.

24. Later biographers followed this line of thought and assumed that Nur Jahan's resources were limited and hence she could not embark on a grand venture such as the late Emperor's tomb. Syed Muhammad Latif, *Lahore: Its History, Architectural Remains and Antiquities* (Lahore: The New Imperial Press, 1892), 106; Shujauddin and Shujauddin, *The Life and Times of Noor Jahan*, 123.

25. Koch, *Taj Mahal*, cited in chapter 8, 84, 88; E.B.A. Havell, *A Handbook of Indian Art* (London: John Murray, 1927), 137; James Fergusson, *History of Indian and Eastern Architecture* (Delhi: Munshiram Manoharlal, 1967), 304–5; Percy Brown, *Indian Architecture, Islamic Period* (Bombay: Taraporevala Treasure House of Books, 1968, 5th ed.), 100.

26. Koch, *Taj Mahal*, 88.

27. Ebba Koch, *Mughal Architecture: An Outline of its History and Development* (1526–1858) (New York and London: Prestel Publishing, 1991), 98.

28. Shujauddin and Shujauddin, *The Life and Times of Noor Jahan*, 124.

29. *Maathir-Ul-Umara*, cited in chapter 2, 1077.

30. *Shah Jahan Nama*, 333–34.

SIXTEEN: BEYOND 1627, AN EPILOGUE

1. Mernissi, *The Forgotten Queens of Islam*, cited in chapter 13; Peirce, *The Imperial Harem*, cited in chapter 13, among other scholars who have written on Muslim women's leadership.

2. L.W.B. Brockliss, "The Anatomy of the Minister-Favourite," in J. H. Elliott and L.W.B. Brockliss (eds.), *The World of the Favourite* (New Haven and London: Yale University Press, 1999), 285. The literature

on the favorite is enormous. Apart from this volume, I have consulted John Elliott, *The Count-Duke of Olivares: The Statesman in an Age of Decline* (New Haven: Yale University Press, 1986); Antonio Feros, *Kingship and Favoritism in the Spain of Philip III, 1598–1621* (Cambridge: Cambridge University Press, 2000).

3. *Nur Jahan Holding a Portrait of Emperor Jahangir*, 1627, is now the crowning glory of the Cleveland Museum of Art collection. For a discussion of this painting, see Ruby Lal, "From the Inside Out: Spaces of Pleasure and Authority," in Sonya Rhie Quintanilla (ed.), *Mughal Paintings: Art and Stories, The Cleveland Museum of Art* (London: D. Giles Ltd, 2016). The attribution to Bishandas is still being considered by Islamic art critic Marcus Fraser. The painting is also mentioned in the following volumes: Beach, *The Grand Mogul*, cited in chapter 1, 159; Philippa Vaughan, "Begams of the House of Timur and the Dynastic Image," in *Humayun's Garden Party*, ed. Sheila R. Canby (Bombay: Marg Publications, 1994), 132, fig. 13; and Linda Komaroff, *Gifts of the Sultan: The Arts of Giving at the Islamic Court* (Los Angeles: Los Angeles County Museum of Art, 2011), no. 59, 177.

4. In Nizami of Ganja's twelfth-century collection there is a story, *Khusrau va Shirin*: a parable of love, unity, and divinity in which the painter Shapur, highly skilled at lifelike presentations, tells the hero, Khusrau, about the beautiful Shirin (literally, "sweet"). Khusrau's grandfather once told him that he would meet a beloved of great sweetness. And so Khusrau asks Shapur to find Shirin. He can only do so through Khusrau's portrait. Shapur, disguised as a monk, goes to Armenia to find Shirin. He finds out from a priest where she and her attendants spend time. Early one morning, he goes to that meadow, paints a portrait of Khusrau, and suspends it on a branch of tree. Shirin and her companions arrive. Her eyes fall upon the portrait. The women bring the portrait to her, and looking at it she becomes absorbed "in rapt contemplation." She embraces it as if it were alive. Fearful, thinking that the portrait was the work of demonic creatures, the women take it away from her. The next day Shapur makes a second painting, exactly like the first. When Shirin sees it, she is overwhelmed, unable to speak. Her companions destroy the painting again, burn rue to

dispel the evil spirits, and move to a new meadow. And yet, Shapur embarks on a third, exactly like the first two. Shirin finds and holds up the portrait. The portrait that Shirin held, says Nizami, "contained her own reflection." "In the mirror (ayina) she saw her own reflection (nishan) when she seized it, she fainted." (Priscilla Soucek, "Nizami on Painters and Painting," in Richard Ettinghausen (ed.), *Islamic Art in the Metropolitan Museum of Art* (New York: The Metropolitan Museum of Art, 1972), 17, 18.

5. "Women seeing portraits" are available in the following museums: Freer Gallery of Art and Arthur M. Sackler Gallery (Washington, DC), F.1984. 43 2 and 1985. 1. 354; Bonhams (London, UK), 3.19. 2012 lot. 1167; and *Jahangir Viewing a Portrait of Akbar*, Louvre (Paris, France), OA 3676 b (1); For further examples and details, see Klaus Ebeling, *Ragamala Painting* (New Delhi: Ravi Kumar, 1973), 76, C26.

6. Afshan Bokhari, "Imperial Transgressions and Spiritual Investitures: A Begum's 'Ascension' in Seventeenth Century Mughal India," *Journal of Persianate Studies* 4 (2011), 94, 95.

7. Ibid., 92.

8. Cited in Ibid., 91.

ILLUSTRATION CREDITS

The mythical Wak-Wak tree: *A Floral Fantasy of Animals and Birds* (*Waq-Waq*), early 1600s. India, Mughal. Opaque watercolor and gold on paper; page: 37.6 × 26.6 (14 13/16 × 10 1/2 in); painting: 19.8 × 12.5 cm (7 13/16 × 4 15/16 in). © The Cleveland Museum of Art. Gift in honor of Madeline Neves Clapp; gift of Mrs. Henry White Cannon by exchange; bequest of Louise T. Cooper; Leonard C. Hanna Jr. Fund; from the Catherine and Ralph Benkaim Collection, 2013.319.

The fort complex at Agra: *Exterior View of the Fort Complex.* IAA107530 © Aga Khan Trust for Culture / Michael Peuckert (photographer).

Nur Jahan surrounded by harem women: *Chiterin: An Illustration of the Nur Jahan Episode*, © Bharat Kala Bhavan, BHU, Varanasi.

Abul-Hasan's remarkable painting: *Portrait of Nur Jahan Holding a Musket*, by Abul-Hasan Nadir uz-Zaman, c. 17th century CE. 10 × 6 cm. Courtesy of Rampur Raza Library.

A clear indicator: *Silver Rupee with Nur Jahan and Jahangir's Names.* H. Nelson Wright, *Catalogue of the Coins in the Indian Museum Calcutta* 3 vols. (Oxford: Clarendon, 1908). Plate 8, 1625–28 CE.

A celebration: *Jahangir and Prince Khurram Entertained by Nur Jahan*, Freer Gallery of Art and Arthur M. Sackler Gallery, Smithsonian Institution, Washington, DC. Gift of Charles Lang Freer, F1907.258.

Nur Jahan: Portrait to Be Worn As a Jewel, seventeenth century. Harvard Art Museums/Arthur M. Sackler Museum, the Stuart Cary Welch Collection. Gift of Edith I. Welch in memory of Stuart Cary Welch, 2009.202.4, Imaging Department © President and Fellows of Harvard College.

Posthumous Portrait of Emperor Jahangir Under a Canopy (recto), c. 1650. India, Mughal, 17th century. Opaque watercolor and gold on paper, borders with floral motifs in colors and gold (recto); page: 35.2 × 22.1 cm (13 7/8 × 8 11/16 in); painting; 20.4 × 8 cm (8 1/16 × 3 1/8 in). © The Cleveland Museum of Art. Gift in honor of Madeline Neves Clapp; gift of Mrs. Henry White Cannon by exchange; bequest of Louise T. Cooper, Leonard C. Hanna Jr. Fund; from the Catherine and Ralph Benkaim Collection, 2013.329.

Mausoleum of I'timad ud-Daula, 19th-century image of the exterior approach to the tomb. IAA110086 © Aga Khan Trust for Culture / Samuel Bourne (photographer).

Maqbara-i Jahangir, General View from the North. IAA107790 © Aga Khan Trust for Culture.

Tomb of Nur Jahan at Shahdara, 2005. © Guilhem Vellut, https://www .flickr.com/photos/o_0/7962186/.

A painting in the Indian and Persian tradition: *Nur Jahan, Holding a Portrait of Emperor Jahangir*, c. 1627. Northern India, Mughal court, 17th century. Opaque watercolor and gold on paper; page: 30 × 22.1 cm (11 13/16 × 8 11/16 in); painting: 13.6 × 6.4 cm (5 3/8 × 2 1/2 in). © The Cleveland Museum of Art. Gift in honor of Madeline Neves Clapp; gift of Mrs. Henry White Cannon by exchange; bequest of Louise T. Cooper; Leonard C. Hanna Jr. Fund; from the Catherine and Ralph Benkaim Collection, 2013.325.

The Mughal Queen Nur Jahan Playing Polo with Other Princesses. Painted by Ustad Haji Muhammad Sharif (1889–1978), property of S. M. Mansoor, visual artist, Lahore, Pakistan.

Mughal Brave Queen Nur Jahan with Her Husband King Jahangir after Killing Tiger with Her Spear. Painted by Ustad Haji Muhammad Sharif (1889–1978), property of S. M. Mansoor, visual artist, Lahore, Pakistan.

Princess Nur Jahan and Attendants, 18th century, India. Gouache on paper; 11 3/4 × 8 5/8 in (29.8 × 21.9 cm). Rogers Fund, 1948, Metropolitan Museum of Art, New York.

Film still: Photographic Still Mounted on Lobby Card. *Noor Jahan,*1967; India. Zenith Productions, directed by M. Sadiq. Courtesy: The Osian's Archive & Library Collection. 0864490/ The Osian's Collection.

INDEX

Note: Page numbers in italics indicate figures.